The Culture of Power in Serbia

Nationalism and the Destruction of Alternatives

Eric D. Gordy

The Pennsylvania State University Press
University Park, Pennsylvania

Library of Congress Cataloging-in-Publication Data

Gordy, Eric D., 1966–
    The culture of power in Serbia : nationalism and the destruction
of alternatives / Eric D. Gordy.
        p.   cm.
    Includes index.
    ISBN 0-271-01957-3 (cloth : alk. paper)
    ISBN 0-271-01958-1 (pbk. : alk. paper)
        1. Serbia—Social life and customs—20th century.   2. Serbia
—Politics and government—1945–   3. Nationalism—Yugoslavia—Serbia
—History—20th century   4. Totalitarianism—Yugoslavia—Serbia
—History—20th century.   I. Title.
DR2043.G67   1999
949.7103—dc21

                                                                        99-22618
                                                                        CIP

It is the policy of The Pennsylvania State University Press to use acid-free paper for
the first printing of all clothbound books. Publications on uncoated stock satisfy the
minimum requirements of American National Standard for Information Sciences—
Permanence of Paper for Printed Library Materials, ANSI Z39.48–1992.

The Culture of
Power in Serbia

Post-Communist Cultural Studies Series

Thomas Cushman, General Editor

The Culture of Lies
Antipolitical Essays
Dubravka Ugrešić

Burden of Dreams
History and Identity in
Post-Soviet Ukraine
Catherine Wanner

*Gender Politics in
the Western Balkans*
Women, Society, and Politics
in Yugoslavia and the
Yugoslav Successor States
Sabrina P. Ramet, ed.

*The Radical Right in Eastern
and Central Europe Since 1989*
Sabrina P. Ramet, ed.

For Ivana and Azra

Contents

Illustrations   ix

1 An Approach to Everyday Life in Serbia   1

2 The Destruction of Political Alternatives   21

3 The Destruction of Information Alternatives   61

4 The Destruction of Musical Alternatives   103

5 The Destruction of Sociability   165

   Conclusion: Destroying and Maintaining Alternatives   199

Bibliography   209

Index   219

Illustrations

1. The Milošević family at the inauguration of Slobodan Milošević as president of SRJ in 1997.   22

2. The leaders of the parties in the *Zajedno* coalition during the
   student and citizen protests, December 1996.   23

3. Vojislav Šešelj, leader of the ultraright Serbian Radical Party,
   confronts his critics in a dramatic manner.   45

4. Volunteers selling a "special edition" of the newspaper *Borba*
   after it was taken over by the regime in December 1994.   66

5. Rambo Amadeus (Antonije Pušić).   116

6. The antiwar band *Rimtutituki* performs at an antiwar demonstration in Belgrade in 1992.   120

7. Turbofolk singer Svetlana Veličković-Ceca in performance.   137

8. Folksinger Dragan Kojić-Keba.   139

9. A street-corner currency dealer offers to exchange large-
   denomination dinar notes for single dollars during the period
   of hyperinflation in 1993.   171

1

An Approach to Everyday Life in Serbia

How does the regime of Slobodan Milošević's SPS (*Socijalistička partija Srbije*) remain in power in Serbia? By most measures of predicting the success or failure of regimes in political power, it ought not to have survived as long as it has. Since legitimizing its power as the successor of Serbia's League of Communists in December 1990, it has engaged in three losing military conflicts, produced over 500,000 refugees whose interests it had come to power promising to protect, presided over the hugest hyperinflation in modern times, and turned back on its original dangerous and defining promise to see "all Serbs in one state." Aside from its long list of failures, the party in power has not once received a majority of votes in an election, and each election after 1990 has seen its support declining further.

Conventional answers to the paradox of Milošević's longevity in power involve enthusiastic response to demagogic nationalist rhetoric, war hys teria, and some mystical form of ethnic hatred that is somehow "centuries old," lies dormant for most of these centuries, then effortlessly awakens at a moment's notice. The mobilization of ethnic hatred is certainly not irrelevant, and these conventional answers may explain some aspects of the Serbian regime's accession to power, but the anomaly still presents itself: How does the regime remain in power?

The answer I have derived from my research into politics, information, sociability, and popular culture in contemporary Belgrade is that the regime's strategies of self-preservation can be found in everyday life—in the destruction of alternatives. Specifically, the regime maintains itself not by mobilizing opinion or feeling in its favor, but by making alternatives to its rule unavailable. The story of everyday life in contemporary Belgrade, then, is that of a regime attempting to close off avenues of information, expression, and sociability, while many outside the regime endeavor to keep those avenues open.

The familiar exhortations to war and the atrocities committed in the war have led some outside observers to draw parallels between Milošević's regime and the National Socialist regime that ruled Germany from 1933 to 1945. The parallel may have some appeal as rhetoric, but it ignores crucial differences. Rather than maintaining power on the basis of a "triumph of the will," Milošević relies on the habituated passivity of that portion of the Serbian population, mostly older, less highly educated, and rural, accustomed to supporting or adapting to the rule of regimes—of any kind. For the rest of the population, a *test* of wills better describes the situation. Therefore, at the center of my research are the many conflicts between the regime and citizens wanting to expand political space, broaden cultural space, or simply live ordinary lives. Although the most apparent factors in the former Yugoslavia are the very public wars in Croatia and in Bosnia-Hercegovina, the research presented here focuses on another, silent war in Serbia—that of the state against the society.

The following chapters present several dimensions of this fundamental conflict. Before discussing the destruction of alternatives, it is necessary to consider first the conventional thesis of "centuries-old ethnic hatred" and then to discuss the two principal elements underpinning the rule of SPS in Serbia: the structure and rhetorical shape of contemporary Serbian nationalism and the manner of rule inherited from the recent Communist past.

Table 1. Question: *With members of which nationality from the former Yugoslavia would you most willingly live as a neighbor?*

With Macedonians	16.4%
With Slovenians	6.7
With Croatians	0.3
With Muslims	0.8
With none of them	25.0
With any one of them	48.6
Don't know	2.1

SOURCE: Unsigned, "Susedi," *Vreme*, no. 223, 30 January 1995, p. 30.

Table 2. Question: *With members of which nationality from the former Yugoslavia would you most willingly drink coffee?*

With Macedonians	15.8%
With Slovenians	5.6
With Croatians	1.1
With Muslims	0.9
With none of them	23.0
With any one of them	50.9
Don't know	2.7

SOURCE: Unsigned, "Susedi," *Vreme*, no. 223, 30 January 1995, p. 30.

"Ancient Ethnic Hatreds" or Long-Standing Social Divisions?

Early in 1995, the independent Belgrade weekly *Vreme* published the results of a survey by the "Partner" polling agency, which set out to test the degree to which "ethnic hatreds," or even ethnic distance, characterize the population of Serbia. The results for two questions posed in the survey are presented in Tables 1 and 2.

The results offer possibilities for comparing levels of ethnic distance. Macedonians seem to be generally more "popular" than Muslims or Croatians. At a more marginal level, drinking coffee with Croatians appears to be nearly four times more popular than living near them, whereas Slovenians seem to be perceived as slightly better neighbors than coffee partners. Such observations, however, miss what seems to be the major finding of the survey. The most frequent responses came from people who refused to make the menu selection of ethnicities that the questions invited. Instead, they answered more generally, "with any one of them" or "with none of them." In doing so, they expressed their general cultural orientation rather than their attitudes toward specific ethnic groups. This crucial difference—between an outlook broadly open to others and one that is closed—represents the greatest division among people in Serbia, with adherence to one of its poles expressed more commonly than any ethnic hatred, "ancient" or newly discovered.

A generation of research on ethnic distance performed before the breakup of the old Yugoslavia (*Socijalistička federativna republika Jugoslavija*, hereafter SFRJ)[1] demonstrated that levels of rejection of other nationalities expressed in surveys were consistently very low indeed.[2] Bora Kuzmanović characterized the findings of this research as showing "little ethnic distance, less than in many other more developed countries of the world."[3] Other indications of softening ethnic boundaries were apparent as well. Ethnically "mixed" marriages increased from 8 to 9 percent of all marriages in the period from 1950 to 1957 to 13 percent of all marriages in the period from 1977 to 1981.[4] The number of people listing their nationality as Yugoslav (as opposed to any specific nationality) in the cen-

1. The contemporary state formed by the federation of Serbia and Montenegro goes by the name of Federal Republic of Yugoslavia (*Savezna republika Jugoslavija*), and is identified in the text as SRJ. SRJ was unrecognized by any country during the period of research and continues to be unrecognized by the United States at the time of writing. My practice in the text is to call all entities and states by the names they use for themselves. This practice is not intended to imply any position on the question of recognition, successorship, or legitimacy.

2. The major studies from 1960 to 1989 and afterward are summarized in Bora Kuzmanović, "Socijalna distanca prema pojedinim nacijama (Etnička distanca)," in Mladen Lazić, Danilo Mrkšić, Sreten Vujović, Bora Kuzmanović, Stjepan Gredelj, Slobodan Cvejić, and Vladimir Vuletić, eds., *Razaranje društva: Jugoslovensko društvo u krizi 90-ih* (Belgrade: Filip Višnjić, 1994), 228–32.

3. Kuzmanović (1994), 228. In fact, the findings on many specific questions do show a lesser degree of ethnic distance in SFRJ than findings for similar questions asked in the same years in the United States, which are presented in the longitudinal study by Howard Schuman, Charlotte Steeh, and Lawrence Bobo, *Racial Attitudes in America: Trends and Interpretations* (Cambridge, Mass.: Harvard University Press, 1985).

4. Ruža Petrović, *Etnički mešoviti brakovi u Jugoslaviji* (Belgrade: Institut za sociološka istraživanja Filozofskog fakulteta u Beogradu 1985), 57.

Table 3. Some social characteristics of "Yugoslavs," "Serbs," and "Croats" in SFRJ (1971 census)

	Yugoslavs	Serbs	Croats
Median age (years)	20.9	31.3	31.3
Principal occupation is agriculture	8.1%	51.4%	35.3%
Percentage illiterate	3.4	17.3	9.9
Percentage with some higher education	10.0	3.5	3.3

SOURCE: Ruža Petrović, *Etnički mešoviti brakovi u Jugoslaviji* (Belgrade: Institut za socio-loška istraživanja Filozofskog fakulteta u Beogradu, 1985), 39, 40, 43, 44.

sus increased from 317,124, or 1.7 percent of the population in 1961, to 1,209,024, or 5.4 percent of the population in 1981.[5]

Because "Yugoslav" was the only positive answer available on the census to people who preferred not to choose a specific nationality,[6] the people who identified themselves in this way are particularly interesting. Table 3 compares some social characteristics of self-identified Yugoslavs with those of self-declared Serbs and Croats. The declaration of nationality in the census was a matter of choice. People who were younger, more urban, and more highly educated were more inclined than others to identify themselves by their citizenship, as Yugoslav, as one way of refusing a narrower national identity.

Not all the people who adopted a more open orientation identified themselves as Yugoslav in the census, nor did all the people who identified themselves as Yugoslav adopt a more open orientation. Yugoslav identity could also indicate other conditions, for example, ideological attachment to the "non-national" ideology promoted by the Communist elite or "mixed" parentage. The social correlates of the Yugoslav identity,

5. Petrović (1985), 30. At that time, the statute on ethnic identification for the Yugoslav census read: "The answer on nationality is filled out according to the freely expressed national identity of the respondent. For children under ten years of age the figure is listed according to the declaration of their parents" (19). Thus nationality was recognized by the census as a subjective category. The option of categorizing oneself as "Yugoslav," however, was not available in the census before 1961. Before that time, the "Yugoslav" category fell under the broader category, "did not express a national identity" (29).

6. The other options were principally negative and included smaller numbers of people. In the 1981 census, 46,700 people were listed as "did not declare a national identity," 25,700 people gave a regional identity as their nationality, and 153,500 people were listed as "nationality unknown" (Petrović, 1985, 32).

however, as well as its growing popularity, suggest two theses about social change in SFRJ before the country fell apart: People were seeking and finding alternatives to narrow national identity, and "Yugoslav" identity constituted one of those alternatives; and this search for alternatives constituted an emergent social force, particularly among the younger, more urban, and more highly educated portions of the population.

Both these theses apply to the period before Slobodan Milošević came to power in Serbia and before the nationalist mobilization on which he founded his rise began to take root in media, politics, and culture. Research by Veljko Vujačić has amply demonstrated that during Milošević's rise, nationalist tendencies were correlated with impulses for Communist restoration and authoritarian forces in such institutions as the military and the academy.[7] Once Milošević had consolidated his place in power, national homogenization became a necessary part of maintaining the regime. The more open orientations emerging in Serbian society and also in the other parts of the former Yugoslavia where nationalist authoritarianism came to power presented the most important obstacles to national homogenization.

Milošević's regime attempted to overcome these obstacles in the way that dictatorships do. This book presents the various strategies by which the Serbian regime endeavored to maintain itself in power by making alternatives unavailable to people in their everyday lives. The following chapters offer varying perspectives on the destruction of alternatives at work—in the political system, in the provision of information, in culture, and in sociability.

None of the efforts of the Serbian regime to make alternatives unavailable in the areas of everyday life examined in this book took place in a social or cultural vacuum. Rather, they drew on the strong social divisions that have long characterized Serbian society as it has experienced its extended and incomplete transition from an agrarian to a modern form. The cultural and social conflicts between older and younger generations, between urban and peasant (as well as urban-peasant) outlooks, and more generally between open cosmopolitan and closed national orientations played roles in each instance of the destruction of alternatives discussed in this research. The combined impact of dictatorial strategies, national

---

7. Veljko Vujačić, *Communism and Nationalism in Russia and Serbia* (Ph.D. diss., University of California, Berkeley, 1995).

homogenization, international isolation, and war made the destruction of alternatives easier by heightening and intensifying social divisions.

Finally, the story of the destruction of alternatives is neither a story of the regime inflaming national passions nor even of the group in power generating public support. Rather, it is a narrative of the production of habituation, resignation, and apathy. It is difficult to gauge more than tentatively the extent to which this process may be regarded as having succeeded. This extent is perhaps indicated by the sentiment of Stojan Cerović, the political commentator for the independent weekly magazine *Vreme*, as he discussed his ambivalent feelings toward both the regime and the opposition: "As far as I am concerned, I do not care much for any of the opposition parties, not even for all of them together. I have nothing against the regime, except that I consider it responsible for the war, the sanctions, for poverty, theft, crime, and the strangling of the free press. It does not seem to me that anybody in the opposition would be any better, only less effective, which is an advantage. It also seems to me that it is too late to hope for any great improvement in the quality of our lives, whoever may come to power."[8] To the degree that the regime succeeded in producing these feelings of defeat, exhaustion, and hopelessness among its potential opponents, its continuation in power was relatively more secure.

An Alternative Account of Serbian Nationalism: What Is Old and What Is New

To describe the process by which the destruction of alternatives and the production of resignation take place, we must ask what kind of regime Serbia has. Its regime has been variously defined by both supporters and opponents. From the side of the regime's supporters come claims to be continuing the legacy left by Josip Broz Tito and also to be pushing long-neglected Serbian national interests and to be developing a socialism for the twenty-first century. Along with these claims come denials that the regime fosters the monopoly of a single party and self-characterizations of the present minority government as a "national unity" government of "experts." Regime opponents have defined it in several different ways, from the association with the darkest periods of Communism indicated

8. Stojan Cerović, "Načelo žrtvovanja," *Vreme*, no. 222, 23 January 1995, p. 8.

by the slogan "Sloba-Stalin" to the association with other contemporary militarist dictatorships indicated by the slogan "Sloba-Saddam." The regime has also been defined in many other ways, from fascist and totalitarian to criminally run and an individual (or family) dictatorship.

The term I have chosen to describe the regime is *nationalist-authoritarian,* a term meant to be more precise than *nationalism* and more generalizable than the currently fashionable *post-Communism.*[9] *Nationalist authoritarianism* refers to a specific set of circumstances in which an authoritarian regime seeks to justify its continuation in power by means of nationalist rhetoric or to secure its future by appealing to nationalist movements. It especially describes the late Communist regimes of East-Central Europe and some of their successor states.

In most cases, these regimes are nominally ruled by either a former Communist party with a new name (as in Serbia) or by a vocally right-wing party whose leadership is largely taken from a former Communist party (as in Croatia and Slovakia). Although they share authoritarian legacies, the regimes are not totalitarian, neither in the sense that they wholly control both everyday and institutional life—an impossibility in any case—nor in the sense that they rely on a consistent and schematic ideological worldview. Rather, they make a show of such pluralistic institutions as they have while seeking to limit their functioning as far as possible. The myths they put forward in their own defense are neither advanced with confidence and conviction nor harmonious with one another.

These ideological and practical inconsistencies allow the regimes, however briefly, to rely on a shifting coalition of conformists, nominally left-wing supporters of the Communist regimes of the past, right-wing nationalists who were formerly opponents of those regimes, and even some liberals who may trust in promises of eventual reform or believe that the regime can be compromised from within. In this regard, they simultaneously represent a continuation of the old regime and a limited departure from it.

The Serbian regime embodies nationalist authoritarianism both in its inheritance from the Communist era and in the contemporary nationalist basis of its justifying rhetoric. The Communist side of its identity pro-

---

9. Neither of these is a category. *Nationalism* refers to a strategy of justification applied to a widely varying number of situations, whereas *post-Communism* does not describe any particular ideology, place, or period.

vides a comfort for the not inconsiderable number of Serbians who became accustomed to and felt at home with the relatively liberal Communist regime that governed Yugoslavia from 1945 on. Its nationalist side dispenses with those aspects of the old regime most hostile to the patriotism of the Serbian peasant spirit—not only the rhetoric of the equality of nations and people but also the urbanist and modernizing tendencies of Communism.[10]

Perhaps most important, the regime's strategies and structure of support have remained consistent even as it has shifted—repeatedly—from Communism to "modern European socialism" to nationalism and back again. Two conclusions follow from this: first, the base of support for the Milošević regime is not necessarily made up of people who are fond of Milošević or of people who agree with the ideological positions his party advocates.[11] Rather, it seems to be made up of those conformist social groups who simply like regimes. The same people supported the previous regime and will likely support the next one when it comes. Second, re-

10. Anti-Communist rhetoric consistently associated Communist regimes with backwardness and charged them with slowing down the processes of modernization in the countries where they were in power. Without intending to speculate on how Yugoslavia might have modernized had it been governed by a different regime from 1945 onward, I note several points about the modernizing influences of the regime it did have. The urban proportion of the population increased dramatically from 1945 onward. The proportion of the population principally occupied in agriculture decreased from 40.7 percent in 1947 to 21.8 percent in 1966; the proportion principally occupied in industry increased from 25.1 percent to 44.3 percent in the same period (Fred Singleton, *Twentieth-Century Yugoslavia* [New York: Columbia University Press, 1976], 246). The population of the city of Belgrade increased dramatically from 843,209 in 1961 to 1,470,073 in 1981 (Miloš Nemanjić, *Filmska i pozorišna publika Beograda: Socijalno-kulturni uslovi formiranja u periodu 1961–1984* [Belgrade: Zavod za proučavanje kulturnog razvitka, 1991], 275). Cultural and educational opportunities increased dramatically, especially for urban residents, as did the ability to travel after 1965. The federal structure of SFRJ encouraged wide communication between urban centers in Yugoslavia. Although the old Communist regime in Yugoslavia may not have been metropolitan in orientation, it favored cities and fostered the development of urban culture.

11. For that matter, descriptions of Milošević as a charismatic leader seem to be off the mark. He did generate a strong public personality in the period of his rise to power, but since consolidating his power he has rarely appeared in public and puts forward his opinions only in the most formalized settings such as prepared press releases. In this regard, he differs greatly from his Croatian counterpart Franjo Tuđman, who frequently speaks at length in public in an effort to establish himself not only as an important historical figure, but also as an academic historian in the grand manner.

gardless of the changes in ideology publicly promoted by the regime, the regime has basically not changed its character over time.

Nonetheless, there are some important differences between the "old" and "new" regimes. The Communist regime regarded peasant culture and its manifestations as backward, associating them with both the deposed Serbian monarchy drawn from the ranks of the peasantry and with the Partisans' wartime rivals in Serbia, the Četniks, whose support was largely drawn from the Serb peasantry in Serbia and in Bosnia-Hercegovina. The Communist ideology of progress was embodied in an alliance between centralized political power and the urban culture, which Tito's regime promoted. Whether or not urban intellectuals supported the Communist monopoly of power, an informal alliance operated, in which the Yugoslav state (in contrast to its Communist counterparts elsewhere in East-Central Europe) did not interfere with the cosmopolitan aspirations of intellectuals and professionals in the urban centers and in consideration for this tolerance, urban denizens offered evidence of the state's liberality and the society's prosperity to the outside world.

The cosmopolitans' own success, however, made maintaining the position they had gained under the Communist regime more precarious. Professionals and intellectuals moved en masse to the larger cities of Yugoslavia, where their isolation from the culture of the villages—and their rejection of it—became complete. If these urbanites did not make their way to other countries, seeking greater opportunity in Western Europe, the Americas, or Australia, their children often did.

Those who stayed behind came to dominate local political and cultural institutions. By the 1980s, the official institutions of the state had lost most of their credibility and appeal, particularly among the younger generation of urbanites. As one Belgrade native who attended Belgrade University during the 1980s described the situation to me, official organizations were regarded as dated, mediocre, and irrelevant by participants in the urban culture:

> The Party was scrounging for members. After years of thinking that Party membership was some kind of rare thing, I remember one meeting at the University for funding of student groups. At one point in the meeting this woman climbed up on a table and yelled, "Who wants to join the Party? Over here to join the Party!" Only the bad students joined the Party. The rest of us just weren't interested; we ignored them instead. Then you'd see the dumb students

who joined a few years later as the leaders of the official student association, writing for the official papers, holding political offices.

The joiners were also more likely to be from the provinces. As Teofil Pančić wrote in his homage to the city of Novi Sad, "[I]n Novi Sad there are no truly awful things, except the local government and the local television, and they aren't from Novi Sad anyway."[12] Although these institutions commanded little prestige in the urban culture, they did eventually attain some popularity among local cultural audiences, principally by articulating the national frustrations their members believed were held by the peasantry. The nationalist rhetoric that came to dominate politics in Serbia by the early 1990s was first voiced not by Slobodan Milošević, as is commonly assumed, but by the Serbian Writers' Union (*Udruženje književnika Srbije—UKS*) and the Serbian Academy of Sciences and Arts (*Srpska akademija nauka i umetnosti— SANU*). These bodies emerged as nationalist voices as a consequence of the weakness of the federal center, which encouraged local institutions to compete with one another on the basis of nationality. As long as no Yugoslav Academy of Sciences and Arts existed, the best position an intellectual who could not reach an international audience could hope for was one of authority in one of Yugoslavia's republics.

With the breakup of Yugoslavia into mutually hostile republics, some continuity was assured by the preservation of local structures of authority and their principally mediocre membership. The group making up the portion of the political and intellectual classes with access to institutions had access to them principally in individual republics, and the breaking of ties between the republics diminished neither the range of this group's authority nor the possibilities open to it. Similarly, although the official ideology rapidly changed from Communism to nationalism, the principle of conformity that defines both these ideologies did not change. Not only is it a small step from Communism's false collective of the popular to nationalism's false collective of the people, it is a step that many Serbian intellectuals had already made before the regime did.[13]

To the extent that the present regime in Serbia represents a departure

12. Teofil Pančić, "Novi Sad," *Vreme*, 16 October 1995, p. 66.
13. For a broader discussion of the easy transition made by elites into the war environment, see Mladen Lazić, "Društveni činioci raspada Jugoslavije," *Sociološki pregled* 28, no. 2 (1994), 155–66

from the previous regime, this departure has to do with the nature of the enemies with which it claims to be surrounded. Where "bourgeois" nationalisms had previously been regarded either as manifestations of the "class enemy" or as examples of the "backward thinking" of the peasantry, the new ideology divided nationalisms into categories—the nationalism of other former Yugoslav nations, which was revanchist, separatist, aggressive, and genocidal, and Serbian nationalism, which was not nationalistic at all but rather a defensive response to "Serbophobia" on the part of other nations, or in the totalized versions of the far-right nationalists, a reaction to the "global conspiracy against Serbia." With nation replacing class as the fundamental ideological principle, opponents of the regime became enemies of the nation.

National thinking in this radical view is narrower than Communist thinking was, admits fewer allies (even self-declared allies are subject to exclusion), and regards opponents as traitors. As its principle of exclusion is nationally based, it assumes "national consciousness" on the part of both its own nation and others and attempts to explain disagreements over political questions through the national key. Hence, it includes charges against domestic opposition political parties of collusion with competing former Yugoslav regimes, charges against independent media outlets of being financed and encouraged by foreign intelligence agencies and the Soros Foundation (rhetorically equated with foreign intelligence agencies), as well as the thesis (which I have heard more than once) that Bill Clinton's opposition to the Serbian regime's projects of conquest in Croatia and Bosnia-Hercegovina can be explained by the speculation that he had a German ancestor.[14]

As the "nation" became the legitimating principle of the regime, an ideological hostility to the urban centers emerged. Particularly identified as a target was the city of Belgrade, which had, as the federal Yugoslavia's capital, hosted many international visitors and residents and which had traditionally been home to people of a wide variety of ethnicities. It was not unique among cities in the region, which as trading and political centers had long been ethnically diverse while the surrounding rural areas

---

14. I must confess to not knowing whether Mr. Clinton has a German ancestor and also to not knowing what the effect would be of his having one or not. When I mentioned to a proponent of the German-ancestor thesis that Mr. Clinton was surnamed Blythe at birth, I received the answer, "You see?"

were more likely to be homogeneous.[15] The "solid peasant" from rural areas, especially from the "Serbian heartland" of Šumadija, came to define the ideal of national identity.[16] In contrast, a view of urban life and culture as unnatural and dishonest came to be promoted. This decidedly negative view of urban life and culture became a major part of the public expression of nationalist politicians.

Arno Mayer attributed such strong feelings of cultural alienation to the "simultaneity of the unsimultaneous,"[17] in which urban and cosmopolitan cultures uncomfortably shared geographic space with rural and traditional ones. Whether or not urban and rural residents belong to different historical periods, the feeling that they do is frequently articulated on both sides of this cultural divide. Sociological studies from a variety of environments[18] confirm the thesis that a wide gulf of values separates villages from cities.

The antiurban emotions of Serbian nationalists were most commonly directed toward Belgrade as the most cosmopolitan of Balkan cities. In addition to representing the essence of urban life for Serbian nationalists, Belgrade had several other roles: as the center of opposition to the war, as the city in which the ruling party always performed worst in elections, and as the place most open to metropolitan culture. As such, it became the target of severe attacks from nationalist ideologues like Dragoslav Bokan, commander of the right-wing paramilitary "White Eagles." In

15. Belgrade is, however, not unique in this regard. In the state currently known as Yugoslavia, the Montenegrin coast had also long been home to people from many nations, the Sandžak region had also been home to many Muslims, and of course Kosovo has long had a majority Albanian population. About the northern province (formerly autonomous) of Vojvodina, with a highly mixed population that before the end of World War II also included many ethnic Germans, I heard the following derogatory rhyme: *Banat, Srem, i Bačka, to je kao Nemačka* ("Banat, Srem, and Bačka, that is like Germany").

16. Marko Živković, "The Turkish Taint: Dealing with the Ottoman Legacy in Serbia" (paper presented at the conference of the American Anthropological Association, Washington, DC, 1995).

17. Arno Mayer, *Why Did the Heavens Not Darken? The "Final Solution" in History* (New York: Pantheon, 1988), 44.

18. See, for example, Claude Fischer, *The Urban Experience* (New York: Harcourt Brace Jovanovich, 1976), and Alex Inkeles and David H. Smith, *Becoming Modern: Individual Change in Six Developing Countries* (Cambridge, Mass.: Harvard University Press, 1974).

his dense verbal attack on Belgrade, Bokan combined images of foreign domination with an implicit attack on Communist "anationalism" and an invitation to consider the national consistency of another city: "Together we have to demonstrate that Belgrade is the Serbian Hong Kong. It doesn't belong to Serbhood, it betrayed Serbhood! That city should have been given the name Titograd, and not honorable Podgorica."[19] Both fans and detractors of Belgrade's cosmopolitan culture regularly warned me, "Belgrade is not Serbia." In the nationalist view, this amounted to the view that "Belgrade is Tito's whore. It sees itself as Yugoslav, cosmopolitan, democratic. The only thing it doesn't want to be is what it is: Serbian."[20]

The nationalist authoritarian regime of Slobodan Milošević thus represents both a continuation of and a departure from the old Communist regime. In its authoritarian use of false collectives as legitimating principles and in its reliance on structures of power dating to the old regime, it strongly resembles its Communist predecessor. Emblematic of this lack of transformation is the regime's continued use of laws and documents, including passports, from the old regime; its insistence on retaining the name of the defunct state of Yugoslavia and the right to succession from it; and the ruling party's retention of everything but the name of the old League of Communists. The principal distinction between the old regime and the new is cultural. Whereas Tito's Yugoslavia relied on the acquiescence, if not necessarily the support, of urban and intellectual elites, Milošević early understood that he could not expect their support and turned instead to rural Serbia and the areas around the "southern railway" (*južna pruga*). In turning to the peasantry and the "small towns" (*palanke*), the regime adopted in part many of the attitudes of these groups, particularly opposition to urban life, urban culture, and the supposed contamination and artificiality of cities. These attitudes form a vital part of the nationalist side of the regime's rhetoric.

The Obstinacy of the Communist Power Monopoly

The Communist power monopoly outlived Communism in Serbia as in the other successor states of the former Yugoslavia, maintaining its ma-

19. Quoted in Sreten Vujović, "Stereotipi o gradu, nacionalizam i rat," *Republika*, 1–15 April 1995, p. ix. The Montenegrin capital Podgorica was renamed Titograd in honor of Josip Broz Tito. The original name of Podgorica has since been restored.
20. The unidentified writer of these words is quoted by Vujović (1995).

chinery and its techniques of distribution long after its carriers abandoned Communist ideology. As a result, nationalist successors share a syndrome: Like their predecessors, they operate governments that are intentionally kept weak as sites of political decision, but that maintain the strong distributive and repressive machinery they inherited from their predecessors. In Serbia, an obvious example is the continued predominance of the police forces, now making up a larger personnel force and commanding a greater budget than the military, which was thoroughly demoralized after several purges of the officer corps and successive defeats in Slovenia, Croatia, and Bosnia-Hercegovina.

The police forces, however, represent only instruments of power—and as the experience of Romania shows eloquently, they are not always dependable instruments. More important in establishing the tenacity of one-party rule in Serbia is the system of power. Far from having achieved the "classless" society of Marx or even the "self-managed" society promoted in Edvard Kardelj's revisionism, Yugoslav Communism functioned effectively through cultivating the patronage of political and economic elites, who were often indistinguishable from one another. Mladen Lazić identified the functional elites of that system as the directors of state-owned corporations who had public capital and the distribution of benefits at their disposal.[21] In addition to these actors, distribution was also controlled by political elites in the system Lenard Cohen memorably described as "devolutionary socialism."[22] These elites may neither have controlled nor had many ideas—they did not need to—but they made their contributions to the preservation of the system by regulating, and in many cases abusing, access to apartments, jobs, vacation sites, and other such ground-level social benefits.

Other aspects of the Communist system of power are widely familiar to students of the politics and economics of the countries of what was once called "real socialism." They include monopolistic control over most goods and services, control of information through either direct ownership of or indirect control of the most important media, and political rule, either in law or in fact, by a single party. Ostensible changes in the regime have done little to alter these areas of control. Little privatiza-

21. Mladen Lazić, *Sistem i slom* (Belgrade: Filip Višnjić, 1994).

22. Lenard Cohen, *Devolutionary Socialism: The Political Institutionalization of the Yugoslav Assembly System, 1963–1973* (Ph.D. diss., Columbia University, 1978), and Lenard Cohen, *The Socialist Pyramid: Elites and Power in Yugoslavia* (Oakville, Ontario: Mosaic Press, 1989).

tion has taken place in Serbia, and where it has, as in Croatia, it has worked principally to the benefit of existing "socialist managers" who became owners, or to members of the ruling party. Because "socialist managers" functioned more or less as owners before, little change can be attributed to such transfers.[23] With regard to the media, the establishment of independent outlets of information has been limited principally to Belgrade and other large cities. The only media available throughout the country, however, continue to be regime controlled.[24] In the field of politics, the introduction of a "plural" political system has had no effect on the ruling party's complete monopoly of executive and judicial positions or on its effective control of the parliament.

Why have these elements of the system of power survived ideological shifts that in any other political system would be considered severe? The current Serbian regime's oscillation between Communism, socialism, nationalism, and reform is hardly unfamiliar to people who recall Tito's swings between Stalinism, "nonparty pluralism," centralism, federalism, and nonalignment. A single structural current runs through all these rhetorical variants: authoritarianism.

As long as authoritarian structures remain untouched, the content of the rhetoric by which they are justified has only temporary importance. This rhetoric has changed so many times in the past few years in Serbia that many observers describe their attempts at following the regime's ideology as producing "dizziness" (*vrtoglavica*). Across all these changes, the one demand that remains consistent is for uniformity at any given moment—as opposed to agreement about anything in particular.[25]

The radical contingency of ideology was generally interpreted by people with whom I spoke as producing apathy and passivity through confusion, but it has another dimension as well. A counterculture activist from Slovenia explained to me why he decided to join the Party, which was for

23. The close relation between political and economic power has not altered much either. In the current government, the post of prime minister is held by the president of Progres, the country's largest import-export firm; the chair of the republican parliament is also head of Jugopetrol, the largest petroleum-products firm; and the coordinating minister in the cabinet is president of Simpo, the largest furniture concern.

24. The situation of information media in Serbia is discussed in detail in Chapter 4.

25. In this regard, the cynical comment of one woman in Belgrade is illustrative: "I love to watch the news on the First Program [of the RTS network]. It's my instructions on what to think for the next day."

the most part hostile to countercultural activity: "These people seemed so strong ideologically, but in fact they thought nothing at all. They were mortally afraid of any kind of difference of opinion. So when they would try to close a punk rock club, I could come into the meeting and tell them, 'You're not Marxist. You are anti-youth chauvinists.' And sometimes I could get them to go along, they were so terrified of dissent." This possibility of openness was not always present, however, and was certainly less available in Serbia than in late-1980s Slovenia, where the youth section of the Communist Party functioned as a center for alternative perspectives (and more important, alternative publications). Although some marginal political players may derive some benefit from holding their perspectives in reserve for potential future use by the regime, this hardly benefits a large portion of the population. At best, it provides the regime with a dependable supply of permutations on the one theme that matters, which is its own continuation in power.

By rotating its cast of ideological surrogates through the musical chairs of power, the regime protects itself from its own positions and actions. Rarely speaking or otherwise appearing in public, Slobodan Milošević can rightly claim that he never advocated nationalist or any other positions. In fact, every major political move of his regime has been announced, defended, and removed from the agenda by surrogates. To the extent that Milošević appears at all on the daily television news, it is nearly always in the same manner: a still photograph of the president sitting on the same sofa in the same position, receiving visitors and delegations that vary from day to day.[26] On occasion, he may emerge to perform a ceremonial duty, such as laying a wreath, although this work too is often performed by surrogates, particularly the strangely featureless federal president.[27] Once, he changed into exercise clothing for a photograph with his wife for the local magazine *Žena*, and once into a domesticity-suggesting sweater for some photographs with his wife for the American magazine *Vanity Fair*.

Otherwise, all the crucial ideological, political, and military work of the regime is performed by surrogates. These surrogates are dispensable, and a round of discrediting articles in regime newspapers suggests the

26. Turned sideways toward the guest, elbow on his knee, chin forward.
27. At the time of research, Slobodan Milošević was the president of Serbia and not of the Federal Republic of Yugoslavia, a post held by Zoran Lilić. Milošević installed himself as federal president in 1997, over considerable protest from Montenegro.

impending arrival of their expiration dates. Chronologically, these surrogates include, in the period of Milošević's rise to power, Miroslav Šolević of the Serbian Resistance Movement in Kosovo, nationalist novelist Dobrica Ćosić, federal president Borisav Jović, and generals Veljko Kadijević and Blagoje Adžić; in the period of war and hard-line nationalism, Croatian Serb military leaders Milan Babić and Milan Martić, respectively, Bosnian Serb leader Radovan Karadžić, "private" militia leaders Vojislav Šešelj and Zeljko Ražnatović-Arkan, respectively, and colorful American businessman Milan Panić; and in the period in which "peace has no alternative," National Bank governor Dragoslav Avramović and neocommunist leaders Ljubiša Ristić and Mirjana Marković, who is also Milošević's wife. All those listed here have been dispensed with by the time of writing, except for Arkan, Ristić, and Ms. Marković.[28]

"Enemies" may be considered as a subcategory of surrogates in developing innovative new rhetorics with which to defend the regime. Croatia's Franjo Tuđman is certainly the prime example, as the heavy-handed national rhetoric of Milošević's regime assured his political future by convincing a plurality of Croatians that compromises were not possible in the Communist system. Tuđman has returned the favor several times by giving crucial assistance to Milošević's election in 1990 with his heavy-handed methods, by justifying the Serbian claim of parity of destruction in Bosnia with his intervention in 1993 and 1994, and by demolishing the Krajina parastate that had become a thorn in the Serbian regime's side in 1995. Although the two figures are presented as opposing each other, the symbiosis of their relationship is clear: They helped create each other's political movements and justified each other's methods.

In broad outline, this is the basic structure of the nationalist-authoritarian system: its organization, its ideological eclecticism, and its internally inconsistent combination of bases of support. At question is how this regime maintains itself in power. So far, the combination of mobilized

---

28. Although it may seem to the casual observer that Milošević would not regard his wife as a dispensable political surrogate, there has been much speculation as to potential political differences between the two, à la Juan and Eva Perón. These speculations have been encouraged in no small measure by the cryptic biweekly magazine column Mirjana Marković writes for *Duga*. Her diary-like entries are subject to hermeneutic interpretation by observers of politics, who believe that Marković uses the column to announce changes in policy before they are officially announced and to reveal allegorical criticisms of her husband's regime.

ethnic hatred and the immobilized conservatism of a portion of the population has apparently been sufficient. However, this combination is inherently unstable; passion and passivity can keep a regime going for some time, but not as long as better alternatives are accessible.

In contemporary Serbia, better alternatives have long been available and continue to be. The regime, always short on legitimacy, has recently been in a weaker position than ever after several years of uninterrupted military, political, economic, and international failure. Since the signing of peace accords in the winter of 1995, it no longer has a war with which to justify its continuation. If patterns of politics had the rigidity of laws of physics, the regime would have fallen long ago.

In the following chapters, I argue that the regime has so far had limited success in prolonging its existence by attempting to destroy, silence, or cut off the expression of alternatives. The analysis looks specifically at four fields of everyday life—politics, popular culture, public information, and sociability—in which this has occurred and at the possibilities that the regime may fail in the future in carrying out its means of control.

2

The Destruction of
Political Alternatives

Vuk Drašković, the leader of the opposition party SPO, tells a story of traveling in rural Serbia during an election campaign. He explained to a peasant why Milošević and SPS are dangerous for Serbia. The peasant nodded his head. "So I can count on your vote?" Drašković asked. "No." "But you agreed with me about everything?" "Yes, I did," the peasant answered, "and when you are in power, I will vote for you."[1]

The continued power of Slobodan Milošević's regime should surprise political observers: The ruling party does not enjoy majority support, has no record of successes to which it can point, and has never successfully addressed the problem of legitimacy from which governments in the former Yugoslavia have suffered since the death of Josip Broz Tito. These flaws would be fatal to any government in a normally functioning parliamentary system. The Serbian regime has survived by systematically destroying the crucial elements of a normal parliamentary system— autonomous and viable alternative centers of power—while ostensibly

1. The story is retold by Mark Thompson, *Proizvodnja rata: Mediji u Srbiji, Hrvatskoj i Bosni i Hercegovini*, trans. Vesna Vukelić (Belgrade: Član 19/ Medija centar Radio B-92, 1995), 127 n. 162. The peasant may have to make good on the promise: SPO abandoned opposition politics in 1999, and Drašković was appointed deputy premier of the federal government.

Fig. 1. The Milošević family at the inauguration of Slobodan Milošević as president of SRJ in 1997. Left to right: Marija Milošević, Mirjana Marković, Marko Milošević, and Slobodan Milošević. Photo courtesy of Petar Vujanić.

maintaining, and even claiming the credit for introducing, the formal aspects of a plural political system. Deprived of alternatives, people opposed to the regime are condemned to political resignation and escape into private life, while the lack of enthusiasm of regime supporters hardly matters. In elections since 1990, the motions of the political ritual have been carried out, for the most part without demonstrable conviction or consequence. (See Figs. 1 and 2.)

It has become commonplace to observe that of all the republics of the former Yugoslavia, Serbia has changed least following the destruction of

Fig. 2. The leaders of the parties in the *Zajedno* coalition pause for a discussion during the student and citizen protests, December 1996. Left to right: Vuk Drašković (Serbian Renewal Movement), Zoran Đinđić (Democratic Party), and Vesna Pešić (Civic Alliance of Serbia). Photo courtesy of Draško Gagović.

the old regime. In this chapter, I shall address the question of why, despite cathartic events—the breakup of the Yugoslav federation, war, and the ostensible introduction of a multiparty electoral system—Serbia has indeed changed so little. As noted in Chapter 1, much of the obstinacy of the Communist power monopoly can be attributed to inertia, habit, and conservatism on the part of a large portion of the population. These elements may be thought of as necessary but not sufficient to explain the longevity of the regime. In addition to the "mobilized passivity" of these elements, there was active effort on the part of the regime to manipulate the electoral system for its own benefit, to discredit political opponents by means of its monopoly over the most important media sources, and to co-opt elements of the right-wing nationalist opposition to its own program.

In addition to these political strategies, the regime indulged in the continuation of politics by other means.

The liberal opposition in Serbia has generally accepted the thesis that war was permitted to happen because if it had not, democratic reforms might have happened.[2] In addition to the lives and monuments it destroyed, the war constituted a vital part of the destruction of alternatives. Inertia alone would not have been powerful enough to help the regime survive the collapse of Communism without war. The war provided the regime with the following possibilities: the ability to categorically disqualify political opponents as treasonous, unpatriotic, and fomenting division when unity is needed; a pretext for severing communication between antiwar and antiregime forces in different republics; dramatic demographic changes, especially the massive exodus of the young and urban populations, enhancing the domination of the more conservative rural and older populations; and a massive shift in economic power from the cities to the rural areas, accompanying the collapse of the industrial and trade economy.

Throughout the "transition" from Communist to nationalist authoritarianism and the wars that followed, there has been considerable opposition both to the regime's monopoly of political power and information and to its use of national rhetoric to justify aggressive and destructive projects in Croatia and Bosnia-Hercegovina. At some points, this opposition has been impressively strong, particularly immediately before the beginning of the war in Croatia. The student protests of 9 March 1991 and the following days mark a turning point, representing both the largest manifestation of democratic sentiment in Belgrade and the moment of its apparently terminal defeat. Milošević entered that March with only a fraudulently obtained parliamentary majority, but emerged with his rule in Serbia consolidated, the military thoroughly compromised with his regime, and a lasting rhetoric that would identify his political opponents as treasonous and destructive. For the preservation of his regime, it was a small and necessary step to finally engage in war, for which the state-run media had been assiduously preparing the ground.

Nationalism: The Search for Credibility

Although the constitution of SRJ defines the system of government as parliamentary, the existence of competing political parties and a parlia-

---

2. See, for example, Nebojša Popov, "Cvet i mraz," *Republika*, no. 112, 16–31 March 1995, p. 1.

ment disguises the monopoly of power, and of administrative positions, by a single party—Milošević's *Socijalistička partija Srbije* (SPS). Indisputably the dominant political party in Serbia, having inherited the property and membership of the formally defunct League of Communists of Serbia (*Savez komunista Srbije*), SPS maintains a complete monopoly over executive positions and control over a majority of the seats in parliament, despite never having won a majority of votes in an election in Serbia.

Popular explanations of the origins of the war in the former Yugoslavia describe Slobodan Milošević as having risen to power on a wave of nationalist euphoria. In fact, he became euphorically nationalist (and inconsistently so) only after acceding to power, and although he did eventually generate significant popularity among several social groups, his rise to power was untainted by popular participation. Milošević gained power over the Serbian party in an intraparty coup involving neither elections nor the political participation of any people outside the leadership of the Serbian Communist party, in December 1987.[3] He acceded to the position of president two years later, again without the benefit of popular election.[4] Popular elections did not occur to ratify his holding that position until December 1990. His party, by then already renamed the Socialist Party of Serbia,[5] failed to receive a majority of votes in that first election and received progressively fewer votes in each subsequent elec-

3. The process and organization of this party coup are described by several sources, perhaps most interestingly by an involved eyewitness, Ivan Stambolić, *Put u bespuće* (Belgrade: Radio B-92, 1995). Stambolić preceded Milošević as president, promoted Milošević to positions of power, and was finally deposed by him. For a description of the balance of political forces in Serbia in the 1980s and the strategies that brought Milošević to power, see Vujačić (1995).

4. A fraudulent election was held, with results reporting an astounding turnout of 104 percent.

5. The Serbian Communist Party (*Savez komunista Srbije—SKS*) has two successors claiming continuity with the old regime. These are the SPS, "founded" in July 1990 and headed by Milošević, and the League of Communists—Movement for Yugoslavia (*Savez komunista-Pokret za Jugoslaviju—SK-PJ*), formed as the "generals' party" in 1990 and headed by Milošević's wife, Mirjana Marković. In 1995, the coalition party United Yugoslav Left (*Jugoslovenska udružena levica—JUL*) was formed, with Marković's SK-PJ as the dominant member. JUL is distinguished by its closeness to the ruling party (sharing in many cases individual members), its access to state-run media, and its access to government positions despite having no parliamentary seats and in fact never having participated in an election. Of the parties that make up JUL, all received far fewer than the minimum number of votes required for parliamentary representation in the elections of December 1993.

tion, despite having several crucial advantages characteristic of single-party systems.

Although most narratives of Milošević's taking and maintaining power in the period leading up to the 1990 elections emphasize the use of the worsening position of Serbs and Montenegrins in Kosovo, and later the tensions between the Serbian party leadership and the party leaderships of Slovenia and Croatia, to associate the ruling party with the national sentiments of people in Serbia, the story develops in a more complex manner. Milošević succeeded a series of nonentities as president of Serbia, being the first among them, as even opponents of his rule admit, to "speak clearly."[6] Offering his support *both* to the nationalist Serbian Resistance Movement (*Srpski pokret otpora*) in its increasingly popular demonstrations against the Kosovo provincial government *and* to the old guard of the Communist party and the military, which feared the consequences of economic and political reform, Milošević formed an insecure coalition of opposites. During this earlier period, although he had already developed the populist "plebiscite-by-rally" strategy that marked his early period of popularity,[7] his rhetoric remained in the Yugoslav Communist tradition of calls to "brotherhood and unity" among people and formal opposition to nationalism.[8]

6. Every account I have seen of Milošević's rise to power cites his response to the police riot against Serb protesters at Kosovo Polje in 1987, in which he pronounced his well-known phrase, "[F]rom now on, nobody has the right to beat you!" Whereas for some this moment encapsulates his adoption of the rhetoric of nationalist movements, for others it represents the populist techniques he exploited with dramatic effect in his years of ascent. All these analyses seem to miss one crucial point: This was one of the first instances in which a leading politician had spoken in public and offered an idea that everybody could understand and who went so far as to encapsulate the message in a single comprehensible sentence. After years of progressively more incomprehensible and dense babble purporting to explain Yugoslavia's unnervingly opaque system of "workers' self-management," such an event was beyond memory for people who opposed Milošević as well as those who supported him.

7. Vujačić (1995) describes in detail the crucial meetings that defined Milošević's political ascent. Ivan Čolović, *Bordel ratnika* (Belgrade: XX Vek, 1994a), offers an analysis of the slogans and other folkloric forms that developed as a part of the populist element of this ascent. Nebojša Popov, *Srpski populizam: Od marginalne do dominantne pojave* (*Vreme*, special supplement to no. 135, 24 May 1993), places Milošević's "plebiscitarianism" in a tradition of populist-national movements in Serbia.

8. See the collection of Milošević's speeches during this period published as *Godine raspleta* (Belgrade: BIGZ, 1989). Čolović (1994a), 30, offers one indication of the sense

Growing tensions between the republics of SFRJ, together with an increased public presence of nationalist intellectuals in a "neutral" alliance with Milošević, led the ruling party to take on an increasingly nationalist cast in both rhetoric and practice. By 1989, Milošević had moved from his rhetoric of equality of people in Kosovo to taking over the government of that autonomous province, as well as the autonomous province of Vojvodina (the takeover of the republican government of Montenegro had already been arranged in January). In response to the opposition to his politics on the part of the Slovenian leadership,[9] Serbia declared a boycott of Slovenian manufactured goods. When multiparty elections brought to Slovenia a government interested in weakening or dissolving the Yugoslav federation and later an aggressively nationalist government to Croatia and a weak coalition of nationalist parties to Bosnia and Hercegovina, Milošević capitalized on the fears of Serbs in the other republics to build an image as their protector—the defender of national interests.[10]

It is important to consider, among the crucial determinants of this move to nationalism in the rhetoric of the ruling party, both the precipitous decline in popularity and credibility of the moribund Communist party and Milošević's consequently increasing reliance on the ideas of nationalist intellectuals who formed the other major portion of his coalition. Desperate to avoid or at least to weaken potential political reform that would threaten the Communists' long-standing monopoly of power, Milošević appropriated positions from the most vocal nonparty public actors: the "nationally conscious" intelligentsia centered around the Serbian Academy of Sciences and Arts (*Srpska akademija nauka i umetnosti—SANU*) and the Union of Serbian Writers (*Udruženje književnika*

in which Milošević presented his politics as a continuation of Tito's in his analysis of the slogans at Milošević's meetings, such as "The entire nation wonders/ when will Slobodan replace Tito" (*Sav se narod, sav se narod uveliko pita / Slobodan će, Slobodan će zamjeniti Tita*).

9. Lenard Cohen, *Broken Bonds: Yugoslavia's Disintegration and Balkan Politics in Transition* (San Francisco: Westview Press, 1995), specifies the many political differences, the extremes of which were represented by the positions of the Serbian and Slovenian leaderships, respectively. Joseph Bombelles offers a view into one of the more important financial aspects of the conflict in "Federal Aid to the Less Developed Areas of Yugoslavia," *East European Politics and Societies* 5 (Fall 1991), 439–65.

10. The borders of the constituent republics of SFRJ were not drawn on the basis of ethnicity, and all republics except Slovenia had ethnically mixed populations.

Srbije—UKS).[11] Zoran Slavujević described this "transitional" period as follows:

> From the point of view of the constitution of the opposition the last years of the single-party system can be divided into two short successive periods. The first could be called the period of "diffuse pluralism," when various cultural institutions, organizations, committees, *ad hoc* groups, and so on appear as the articulators of alternative political positions, and which lasts until the beginning of 1990. The second could be called the period of "wild pluralism," from the founding of the first opposition parties to the legalization of the multiparty system and the registration of the first opposition parties, from the beginning to the middle of 1990. During this entire period, the opposition appears insufficiently organized, with only roughly defined ideological and programmatically heterogeneous positions. SKS takes advantage of this, as the only organized political power, to *appropriate several oppositional political proposals* and to impose itself as the *leader of a broad national movement*.[12]

From this point on, the political scene in Serbia begins to take on the characteristics that define it until the beginning of war in 1991: a regime associating itself with nationalist sentiments with increasing intensity and enjoying an aggressive monopoly of both political power and the most important media sources, which survives the shift to "pluralism."

Milošević's populist mobilization of national sentiment, both in Serbia and among the Serbian populations of Croatia and Bosnia and Hercegovina, has been well documented in existing research.[13] During the same period, the ongoing political and economic crises in Yugoslavia, marked by hyperinflation and the increasingly evident paralysis of the federal government, gave increased impetus to demands for reform or replacement of the Communist system in all parts of the country.[14] Ante Mar-

---

11. See Vujačić (1995), for an account of the political activity originating in these two institutions.

12. Slavujević, in Vladimir Goati, Zoran Slavujević, and Ognjen Pribićević, *Izborne borbe u Jugoslaviji, 1990–1992* (Belgrade: Radnička štampa, 1993), 73.

13. See especially Vujačić (1995), Cohen (1995), and Sabrina Ramet, *Nationalism and Federalism in Yugoslavia, 1962–1991* (Bloomington: Indiana University Press, 1992).

14. Especially evident since the death of Josip Broz Tito in 1980 was the paralysis of the federal presidency, made of a rotating titular "President of the Presidency" and

ković, who became Yugoslavia's last federal prime minister, attempted to reconcile the republican governments and began to promise privatization and the introduction of political pluralism. Although the brief period of prosperity that Marković's economic reforms brought about made him personally popular, he was undermined both by hard-line Communists and later by the elected governments of all Yugoslavia's republics.

Demands for an end to the Communist monopoly of power became irresistible in the course of two events. First, in the fall and winter of 1989, Communist dictatorships fell from power throughout East-Central Europe. In some instances, these were nonviolent "velvet" revolutions as in Czechoslovakia, but some were more dramatic and violent, like the abrupt end of the Ceauşescu regime in neighboring Romania. Second, the political conflict between Yugoslavia's two political poles, Serbia and Slovenia, came to a head in January 1990, when the extraordinary Fourteenth Congress of the League of Communists of Yugoslavia (*Savez komunista Jugoslavije—SKJ*) ended with the Slovenian delegates leaving the congress and the party. The independent daily newspaper *Borba* reported the event under a dramatic headline: "The SKJ no longer exists."[15]

The first multiparty elections in Yugoslavia occurred in Slovenia in April 1990. The center-right coalition DEMOS won a convincing majority, gaining 55 percent of the vote and forty-seven out of eighty seats in the new parliament. The Communist president of Slovenia, Milan Kučan, was confirmed in the position of leader of the renamed League of Communists of Slovenia—Party of Democratic Reform (ZKS-SDR). Whereas Kučan spoke moderately of a looser confederation of the republics of Yugoslavia and of "Slovenia's right to self-determination in a non-disruptive manner,"[16] his rivals in DEMOS more openly claimed that "Yugoslavia as a concept is exhausted."[17]

---

eight representatives from each of the six republics and two autonomous provinces of Yugoslavia. Ramet (1992) chronicles the shifting coalitions in voting in the presidency on several important questions. With Milošević's takeover of the autonomous provinces of Kosovo and Vojvodina in 1989, the presidency was evenly split into two blocs: one (Serbia, Montenegro, Kosovo, and Vojvodina) controlled by Milošević and another (Slovenia, Croatia, Macedonia, and Bosnia and Hercegovina) generally opposed to Milošević. With this balance of forces, neither bloc was consistently able to garner a majority of votes, but both were able to consistently block the initiatives of the other.

15. Ivan Mrđen, "Osvetoljubivost uvređenih," *Dosije Borba* (special edition), 22 November 1994.

16. Quoted in Cohen (1995), 94.

17. Quoted in Cohen (1995), 90.

Closely following on the elections in Slovenia, elections were held in Croatia in two rounds in April and May 1990. These ended in victory for the right-wing nationalist Croatian Democratic Union (*Hrvatska demokratska zajednica—HDZ*), which was heavily financed by Croatian émigrés living outside the country. HDZ's leader, who became president of Croatia, was the controversial former general and historian Franjo Tuđman. Although widely regarded as a prominent dissident in Croatia, especially among émigrés whose support he had been cultivating for a decade,[18] his nationalist views made him generally feared among Croatia's Serbian minority.[19] He did not increase confidence among the Serbian minority during his campaign, in which he sought to rehabilitate the image of Croatia's wartime fascist regime, openly discussed territorial claims to Bosnia and Hercegovina, and argued that Serbs were over-represented in political, law enforcement, and media institutions.[20] HDZ won a bare plurality in the elections, gaining 41.8 percent of the vote in the first round and 42.2 percent in the second—closely followed by the "re-formed, renamed" Communist party (*Savez komunista Hrvatske-Stranka demokratskih promjena—SKH-SDP*) with 34.5 percent in the first round and 37.3 percent in the second. However, this plurality translated into fifty-four of the eighty seats in parliament, or 67.5 percent of parliamentary seats, for HDZ.

Elections held in Bosnia and Hercegovina in November and Decem-

18. See his promotional pamphlet *Croatia on Trial: The Case of Croatian Historian Dr. F. Tuđman* (Amersham, England: United Publishers, 1981).

19. Tuđman argued in his two major publications, *Bespuća povijesne zbiljnosti* (Zagreb: Matica Hrvatska, 1989), and *Nationalism in Contemporary Europe* (New York: Columbia University Press, 1981), that the figures commonly given for the number of victims of the Holocaust in World War II are grossly overstated in a campaign to smear the nations implicated. Most famously, he sought to minimize the number of Serbs, Jews, and Gypsies murdered by Croatia's *Ustaša* regime between 1941 and 1945, but he went on to claim that figures of Holocaust victims are grossly overstated generally. Although HDZ has largely succeeded in presenting itself to international observers as "liberalizing" and "pro-Western," especially in the period immediately leading up to the war in Croatia, the situation is quite different. It is worth taking into account Jim Seroka's observation: "It has taken a long time for Western publics, particularly in North America, to appreciate the differences between anti-communism and democratic pluralism, and even more, the inherent similarities between authoritarianism of the Left and authoritarianism of the Right." In Jim Seroka and Vukašin Pavlović, eds., *The Tragedy of Yugoslavia: The Failure of Democratic Transformation* (New York: M. E. Sharpe, 1992), 68.

20. See Cohen (1995), 97, and Vujačić (1995), 411–12.

ber 1990 ended with a fragile coalition of three nationalist parties, which later came to be known as "warring factions": the Serbian Democratic Party (*Srpska demokratska stranka—SDS*), the Bosnian affiliate of HDZ, and the Muslim Party of Democratic Action (*Stranka demokratske akcije— SDA*). In Macedonia, elections were also held in November and December, with no party winning a majority of seats.

In his efforts to cement his new nationalist coalition, Milošević could not have wished for better assistance than he received from Tuđman's victory in Croatia. In addition, with two major republican power centers in Croatia and Slovenia advocating a severe weakening or dissolution of the Yugoslav federation and federal prime minister Marković advocating pluralism, the military and Communist portions of Milošević's coalition had nowhere else to turn but to him. The apprehensions of people in Serbia probably made Milošević genuinely popular during this time. The regime massively engaged the media under its control to encourage fears, to develop and to revive memories of atrocities committed by the Independent State of Croatia (*Nezavisna država Hrvatska—NDH*) during the Second World War, and to associate HDZ with the puppet regime of that period. A similar media campaign in Croatia assured that national passions were fired on both sides and that tension between Serbia and Croatia rapidly developed to a dangerous level. As Zoran Slavujević described the period:

As one nationalism feeds another, so one set of nationalist propaganda offers content, "arguments," criteria of value for reality and events and so on to another, hurtling into an ascending spiral of mutual hatred. On this basis it was possible to begin a "propaganda war," which, in the space it covered, variety of shape and content, length of time it lasted, volume and intensity, in its engagement in (*preplitanje*) international and domestic politics, and especially in its effects, represents *the largest propaganda campaign in the country in the last decades.*[21]

The "public enemies" in this propaganda campaign included not only the nationalist governments elected in other republics (especially Slovenia and Croatia), but also Prime Minister Marković's reformist federal

21. Slavujević (1993), 105.

government, which was accused of weakening the Yugoslav federation and acting in the interest of the other republics.[22]

Even after elections had been held in Slovenia and Croatia, it was not certain that there would be multiparty elections in Serbia and Montenegro. The ruling SKS publicly accepted the formation of a multiparty system only in November 1989, with the somewhat equivocal statement at its Eleventh Congress that "the SK of Serbia has neither reason nor desire to administratively impede the formation of political parties."[23] Although opposition parties began appearing in early 1990, the law legitimizing multiparty elections was not passed until July of that year. In September, an election law regulating the selection of parliamentary deputies was passed, as was a new constitution for Serbia,[24] by the single-party parliament. After several conflicts with opposition parties over the election law, the law was changed only two weeks before the election. At the same time, confusion remained as to whether opposition parties would participate in the elections—in the course of a single week in November, opposition parties declared an election boycott, began an antielection campaign designed to discourage people from voting, and abandoned the campaign in consideration of the final changes in the election law.[25] The disorganization and confusion of the opposition probably contributed to its poor showing in the elections.

22. If the Croatian and Serbian regimes agreed on one substantive point during this period, it was on opposition to the federal government and to Ante Marković personally. Although Marković's advocacy of privatization and political pluralism placed him in opposition to the Serbian regime, local propaganda presented his Croatian nationality as evidence of "whom he was really working for." In Croatia, as the only representative of Yugoslavia with any legitimacy or popularity, he represented an obstacle to separation from the country and was presented as a tool of "Greater Serbia." Marković eventually organized a political party, but too late to compete in the Croatian or Slovenian elections. In Bosnia and Hercegovina and Serbia, the party received considerably less support than expected.

23. In *Komunist*, 22 November 1989. Quoted in Goati, "Višepartijski mozaik Srbije," in Miroslav Pečuljić, Vladimir Milić, Vladimir Goati, Srbobran Branković, and Miladin Kovačević, *Rađanje javnog mnjenja i političkih stranaka* (Belgrade: Centar za javno mnjenje i marketing "Medium," 1992), 160.

24. In Serbia, it is widely argued that Slovenia provided the first impulse for the dissolution of Yugoslavia in its declaration, in July 1990, that in the event of a conflict between federal law and the law of the Republic of Slovenia, republican law takes precedence. It bears noting that the Serbian constitution declared two months later contains a similar provision.

25. For a more detailed discussion, see Slavujević (1993), 84–85.

Also significant was the use of state-controlled media in the pre-election period. Milošević's Socialist Party of Serbia,[26] as the party in power, used its control over most important media sources to present itself as moderate, experienced, and in tune with the aspirations of the Serbian people—under the slogan "with us, there is no uncertainty" (s nama nema neizvesnosti). Opposition parties were presented as disorganized, corrupt, fighting among themselves, and opposed to the national interest. In the state television's report of the first meeting of opposition parties on 13 June 1990, which was attended by around 50,000 people and ended with police intervention, the following commentary was offered to viewers:

> The meeting passed, and from its size and the response of the people there remained only great words. So it happened that on Republic Square, in the middle of the day, in public, it was shown that the united Serbian opposition has no legitimacy among the Serbian people. Not even the throwing of mud at the government or the flood of primitive anticommunism helped. The united Serbian opposition showed clearly that in the name of the struggle for power it would sacrifice both true democracy and the constitutional unity of Serbia, and even its territorial integrity. In their blindness and desire to come to power by any means, they would sacrifice Kosovo as well. So the moral of today's meeting in Belgrade is that not one party in Serbia, no matter how it dresses up its supposedly democratic wings, and hence neglects the vital national interest of its own state, can receive the support of the Serbian people.[27]

Zoran Slavujević offered an example of the tone of political coverage on the state television, in which a leading member of an opposition party appeared, "directing severe criticisms toward [his own party] and finally, apologizing to the Serbian people!"[28]

Finally, highly charged nationalist rhetoric on the part of an important member of the opposition undoubtedly improved Milošević's position in

26. The party acquired its new name on 16 July 1990.

27. Quoted in Lazar Lalić, Tri TV godine u Srbiji (Belgrade: Nezavisni sindikat medija, 1995), 11–12. According to research conducted in 1992, over 60 percent of the population of Serbia watches the principal news program on the state television, "TV Dnevnik II"; 2 percent reads newspapers. Cited in Miklòs Biro, Psihologija postkomunizma (Belgrade: Beogradski krug, 1994), 84.

28. Slavujević (1993), 100.

the elections. The largest party to emerge as opposition to SPS was Vuk Drašković's Serbian Renewal Movement (*Srpski pokret obnove—SPO*). The novelist Drašković[29] cut a Dostoevskian figure with his long hair and full beard, and although he later became an opponent of the war and an advocate of political liberalism,[30] at the time his party advocated extreme national positions—including the "unity of all Serbian lands" and several specific territorial claims against Croatia.[31] Milošević's party benefited tremendously from SPO's extremism in 1990 and gained the ability to dismiss pro-European liberal parties as subject to "foreign elements," appeal to nationalist sentiment, and appear to be moderate at the same time.[32]

March: From the First Elections to the First War

Serbia's first multiparty elections occurred in an environment of uncertainty and instability. It was by no means clear that the elections would

29. For a discussion of Drašković's major novel *Nož* (*The Knife*), see Vujačić (1995), chap. 4.

30. The Civic Alliance of Serbia (*Građanski savez Srbije—GSS*) can also lay claim to the title of having been consistently liberal and antiwar, but it has been and remains a very small party, made up principally of Belgrade intellectuals and unlikely to gain much popular support. The only party to use the word "liberal" in its name was the right-wing Serbian Liberal Party (*Srpska liberalna stranka—SLS*), led by Nikola Milošević and Kosta Čavoški. The Democratic Party (DS) itself did not take a clear position on "national" questions in the beginning, claiming that it was more interested in economic reforms and that the questions involved are "questions of democracy" (Goati, 1992). After several internal conflicts in which more nationalistic wings of the party split off, the DS finally opted in favor of full support for the nationalist militias in Bosnia-Hercegovina and Croatia. Its first president, Dragoljub Mićunović, was replaced by Zoran Đinđić, who later ejected Mićunović from the party.

31. See Goati (1992), 168. When armed conflict in Kosovo began in 1998, Draškovič revived the nationalist cast he had abandoned after the beginning of the war in Bosnia-Hercegovina.

32. So, for example, an ethnic Serbian party in Croatia was able to organize a "referendum" on the autonomy of portions of Croatia on 19 August 1990 with the full and vocal support of Milošević (see the text of his letter reproduced in Lalić, 1995, 15)—assuring his association with the separatist movement well in advance of the beginning of electoral efforts on the part of other parties. Milošević received support and endorsements from such outside actors as Radovan Karadžić, president of Bosnia and Hercegovina's SDS, who charged Drašković with causing SDS to lose votes in the Bosnian election (Lalić, 1995, 28).

be carried out honestly or that their results would be respected by the ruling party. At the same time, the various opposition parties, in their disorganization and disunity, had not dispelled uncertainty about whether they would participate in or boycott the elections. With the elections scheduled for December, by November there was still active debate as to whether opposition parties should accept an election carried out under a law on which they had not been consulted and under a new constitution that had been rushed through the single-party parliament. Elections were finally held, and the opposition did participate, but the result offered no convincing victory or defeat for the regime, which continued to operate like its unstable single-party predecessor. The ultimate victory of the regime over the democratic opposition would not occur in an election, but on the streets of Belgrade three months later.

When elections were held on 9 December 1990, SPS emerged as the largest vote-getter, but did not receive a majority of votes. Its 46.1 percent of the popular vote, however, gained it in an overwhelming majority of seats in the Serbian parliament: 194 seats, or 77.6 percent of all seats. A sense of the imbalance in returns can be gained by comparing votes per seat for the two leading parties. SPS gained one parliamentary seat for each 11,962 votes; SPO received one parliamentary seat for each 41,831 votes, a ratio of nearly 1:3.5. Table 4 presents the results of the election.

With SPS transforming its electoral plurality into an overwhelming parliamentary majority, the elections did not mark a transition from a single-party to a plural-party system. Slavujević described the resulting control of SPS over the Serbian parliament as a "predominant-party" system,[33] in which SPS deputies were able to cut short debate and pass any and all laws and resolutions without any consideration of the positions of opposition parties. Vladimir Goati described the parliamentary situation:

> Possession of a convincing majority relieved the Socialist Party of Serbia of the obligation to gradually win over and persistently persuade other parties in the rightness of its measures and decisions, and to correspondingly be prepared for giving in and for compromises. Instead, they were able to impose their political orientation in the Parliament without any difficulty by outvoting the minority. That easily led to the illusion on the part of deputies of the ruling

33. Slavujević (1993), 103.

Table 4. Votes and parliamentary seats received, 1990 election

Party	Number of Votes	Percentage	Number of Seats	Percentage	Difference (Percentage)
SPS	2,320,587	46.1	194	77.6	+31.1
SPO	794,789	15.8	19	7.6	−8.2
Independent candidates	456,318	9.1	8	3.2	−5.9
DS	374,887	7.4	7	2.8	−4.6
DZVM	132,726	2.6	8	3.2	+0.6
SDA	84,156	1.7	3	1.2	−0.5
SRSJ/V	71,865	1.5	2	0.8	−0.7
NSS	68,045	1.4	1	0.4	−1.0
SSSS	52,663	1.0	2	0.8	−0.2
SDS	32,927	0.6	1	0.4	−0.2
UJDI	24,982	0.5	1	0.4	−0.1
DSH	23,360	0.5	1	0.4	−0.1
PDD	21,998	0.4	1	0.4	0
SJ	21,784	0.4	1	0.4	0
DRSM	3,432	0.1	1	0.4	+0.3
Others	341,732	6.8	—	—	—
Invalid ballots	205,212	4.1	—	—	—
Totals	5,031,463	1	250	1	

SOURCE: Vladimir Goati, Zoran Slavujević, and Ognjen Pribičević, *Izborne borbe u Jugo-slaviji, 1900–1992* (Belgrade: Radnička štampa, 1993), 197.
NOTE: SPS = Socialistička partija Srbije (Socialist Party of Serbia); SPO = Srpski pokret obnove (Serbian Renewal Movement); DS = Demokratska stranka (Democratic Party); DZVM = Demokratska zajednica vojvođanskih Mađara (Democratic Union of Vojvodina Hungarians); SDA = Stranka demokratske akcije (Party of Democratic Action); SRSJ = Savez reformskih snaga Jugoslavije (Union of Reform Forces of Yugo-slavia); NSS = Narodna seljačka stranka (People's Peasant Party); SSSS = Srpska svetosavska stranka (Serbian St. Sava Party); UJDI = Udružena jugoslovenska demo-kratska inicijativa (United Yugoslav Democratic Initiative); DSH = Demokratski savez Hrvata (Democratic Union of Croatians); PDD = Partija demokratskog delovanja (Party of Democratic Practice); SJ = Stranka jugoslovena (Yugoslav Party); DRSM = Demokratska reformska stranka Muslimana (Democratic Reform Party of Muslims).

party that the Parliament was comprised only of the majority, and not of the majority and minority both.[34]

Consequently, although Serbia could boast of having held elections in which more than one party participated and of having opposition repre-

34. Goati (1992), 178.

sentatives in its parliament, the parliament could not be described as democratic. SPS's narrow plurality in the 1990 elections did not resolve its problem of legitimacy, nor did it force the regime to adjust to the new reality of a pluralistic political system. In practice, such a system did not exist.

Milošević, for his part, was confirmed as president of Serbia in the elections and went on to govern principally by executive power.[35] SPS maintained its monopoly over all ministries and all executive positions and continued to extend its control over the two institutions that would continue to be most important to its rule: the police and the state television network.

The two elements came together most strongly in the events of 9 March 1991 and in the following days. In the demonstrations of 9 March, which ended with the first use of military power against civilians in Yugoslavia's post–World War II history, the die was cast for war to begin as the only way for Milošević's regime to persuasively assert its power over Serbia. The student demonstrations and "Terazije Parliament" of the following days represented a strong effort to transform the Tiananmen Square experience of 9 March into a "velvet" Wenceslas Square. The transformation proved as practically difficult as it was geographically improbable. The students succeeded in exposing the regime's failure of legitimacy, but their failure to develop their public display into a new balance of political forces augured the definitive defeat of the possibility of democratic transformation in Serbia. The regime emerged with the military thoroughly compromised; the army discredited itself as an independent force by placing the first mark on its record of violence against civilians. This development not only made war between the republics possible; war also became necessary as the only means of preserving a power that had been openly challenged and exposed.

The demonstrations were called as a response to months of exclusion of the opposition parties from television news coverage on the state chan-

---

35. The Serbian regime is not unique in this capacity. As Vučina Vasović points out, "In Serbia, Slovenia, and Croatia . . . (the presidents) have the right to dissolve parliament and the right to issue executive orders that have the force of law. In addition, they have the right to constitute judicial proceedings, intervene in the judicial process, and name judges to the constitutional courts. Further, the presidents are the military commanders-in-chief; they have the right to approve international agreements without the ratification of parliaments; they can retain their party functions; and they can suspend the civil rights of individuals for national security reasons or declare martial law." In Seroka and Pavlović (1992), 186.

nels[36] and of the use of the state television to present one-sided reports of intensifying national conflicts in Yugoslavia.[37] In the name of a coalition of opposition parties, Vuk Drašković announced demonstrations to demand the resignation of the directors of the state television stations.[38] The demonstrations were banned, and while Drašković's SPO bused in supporters from throughout the country, Milošević prepared by bringing in police officers from throughout the country.

On the morning of 9 March, the police attempted to block entry to Republic Square where the meeting was to take place, set up checkpoints for automobile traffic going to the city, and tried to redirect cars to New Belgrade. Nonetheless, people entered the square. The attempt to block the procession, led by Drašković, from the SPO offices to Republic Square, also failed. By 11:45 A.M., with a large crowd having assembled at Republic Square and Drašković and other opposition leaders having assembled around the monument to Prince Michael in the square, police attempted to disperse the crowds—first with tear gas, which did not succeed as the gas was blown away by the wind, and next with water cannons.

36. The government directly controls three television stations: RTS (*Radio-Televizija Srbije*) channels 1, 2, and 3. The first two offer principally news, sports, and dramatic fare, while the third is dedicated principally to "relatively independent" music and film presentations. In the city of Belgrade, the local station Studio B was independent at the time.

37. For example, one week before the demonstrations, on 2 March 1991, armed conflicts between the Yugoslav People's Army (*Jugoslovenska narodna armija—JNA*) and Croatian police occurred in the Slavonian town of Pakrac. RTS carried the official reaction of the Belgrade SPS organization condemning the "brutal attack by the Croatian government on the population of Pakrac [using] violent and fascist methods," followed by an invitation to attend "protest meetings against the violent behavior of the Croatian, HDZ government." The report ended with a report of threats against journalists in Ljubljana and Zagreb and the ominous commentary "It is fortunate that our colleagues from Slovenia and Croatia who report from Serbia do not experience similar unpleasantness in our area." Quoted in Lalić (1995), 40. Earlier, on 16 February, Drašković had been "accused . . . of maintaining secret contacts with Tuđman's Croatian Democratic Union (HDZ)" (Misha Glenny, *The Fall of Yugoslavia: The Third Balkan War* [New York: Penguin Books, 1993], 45) and not permitted to reply to the "charge" of negotiation. The association of Drašković with the Croatian regime can, in a way, be taken as a measure of how far he had moved in the intervening time from the extreme national positions he had held one year before.

38. The directors in question were Dušan Mitević, general director of Belgrade Radio-Television (RTB), Predrag Vitas, editor-in-chief, Sergej Šestakov, director of TV Belgrade, and the editors Slavko Budina and Ivan Krivec.

After Drašković had addressed the crowd from the balcony of the National Theater, police received the order to try to disperse the crowd again. Miloš Vasić described the atmosphere in the square around 1:30 P.M.:

> The combination of two factors—too many people in a small space (over 100,000 citizens were in Republic Square at the time) and the space for exit being cut off [by police cordons] led to the worst possible result: the citizens, squeezed into the space and attacked without having the possibility to retreat—received new and unexpected energy, which showed itself through ignoring danger and through heroism. The swift counterattack on the part of the citizens forced the police to retreat toward the Army Hall and there neither their water cannons nor their armored vehicles helped.[39]

Although police received orders to counterattack, the effort was set back by two factors. First, the mounted units found that their horses were more sensitive to tear gas than the demonstrators were, and second, one unit of police refused the orders to counterattack and instead joined the demonstrators.[40]

Around 2:00 P.M., the demonstrators began making their way toward the street and the park between the parliament building and the Serbian presidency building. Police received an order to regroup in two places: around the building of the state television on Takovska street, and in the area around the presidency and parliament. The demonstrators arrived first at the government buildings, and the police arrived first to the television headquarters. While demonstrators occupied the parliament, the police formed a cordon around the television headquarters, from which the children's educational program was being broadcast at the time. The one area that police successfully protected was the television headquarters, which was henceforth informally known in Belgrade as "the Bastille."

As demonstrations continued around the parliament, and both police and demonstrators continued violence, police from outside Belgrade who had not been trained in crowd management and had little idea of what to

39. Vasić, in Kamenko Pajić, *9. mart 1991* (Sremčica: Kamenko, 1991). Pages are not numbered in Pajić's book.

40. This tact led SPS Deputy Pavić Obradović to suggest that an "analysis of the party memberships of the security forces" be carried out. Quoted in Vasić (in Pajić, 1991).

expect from demonstrators showed their confusion. A busload of police from the town of Požarevac, who had come without briefing and received no orders, were sent to the street corner known as "London," where Knez Miloš street meets the former Marshal Tito street (now known as Serbian Rulers' street). Miloš Vasić described their encounter with the demonstrators: "[A] group of one hundred or so demonstrators headed downhill from 'London,' throwing stones and brandishing sticks and cafe tables. The Požarevac policemen, as it was later established, did not have shields or chemical preparations. Worst of all, they did not have radio contact with the headquarters of the Serbian Ministry of the Interior either, nor any means of communication with them. It is not known whether the policemen from Požarevac had been given the Interior Ministry orders that firearms were not to be used."[41] The police met the group of demonstrators with gunfire—some firing into the air, and some not. Five demonstrators were wounded by bullets, and Branivoje Milinović, an eighteen-year-old student, was killed. Elsewhere, a police officer died under circumstances not fully explained. State media claimed that fifty-four-year-old Nedeljko Kosović was beaten by demonstrators, but others claim that he died in a fall while trying to retreat over a concrete wall. No witnesses to the event have offered conclusive evidence of either version. At the parliament building, over one hundred demonstrators were arrested, among them Vuk Drašković.

As the day wore on, the inability of the police to maintain order became increasingly apparent and the government became panicky. By 6:30 P.M., the president of the Yugoslav federal presidency, Borisav Jović, called units of the army to Belgrade. Milošević issued a statement claiming that "the powers of chaos and madness in Serbia must be opposed by all constitutional means."[42] Within the hour, police entered the offices of the independent television station Studio B and the youth radio station Radio B-92, the only two media sources that had been covering the events on the streets, with orders to cease transmission. Although Interior Minister Radmilo Bogdanović accused the stations of "calling for resistance to the government,"[43] the next day the stations began broadcasting again as federal prosecutors refused to press charges against them.

41. Vasić (in Pajić, 1991).
42. Quoted in Lalić (1995), 44.
43. Vasić (in Pajić, 1991).

The first television reports presented the demonstrations as mayhem on the part of Drašković's followers. Reports showed the grief of the family of the police officer Nedeljko Kosović, but did not mention the death of the student Branivoje Milinović. The evening news on the state television introduced its report with: "The peaceful demonstrations which were called in Belgrade today by Vuk Drašković turned into violence, threats to the lives of uninvolved people, destruction of everything in its path, demonstrators' terror unseen in these parts. It was an attempt to destroy the constitutional order and to bring down the legitimate government."[44] Nationalist rhetoric made its way into condemnations of the protests as well, as the state television turned to a message of support for the regime from Milan Babić, leader of the secessionist Serbs in Krajina. Babić claimed, "[T]he task in which Tuđman has not succeeded, to disunify the Serbian people, Vuk Drašković does a better job of carrying out for him."[45]

The next day, arrests and beatings by the police continued. In the student residences, students decided to gather on Terazije in the center of town to voice their concerns. Stopped momentarily by police and attacked with tear gas on the way to Terazije, the students eventually arrived. One group was protected from the police by taxi drivers, who drove in file beside them. The group that was stopped on the bridge from New Belgrade arrived with a new slogan, "[W]e have more tears than they have tear gas."[46] Throughout the night and for the following four days on Terazije, the crowd swelled as speakers climbed up onto the fountain to address the crowd, now calling itself the "Terazije Parliament." The students formulated a list of demands to the government, including the original demands of the disastrous 9 March rally, along with calls for the release of all people arrested on 9 March, including Drašković, and for the resignation of the Interior minister, Radmilo Bogdanović, who had

44. Quoted in Lalić (1995), 43.
45. Quoted in Lalić (1995), 44. Babić's statement is especially ironic in view of the "defense" of the Serbs of Krajina offered by the leaders of that area when it was retaken by Croatia in August 1995. At that time, Babić's successor Milan Martić released rumors of his own death to cover his flight from the front lines; the cowardice of the Krajina leadership succeeded in helping Tuđman accomplish what NDH never had. As for Babić himself, he held the title of minister of foreign affairs of Krajina at the time.
46. Vasić (in Pajić, 1991).

commanded the police in their violence.[47] Most of the students' demands were met as the "Terazije Parliament" went on.[48]

An attempt was made to meet the students' popular demonstration with a pro-regime demonstration. On 11 March, the regime-sponsored Women's Movement for the Preservation of Yugoslavia" (*Pokret žena za očuvanje Jugoslavija*) invited people, over the state television, to attend its meeting at Ušće, across the Sava river in New Belgrade, at which it promised to "defend Serbia and the president of the Republic of Serbia who is today more threatened than ever by a conspiracy of all the enemies of Serbia."[49] Several thousand SPS supporters came to Ušće, where they heard speeches of government officials and supporters. Consistent with the accusation that opposition to the government was "anational" and with the thesis of a global conspiracy against the Serbian government, the Belgrade mayor accused "the Albanian alternative, HDZ, and foreign intelligence services" of organizing the student manifestation.[50] A call at the meeting by Industry Minister Dušan Matković for the assembled SPS supporters, mostly older people, to cross the river and forcefully disperse the students met with no response.

Among the students' demands was a call for the holding of a special session of parliament, which did occur. At this session, Bogdanović offered his resignation as Interior minister, and Jović offered his resignation as federal president, which he withdrew six days later. However, implicit calls for the resignation of Slobodan Milošević were rejected, not to be revived by opposition forces until the force of the demonstrations had dissipated.

Regime supporters summarized the events of 9 March and afterward as a "visitation of destruction," which fully demonstrated the bad intentions of the opposition. Regime opponents referred to it as "Serbia's last cry" before war made the regime invincible and opposition was equated with treason.[51] Without staking out a position on either end of that con-

---

47. The full list of demands of the "Terazije Parliament" is reproduced in Glenny (1993), 53–54.

48. The director of the state television network, Dušan Mitević, whose resignation was the original demand of the demonstrators on 9 March, was replaced by Ratomir Vico. For more on Vico, see Chapter 3 on the takeover of independent media in 1994 and 1995.

49. Quoted in Lalić (1995), 47.

50. Quoted in Lalić (1995), 48.

51. As expressed by Ljubomir Tadić, the former "dissident" who presents his sup-

tinuum, some medium-range conclusions are probably possible. The key outcome of the 9 March demonstrations and the events of the following days was, first of all, that the generational division of Serbian society became graphically apparent. As the independent newspaper *Borba* put it on 11 March, parents were at Ušće and their children were on Terazije.[52] The scene was repeated in the large student protests of the following year.[53] Second, by bringing the JNA into Belgrade against the demonstrators on the night of 9 March, Milošević succeeded in irredeemably compromising the army's independence from political forces and placing it in obligatory coalition with his regime. Although his attempt to declare a state of emergency and to impose martial law throughout Yugoslavia in the following week did not succeed, the co-optation of the military strengthened his regime as Yugoslavia descended into war.

Serbia After March: Consolidation and War

As the curtain closed on the students at Terazije, it opened on the war in Croatia. The relation of the two events is anything but coincidental. Tensions between Serbs and Croats in Croatia could be said to have been "brewing"[54] for some time, but the active engagement of militias and military forces sprang up not organically but by administrative decision. War presented itself as a means to preserve the dictatorship that had been compelled to resort to force in the demonstrations, to make the complic-

---

port for Karadžić's forces in Bosnia as an example of his concern for democracy and human rights, diversity of opinion has its limits, which are severe: "In Serbia, thank God, we are not unanimous, although unanimity has to exist in moments of defense of the bare existence of the people, and whoever is not with his people is nothing more than a traitor." Quoted in Vukić (1994), 18.

52. *Borba's* headline to that effect is quoted in Nada Kovačević, "Tako je pisala 'Borba,'" *Dosije Borba*, 22 November 1994, p. 11.

53. The 1992 student protests are exhaustively analyzed in the collection edited by Bora Kuzmanović, *Studentski protest 1992: Socialno-psihološka studija jednog društvenog događaja* (Belgrade: Institut za psihologiju, 1993).

54. The term *brewing* seems to be a favorite of journalists who claim that the onset of war in the former Yugoslavia followed inevitably from the character of the people and their cultural differences. It should be obvious from this work that I do not share that opinion. The implicit analogy is not apt, either: Workers in the beer and tea industries can confirm that brewing does not occur by itself, but only by the engaged involvement of humans.

ity of the army in preserving the regime irredeemable, and to convincingly disqualify Serbia's opposition with the label of treason. The ground for war had been exhaustively prepared in the official media in Serbia as in Croatia, and the actual outbreak of war constituted a fulfillment of the state media's prophecy of inevitable conflict—perversely justifying the media's dominance that had been one of the original impulses for the March demonstrations. With war too came demographic change. Added to the general poverty and misery that came with economic collapse was the massive refusal of military service, which meant that many young people were leaving the country or living underground. Within a few years, a good portion of the students who had made up the "Terazije Parliament" was living in other parts of the world.

Overcoming both his distaste for opposition political parties and his ostensible antipathy to the extreme right, Milošević found the "opposition" politician to be his principal public support in discrediting and defeating opposition parties and in carrying out the war that soon began in Croatia. As leader and "duke" (*vojvoda*) of the tiny "Serbian Chetnik Movement" (*Srpski četnički pokret*), Vojislav Šešelj, a former professor of "the nonexistent science of 'People's Self-Defense,' "[55] was a little-known and marginal political figure. (See Fig. 3.) In the intervening period, however, Šešelj organized a private army in Krajina and transformed his movement into a political party—audaciously naming the party after the dominant political party of the first half of the twentieth century, the Serbian Radical Party (*Srpska radikalna stranka—SRS*). He began to receive tremendous favorable publicity in the state media and took positions appropriate to a darling of the regime. After the demonstrations of 9 March, Šešelj declared that the demonstrations were "a great fraud perpetrated on the Serbian people. The ninth of March in Belgrade was organized by Ante Marković and foreign intelligence services."[56] Milošević responded in kind, pronouncing Šešelj his favorite opposition politician.

Šešelj made his way into the parliament in April 1991 in a special election in the Belgrade district of Rakovica, in which he defeated the DS candidate, the well-known novelist Borislav Pekić. Together with forces

55. Branko Milanović, *Protiv nacizma* (Belgrade: Radio B-92, 1994), 129. Šešelj could also lay claim to the title of "dissident," having been imprisoned in 1984 for the contents of a magazine he edited, which never reached publication.
56. Quoted in Vukić (1994), 11.

Fig. 3. Vojislav Šešelj, leader of the ultraright Serbian Radical Party, likes to confront his critics in a dramatic manner. Slobodan Milošević declared Šešelj his favorite opposition politician. Photo courtesy of *Vreme*.

of the Krajina Serbs (called *"martićevci"* after the Krajina Serb commander Milan Martić), several other paramilitary forces, and the JNA,
Šešelj's "Chetniks" fought in Croatia, where war had begun in earnest.[57]
In the parliament and in public pronouncements, Šešelj came to be
closely associated with the regime, emerging as a "counteropposition"[58]
attacking antiwar forces with a vehemence that the ruling party saw as
beneath its own dignity. His extreme national positions meshed perfectly
with those of the regime and its clients in Croatia and Bosnia-Hercegovina as the war spread to that other republic in April 1992. Commentators
like Branko Milanović refused to differentiate him from Milošević himself, personifying the regime and its most visible ideological supporter as
the entity "Milošešelj."[59]

This position was confirmed in the parliamentary elections of 1992.
SPS once again emerged as the largest party, but the inflation of its 28.8
percent of the votes did not bring it a majority of parliamentary seats.
Šešelj's SRS, which had received an insignificant number of votes in the
previous elections—before it began to receive publicity in the state
media—emerged in second place with 22.6 percent of the votes. SPS
entered into a coalition with SRS and assured itself control of 69.8 percent of all parliamentary seats. As mismatched as the nominally left-wing
SPS and the militantly right-wing SRS may have appeared, at the time
they were closely associated in the minds of their supporters. One survey
indicated that at the time of the 1992 elections, "38 percent of SPS supporters expressed a willingness to vote for SRS, while 39 percent of Radi-

57. Several "private" paramilitary forces fought on the side of the Krajina seces-
sionists—there were also several minor forces. A detailed discussion of the various paramilitary forces operating in Croatia and Bosnia-Hercegovina lies outside the scope of
the present study, although several are described in Glenny (1993). Šešelj could not
resist expressing his unique perspective toward urban culture in his pronouncements
about his paramilitary forces in Croatia, which tempered his characteristic bombast,
strangely: "I guarantee that with one division of ten thousand Chetniks I would make
it to Zagreb in 48 hours. Understand, though, I would not allow the Chetniks to enter
Zagreb, because I would be afraid that they might get lost in the streets there. After all,
it's a big city!" (in Vukić, 1994, 14). For a discussion of the role of peasant ideology
against urban culture and its use in justifying the bombardment of the cities of Dubrovnik, Vukovar, and Sarajevo, see Čolović (1994a), Bogdan Bogdanović, *Grad i smrt* (Belgrade: Beogradski krug, 1994), and Vujović (1995).
58. Slavujević, (1993), 129.
59. Milanović (1994), 136. The inscription on a wall near the Student Cultural
Center of Belgrade might be more to the point: "Milošescu."

Table 5. Votes and parliamentary seats received, 1992 election

Party	Number of Votes	Percentage	Number of Seats	Percentage	Difference (Percentage)
SPS	1,359,086	28.8	101	40.4	+11.6
SRS	1,066,765	22.6	73	29.2	+6.6
DEPOS	797,131	16.9	50	20.0	+3.1
DS	196,347	4.2	6	2.4	−1.8
DZVM	140,825	3.0	9	3.6	+0.6
SSS	128,240	2.7	3	1.2	−1.5
KDR	71,865	1.5	2	0.8	−0.7
Arkan	17,352	0.3	5	2.0	+1.7
DRSM	6,336	0.1	1	0.4	+0.3
Others	663,903	14.0	—	—	—
Invalid ballots	275,861	5.8	—	—	—
Totals	4,723,711	1	250	1	

SOURCE: Republički zavod za statistiku, *Statistički godnišnjak Srbije 1993.*
NOTE: The 1992 election saw the participation of the following parties, which either did not exist or did not run at the time of the 1990 elections: SRS = Srpska radikalna stranka (Serbian Radical Party); DEPOS = Demokratski pokret Srbije (Democratic Movement of Serbia, a coalition of SPO, part of DS, SLS, and Nova Demokratija [ND]); SSS = Seljačka stranka Srbije (Peasant Party of Serbia); KDR = Koalicija demokratske stranke i reformske demokratske stranke Vojvodine (Coalition of the Democratic Party and Reform Democratic Party of Vojvodina).
    "Arkan" is the nickname of the paramilitary commander Željko Ražnatović, who ran as an independent candidate in 1992. He later formed the Party of Serbian Unity (Stranka srpskog jedinstva—SSJ).

cals considered SPS as their reserve party."[60] Table 5 presents the results of the election.

Šešelj and his radicals performed their counteroppositional role with relish and effectively relieved the ruling party of the need to involve itself on the domestic political terrain against antiwar opposition. His bombastic style—he assaulted political opponents several times and frequently waved around a pistol while he spoke—was certain to attract attention, but as Milan Milošević pointed out:

Šešelj's most effective appearances were those when he had as listeners and as his cheering section the Socialist deputies in the Serbian

60 Milan Milošević, "Moć srpskih radikala," *Vreme,* no. 223, 30 January 1995, p. 11.

Parliament—who appeared well pleased that they had in him a verbal Praetorian Guard against the *"deposovci"* [members of the opposition coalition DEPOS], rebellious students, and "defeatists." Among his successes are counted the removal of president Ćosić and the personnel changes in the command of JNA, simply because the Socialists did not want to do those things by their own hands.[61]

With time, however, the love between Milošević and Šešelj faded. In August 1993, Milošević shifted his position from opposition to advocacy of the Vance-Owen peace plan and placed himself for the first time in opposition to the Bosnian Serb forces that had been his clients. He attempted to break off contact and cooperation with Karadžić's forces, but reversed himself after one week. Faced with rebellion and charges of "treason" from Šešelj, Milošević responded with charges of fascism and war crimes. Rather than face a vote of confidence, Milošević dissolved the parliament on 20 October 1993 and set new elections for December. The catastrophic economic conditions in Serbia continued to weaken the credibility of the regime.[62]

SPS's performance in the December 1993 elections was its weakest ever. Although it received more votes than it had in 1992, it could not count on support from its former coalition partner, now bitter enemy, the Radical party. The effort of the regime to promote the newly formed Serbian Unity Party (SSJ), led by organized-crime boss and paramilitary commander Željko Ražnatović-Arkan,[63] as a substitute for SRS failed miserably. Arkan received fewer votes than he had in 1992 and did not win a single parliamentary seat. SPS found itself short of a parliamentary ma-

61. Milan Milošević, "Moć srpskih radikala," *Vreme*, no. 223, 30 January 1995, p. 12. I would also add among Šešelj's "successes" for SPS the removal of the federal prime minister, Milan Panić, who had become the leading opponent of the regime and contested the presidential elections in December 1992.

62. For more on the astronomical hyperinflation of 1993–94 and the effects of international sanctions, see Chapter 5.

63. In addition to being charged with war crimes in Croatia and Bosnia-Hercegovina, Arkan is also wanted for bank robbery by four European countries. For his own part, he lists his profession alternately as "state security" (at a firearms trial in 1986) and as "businessperson" (he owns a bakery in Belgrade) and is further distinguished as president of the fan club of the football team Red Star (*Crvena zvezda*), from whose ranks he recruited his paramilitary forces. His party's posters in the 1993 campaign featured his portrait over the slogan *Mi držimo reč* ("We keep our word"); graffitists altered the slogan to *Mi držimo reket* ("We run the racket").

Table 6. Votes and parliamentary seats received, 1993 election

Party	Number of Votes	Percentage	Number of Seats	Percentage	Difference (Percentage)
SPS	1,576,287	36.7	123	49.2	+12.5
DEPOS	715,564	16.7	45	18.0	+1.3
SRS	595,467	13.9	39	15.6	+1.7
DS	497,582	11.6	29	11.6	0
DSS	218,056	5.1	7	2.8	−2.3
DZVM	112,456	2.6	5	2.0	−0.6
PDD/DPA	29,342	0.7	2	0.8	−0.1
SSS	65,623	1.5	—	—	−1.5
Others	314,909	7.3	—	—	—
Invalid ballots	171,824	4.0	—	—	—
Totals	4,297,110	1	250	1	

SOURCE: Republički zavod za statistiku, *Prevremeni izbori za narodne poslanike Narodne skupštine republike Srbije 1993, konačni rezultati.*
NOTE: A new party appearing in the 1993 elections is DSS = Demokratska stranka Srbije (Democratic Party of Serbia).

jority for the first time and parlayed its 36.7 percent of the popular vote into only 49.2 percent of parliamentary seats, or 123 seats—three seats short of a majority. Table 6 presents the results of the election.

For several days, it was uncertain whether SPS could form a government at all—at the same time, the severe division of the opposition made it extremely unlikely that any party could take advantage of SPS's failure to form a government on its own part. The clearest divisions appeared between SRS and the other parties; SRS was essential to any opposition coalition, but this possibility was precluded both by programmatic differences with the antiwar DEPOS coalition and by a general aversion to forming a coalition with a party that until several months earlier had acted as the regime's attack dog. The small parties of the Albanian and Hungarian minorities, DZVM and the coalition of PDD and DPA, also refused to form a coalition with SPS.[64] Finally, SPS succeeded in breaking off the small New Democracy Party (*Nova demokratija—ND*) from DEPOS. Later, a group of seven Radical deputies broke off from SRS to form another pro-regime bloc.

64. The overwhelming majority of the Albanian population in Serbia boycotted the elections.

Prospects for a strong and unified opposition bloc were weakened by changes in the Democratic party. Its first president, Dragoljub Mićunović, was defeated and replaced by his vice president, Zoran Đinđić. Although under Mićunović the DS had been vague on the question of nationalism—generally claiming that as a party of economic liberals the question was not on its "natural terrain"—Đinđić moved the party's position clearly in favor of the Serb militias in Bosnia-Hercegovina and Croatia.[65] The move partly constituted a recognition that antinationalist positions did not bring DS far from its political base of urban intellectuals and partly sprang from a desire to pick what they assumed was the political corpse of SRS. The shift made extremely unlikely the formation of a proposed "3D" coalition of the three self-described "democratic" parties—DS, DEPOS, and DSS—which in a coalition with the ethnic minority parties could present a credible opposition to SPS.[66] Instead, opposition parties generally continued their infighting and failed to take advantage of the weakness demonstrated by SPS.

The parliament continued to function as the sole reserve of SPS, but had few serious functions. Much of the time, the chamber's work was suspended, and the presiding officers discharged the parliament to avoid debates and votes of confidence. Nor did opposition members protest too vehemently in October 1994 when Vojislav Šešelj received a three-month prison sentence for insulting the presiding deputy on the floor of the parliament.[67] As widely despised among his colleagues as Šešelj was, the

65. Đinđić had previously been identified with the "left" of DS; Vojislav Koštunica, whose DSS had already split off from the DS, was identified with the "right" (see Glenny, 1993, 40). In breaking with his past positions in this way, Đinđić could also be seen as breaking with his erstwhile intellectual mentor Jürgen Habermas. Although Habermas has for the past several years polemicized against "Holocaust revisionists" in his native Germany, Đinđić paid highly public visits to Radovan Karadžić at his military headquarters in Pale. Mićunović, for his part, formed the independent Democratic Center, an organization not expressly identified with any party. However, since Mićunović was expelled from DS in 1995, speculation has arisen that the Center may be transformed into a political party.

66. The possibilities are explored in Dragoslav Grujić, "Post festum izbori 93: Naknadna pamet," Vreme, no. 167, 3 January 1994, pp. 20–21. DS and DSS later formed, in 1995, a short-lived and inactive coalition with Šešelj's Radicals.

67. One DS deputy, Desimir Tošić, voted in favor of lifting Šešelj's parliamentary immunity so that he could be arrested. As for the presiding officer Radoman Božović, there was much to insult: His comically heavy-handed manner was designed to prevent opposition deputies from speaking at inconvenient moments or on inconvenient topics.

act constituted an open challenge to the ability of opposition deputies to carry on debate in the chamber. Instead, much of the opposition concentrated on obstructing parliamentary proceedings—drawing out debate on the prime minister's report on the year's work of the government for several weeks in March and April 1995, for example. Finally achieving unity on the nonfunctioning of the parliament, all the opposition parties walked out of the chamber in January 1996[68] and declared that they would hold their own "parallel parliament." Vesna Pešić, leader of the opposition GSS, summarized the parliamentary situation in which the use of political substitutes by SPS throughout its communist, nationalist, and "peacemaking" periods had finally broken down: "[H]ere it is established that in Serbia there is no sovereignty of peoples, there is no parliamentary life, there are no civil or minority rights, there is not even a regime or a state, the governing group is neither communist as the Radicals assert, nor nationalist as the Civic Alliance asserts, nor peacemaking as SPS asserts about itself, but rather it is simply a family-run thieving society."[69] Other observers might have correctly pointed out that this realization by opposition parties came late. SPS did not receive the support of the majority of Serbians either in the first elections or thereafter, and the multiparty parliament had never functioned as a chamber in which debate was seriously engaged or decisions taken.   \

Social Bases of Regime Support

To the extent that political divisions in Serbia not apparent in its institutions of government are apparent in the electoral behavior of its citizens, it is possible to answer the question of what groups have consistently supported the regime and have provided the measure of legitimacy that it has enjoyed. Analysis of the existing political research and of election results brings out three factors: the deep social division of the country between older and younger people, between urban and rural people, and

---

Šešelj, for his part, would be imprisoned again in May 1995 on charges of holding an illegal public meeting.

68. The immediate reason for the walkout was the curtailment of live television broadcasts of the proceedings of the parliament, which, although often laughable, constituted the only means for opposition party deputies to appear on the state television.

69. Milan Milošević, "Skupština Srbije: Zatvorena zbog krečenja," *Vreme*, no. 271, 30 December 1995, p. 9.

Table 7. Party preference by age, 1990 and 1991

	1990		
	Under 26 Years	26–46 Years	Over 46 Years
SPS	22.8%	33.3%	59.4%
SPO	27.6	14.7	5.6
DS	8.9	6.5	5.6
UJDI/Reform	5.7	4.4	5.6
	1991		
	Under 26 Years	26–46 Years	Over 46 Years
SPS	11.9%	25.2%	43.4%
SPO	12.9	7.6	3.3
DS	15.0	13.0	10.8
SRS	24.8	15.1	11.4

SOURCE: Vladimir Milić, "Socijalni lik političkog javnog mnjenja," in Pečuljić, Milić, Goati, Branković, and Kovačević (1992), 113–14.

NOTE: The group identified by Milić as the UJDI/Reform coalition appears in two places in the 1990 election results in Table 4 of this chapter, under UJDI and SRSJ/V.

between the small group of highly educated people and the much larger group of less educated people. Dragoslav Grujić introduced his discussion of the December 1993 elections with the observation that "the south defeated the north, the undeveloped defeated the developed, the province defeated the metropolis, and the village defeated the city."[70] The same could be said for the other elections that have taken place since 1990.

The first major division that has structured political distinctions in Serbia is age. Support for the ruling party is highly concentrated among the older generation and decreases with age. Surveys cited by Vladimir Milić graphically demonstrate this tendency, as well as its converse, that support for opposition parties declines with age. The figures are shown in Table 7. The relation becomes clearer when the figures are collapsed to indicate preference for SPS as opposed to support for opposition parties. The pattern is consistent—SPS is the clear favorite of the oldest generation, while opposition parties gain the most support among the younger generations, as seen in Table 8.

Although Milić interpreted these figures with measured optimism and speculated that "taking into account the size of [the younger] generation

70. "Naknadna pamet," *Vreme*, no. 167, 3 January 1994, p. 20.

Table 8. SPS and opposition, by age, 1990/1991

	1990		
	Under 26 Years	26–46 Years	Over 46 Years
SPS	22.8%	33.3%	59.4%
Opposition	42.2	25.6	16.8
	1991		
	Under 26 Years	26–46 Years	Over 46 Years
SPS	11.9%	25.2%	43.4%
Opposition	52.7	35.7	25.5

SOURCE: Vladimir Milić, "Socijalni lik političkog javnog mnjenja," in Pečuljić, Milić, Goati, Branković, and Kovačević (1992), 113–14.

and its role in society, this can indicate a change in the near future and a chance for the opposition in some coalition to come to power,"[71] such an event clearly has yet to happen. While subsequent elections have seen a decrease in the popularity of SPS among all generations, several factors make this development unlikely. First, the regime has yet to demonstrate much tolerance even for the limited pluralism that already exists in Serbia, and it remains open to question whether a democratic transfer of power could take place.[72] Second, the sometimes wide margin of difference between the number of votes received and the number of parliamentary seats awarded in elections to date indicates that the results of elections are open to manipulation in favor of the ruling party. The repeated failure of the opposition to unify at election time makes such a prospect more unlikely. Finally, the youngest generation is not only the most likely to emigrate, but also the most likely to abstain from voting. The abstention rate for those under 26 years of age in 1990 was 26.3 percent, as opposed to 14.4 percent for those over 46.[73]

Political differences are also apparent between the urban and rural populations, with urban residents less likely to support SPS. Ognjen Prib-

71. Milić (1992), 113.

72. For an example from a similar regime, consider the most recent election in Croatia. In the city of Zagreb, an opposition coalition won 65 percent of the vote and has to date been unable to place a mayor at the head of the municipal government—as all its choices have been vetoed by the president.

73. Milić (1992), 114–15. Abstention has increased among all generations since the 1990 elections.

ićević developed a table of the percentage of votes won by SPS in the ten most- and ten least-developed boroughs (*opštine*)[74] of Serbia in 1990 and 1992, and I have extended the calculation to include the 1993 elections. The results are shown in Table 9. The pattern emerging from the returns clearly demonstrates an intense and relatively stable concentration of SPS support in the least-developed parts of the country. The pattern becomes clearer when comparisons are made within the city of Belgrade: the central districts of the city show the lowest levels of regime support, while support is higher in the suburban and rural surrounding areas. The comparisons are shown in Table 10. Similar differences can be observed between the more developed north of the country and the acknowledged power base of SPS along the agricultural "southern railway" (*južna pruga*). While some of the difference may be explained by cultural factors, particularly the resentment of urban culture and intellectuals in rural areas, it is probably also important to note that independent media in Serbia are for the most part limited in circulation to the major urban centers.

Support for SPS similarly declines with education. Miroslav Pečuljić cited research from 1991 showing a linear decrease in support for SPS and generally increasing support for opposition parties with educational attainment. The figures are shown in Table 11. Although the figures are partly an artifact of the previous two categories—members of the younger generations and urban residents are also more likely to have completed more years of education—they also indicate the class base of the ruling and oppositional parties. Workers in state-owned industries, who make up the vast majority of workers in Serbia, offer their support to the party on which they depend and whose members are more likely than not the directors of the companies for which they work.

74. A word of caution: "Developed" districts are not necessarily the same as "urban" ones. The category of "developed" is likely to include industrial suburbs, displacing city neighborhoods. Hence, for example, no boroughs in the urban district of Novi Sad appear on the table. Also, the concentration of electoral abstention by ethnic Albanians in the district of Priština, most of whom boycotted elections, has forced statisticians to discount the district, which is largely "undeveloped," in calculating electoral results, because the figures for Priština do not describe the voting behavior of most of the population. The results for 1992 are further distorted by virtue of the fact that many pro-regime citizens voted for regime partner SRS rather than the ruling SPS in the 1992 election, making the SPS total representative of only a part of the entire pro-regime vote.

Table 9. SPS vote by developed and undeveloped boroughs

Developed Boroughs			
Borough (District)	1990	1992	1993
Bor (Niš)	40.9%	28.1%	31.2%
Savski Venac (Belgrade)	47.5	23.3	30.5
Stari Grad (Belgrade)	34.4	18.8	25.0
Užice (Užice)	42.0	33.9	25.8
Valjevo (Užice)	43.3	30.1	34.9
Vračar (Belgrade)	34.4	19.4	26.3
Majdanpek (Niš)	48.7	34.1	41.5
Lazarevac (Belgrade)	52.7	21.1	37.7
Obrenovac (Belgrade)	48.0	26.6	35.4
Trstenik (Kragujevac)	33.4	20.3	39.0
Average	42.5%	25.5%	32.7%
Undeveloped Boroughs			
Borough (District)	1990	1992	1993
Dimitrovgrad (Niš)	51.9%	42.4%	51.4%
Žagubica (Smederevo)	53.7	37.1	34.8
Surdulica (Leskovac)	77.7	54.8	64.5
Vlasotince (Leskovac)	63.8	52.4	67.8
Prokuplje (Leskovac)	60.3	40.7	56.6
Varvarin (Smederevo)	63.1	30.6	42.0
Medveđa (Leskovac)	47.9	38.3	47.7
Doljevac (Niš)	53.3	37.4	53.2
Malo Crniće (Smederevo)	52.2	37.2	46.7
Trgovište (Leskovac)	53.9	31.2	75.6
Average	57.8%	40.2%	54.0%

SOURCE: Ognjen Pribićević, "Politička kultura i demokratska stabilnost," in Goati, Slavujević, and Pribićević (1993), 176; Republički zavod za statistiku, *Prevremeni izbori za narodne poslanike Narodne skupštine republike Srbije 1993, konačni rezultati.*

In addition to those groups that have supported SPS, its opponents also provide it with crucial support in maintaining its power. Not least among these are the opposition parties. The above discussion detailed several instances in which the inability of the opposition to unify into effective coalitions has reduced its power and has allowed SPS to maintain its position as the largest party despite its repeated failure to capture a majority of votes. In addition, some basic inconsistencies in the opposi-

Table 10. Percentage of votes received by SPS, Belgrade District, by borough, 1993

Central Boroughs		Outlying Boroughs	
Čukarica	30.0	Barajevo	40.4
Novi Beograd	34.6	Grocka	34.0
Palilula	28.8	Lazarevac	37.7
Rakovica	30.3	Mladenovac	38.4
Savski Venac	30.5	Obrenovac	35.4
Stari Grad	25.0	Sopot	39.5
Voždovac	28.9		
Vračar	26.3		
Zemun	30.9		
Zvezdara	26.4		

Total percentage received in Belgrade district: 30.1

SOURCE: Republički zavod za statistiku, *Prevremeni izbori za narodne poslanike Narodne skupštine republike Srbije 1993, konačni rezultati.*

Table 11. Party preference by educational attainment, 1991

Party	Low	Middle	High
SPS	52.3%	39.4%	21.4%
DS	5.9	11.0	7.1
SPO	19.1	15.9	28.6

SOURCE: Miroslav Pečuljić, "U začaranom krugu politike," in Pečuljić et al. (1992, p. 75).

tion, from SPO's early shift from nationalism to antiwar politics to DS and its spinoffs' shift from economic liberalism to extreme nationalism, have served to frustrate and confuse its supporters while generally weakening its credibility. The groups most likely to support the opposition—young, urban, educated people—have been emigrating in large numbers since the beginning of the war.

Also assisting SPS in maintaining control over elected positions is the group against whom Milošević first organized his popular support as he was coming to power: the Albanian minority. Although some ethnic Albanians have supported the ethnic parties, DPA and PDD, which did participate in elections, the overwhelming majority of this group followed the election boycott declared by the Kosovo Albanian leader Ibrahim Rugova. The two districts (*jedinice*) with the largest Albanian populations were the only two of Serbia's nine electoral districts[75] in which SPS received a majority of votes—receiving 53.2 percent of the vote in the Leskovac district and 64.9 percent in the Priština district. These were also the districts with the lowest level of electoral participation: the turnout throughout Serbia in 1993 was 61.3 percent, 53.0 percent in Leskovac, and 15.6 percent in Priština. SPS received twenty-one parliamentary seats for its 59,951 votes from the Priština district, more than from any other district in the country. By comparison, it received sixteen seats for 255,071 votes in the Belgrade district, making the "cost" of an SPS parliamentary seat 15,942 votes in Belgrade and 2,855 votes in Priština. The seats from the Priština district, coming 5.6 times "cheaper" to SPS than its seats from the Belgrade district, can be seen as a gift to the regime from the groups that organized the boycott.

Political culture can also be seen as playing a role in the support the ruling party receives. Although much has been made by mainstream authors of "democratization" in East-Central Europe, the process seems to have been—rightly—not taken seriously by many Serbians. As Miklos Biro described the patterns of electoral behavior that persisted after the Communist regime declared its own end, "[V]oters had been accustomed to voting, and not to choosing."[76] Nor did the events that followed the hurried and halfhearted introduction of "democracy" serve to change many minds. Biro cited psychological research in which respondents were asked to give associations for the word "democracy." He detailed responses: "the breakup of Yugoslavia," "Tuđman," "anarchy," "the Serbian Parliament," "worthless freedom, and you don't have anything to eat."[77] If the events in the area since 1990 are any indication of what happens when "democracy" arrives, it should hardly be surprising that its arrival is not hailed.[78] These attitudes particularly define the population from which SPS draws its support—older, rural, and less educated voters who do not welcome change in the social order. Combined with

75. The nine districts are Belgrade, Zrenjanin, Kragujevac, Leskovac, Niš, Novi Sad, Priština, Smederevo, and Užice.

76. Biro (1994), 57.

77. Biro (1994), 82.

78. During the course of my research, I heard many times, especially from older people, discussions of some current scandal or conflict punctuated by statements like, "If this is democracy, then I don't like it." It probably would have been pointless to offer my view that it is not.

this is the folk political philosophy, born of decades of authoritarian rule, described to me by Slobodan Naumović, a Belgrade anthropologist: "People believe that somebody should be the guy in charge and that everything is that guy's fault."

Another dimension of the lack of enthusiasm for democracy is that in a state where political party membership has economic consequences, the ruling party does in fact rule. Hence throughout 1995 and 1996, in a period in which SPS's public support continued to decline, its membership increased, and this increase was publicized in ceremonies in which new members were admitted to the party, reports of which appeared in regime-controlled newspapers and on the state television news program. The secret? The leader of a local SPS branch explained, "[W]hat do you expect when SPS has something to offer?" An opposition leader in the same area explained it differently by saying that his party counsels its supporters to join SPS "if a job is in question" and hopes that in the next election the ruling party will have "fewer votes than members."[79]

The wars in Croatia and in Bosnia-Hercegovina, although they have discredited nearly all the political figures and institutions involved, have also strengthened the regime by making the development of an independent political culture nearly impossible. If, as most Serbian liberals surmise, the purpose of the war was to make democratic transformation impossible, on its own terms it can be said to have succeeded. War propaganda emphasized fears of the other parties in the war[80] and advanced the line that the existence of the Serbian people was threatened. In such an environment, for people who believed such claims, any opposition was equivalent to betrayal of the "nation"; conditions required unity in spite of any objections. Opposition politicians, especially from those parties that did not question many of the official positions on "national" questions, were acutely aware of the risk involved in presenting too vehement a critique. One spring afternoon, I walked with an opposition parliamentary leader, and we discussed potential new formations and coalitions that might develop in the coming year. I asked what would happen if, as seemed possible at the time, events were to bring Serbia and Croatia into direct military conflict once again. His answer was simple: "Of course, if there is a war, there won't be any politics."

79. Dragan Todorović, "Rekord 606 u Lazarevcu: Ponuda i potražnja," *Vreme*, no. 275, 27 January 1996, p. 11.

80. For the record, it should be noted that the official public position of Serbia was that it had not participated in any war.

If there had been no wars in Croatia and Bosnia-Hercegovina, would the inertia and conservatism of some parts of the population have been enough to keep the regime in power? In a way, the answer is self-evident—if these factors were sufficient, there might not have been any wars. Although a large propaganda campaign was under way, war was not engaged until the Serbian regime was seriously threatened by its own internal opposition. The ideological dimension of this move is clear enough; war made it possible to mobilize, around a sense of imminent danger, people who might not have been mobilized in favor of the regime's politics. There is a more drastic dimension as well: war enhanced the dominance of the pro-regime parts of the population by changing its structure. The exodus of the young, the urban, and the educated made the regime's reliance on the old, the rural, and the less educated more secure. At the same time, war conditions made it possible for those anti-war people who remained to be isolated from their antiwar counterparts at home and in other republics and cut off the rest of the population from alternative sources of information. In this regard, war can be seen as one of the elements, perhaps the most important, of what regime critics have labeled "the destruction of society."[81]

The failure of "transition" in Serbia led to the combination of a regime that most people in the country find distasteful and an opposition that is thoroughly discredited, not only by regime-sponsored media but also by its own failures and inconsistencies. The result is a resignation on the part of people who would otherwise look for channels through which to change the regime. One person with whom I spoke described a common perception: "Our opposition practically doesn't exist. It's just a handful of small leaders competing with one another for position. If there were a real opposition party we could really change things." Another person, having been through three election campaigns, said: "I think I'll probably never vote again in my life." The supporters of the regime, who began as a coalition of the conventional and the desperate,[82] are more

---

81. The phrase is used as the title of a collection of studies of contemporary Serbia. Mladen Lazić, ed., *Razaranje društva: Jugoslovensko društvo u krizi 90-ih* (Belgrade: Filip Višnjić, 1994).

82. The alliance of Communist and nationalist elements has been variously described in Russia as a "Red-Black" coalition and elsewhere (for example by Vujačić, 1995) as a "Left-Right" coalition. I am not inclined to repeat this terminology as I fail to see the "left" elements in a Communist power structure composed principally of military leaders and the directors of state-owned corporations. Rather, I am inclined to

inclined to continue their support from habit rather than from belief—paradoxically justifying support for Milošević on the ground that "we lived well under Tito." In a political environment defined by the nominal existence of party plurality and the undeniable fact of single-party rule, the existence of political alternatives and hopes for change are subject to constant pressures. The people who depend on these alternatives and hopes are subject to constant disappointment and frustration. What remains for people is to find a way to live inside a system for which they have no respect.

---

believe, with Max Horkheimer (in his *Critique of Instrumental Reason* [New York: Seabury Press, 1974]), that a regime need not be defined as being of the left simply because it repeats Marxist slogans.

3

The Destruction of Information Alternatives

In the old time when everybody believed, thought, and spoke alike, there were, after all, some who did not. People who were young then should know that even then, when nothing was possible and everything was obligatory, the occasional person managed to carry himself differently. The occasional person did or said something which others did not, or refused something which the majority would not. These people had to have courage and, of course, to pay a certain price.

After that, national homogenization came to power in Serbia. It was not completely obligatory, but again nearly everybody thought alike, and again for the people who did not it was not easy.[1]

In the time of SFRJ, Yugoslav media were, according to Mark Thompson, "much richer, more diverse, and freer than in any other Communist state."[2] They were also much richer, more diverse, and freer than they became with the rise of nationalist authoritarianism. Although Miloše-

---

1. Stojan Cerović, "Loš, gori, najluđi," *Vreme*, no. 228, 6 March 1995, p. 8.
2. Thompson (1995), 5. The comparison need not lead to exaggerated celebration of the former Yugoslavia's ostensible press freedom. Thompson goes on to detail several articles of the former Yugoslav constitution, as well as portions of the criminal law, which specified some strong restrictions on the freedom of the press (8–11). In addition to legal restrictions on content, privately owned media did not exist in practice during most of SFRJ's history. It may also be worthy of note that public figures like Franjo Tuđman and Vojislav Šešelj, who later became leaders of nationalist movements, first achieved international notice as "prisoners of conscience," prosecuted on the basis of material they had written.

vić's regime inherited from its Communist predecessor a large state-controlled publishing and broadcasting empire, including Serbia's most important and widely diffused media outlets, it set out to use them more openly for political purposes than its immediate predecessor had. In addition to state media, the period of Milošević's rule saw the rise of several independent media outlets, as well as several campaigns by the regime to marginalize and silence these outlets.

The role of the media monopolies in the republics of the former Yugoslavia as instruments of regimes and as catalysts of war has been widely noted in existing research. Particularly in Serbia, each major phase of development of the Milošević regime has been accompanied by the takeover or destruction of some important media outlet. Both Milošević's rise to power and the path to war were eased by the takeover of the newspaper *Politika*, the weekly magazine *NIN*, and the state radio and television network RTS. The Belgrade protests of 9 March 1991 centered on the ruling party's control of RTS (which was henceforth referred to in opposition circles as TV Bastille) and saw the temporary silencing of the independent television station Studio B and the independent radio station B-92. With the beginning of the war came the cooperative destruction by the governments of Serbia and Croatia of the federal Yutel television station.[3] As the Serbian regime made its public turn away from nationalism, it took over the daily newspaper *Borba* and the independent television station Studio B and quietly set about shutting down nationalist magazines and local radio stations that it had encouraged during its rise to power. Probably one of the crucial moments in the antiregime demonstrations that began in November and December 1996 involved the regime's closing, then being forced to reopen, the independent Radio B-92 and the student station Radio Indeks.

In addition to examining regime-controlled and independent media institutions in Serbia, I also seek to examine the audiences for these media. The process of information relies not only on institutional factors at the site of production of information, but on motivational and orientational factors at the site of reception as well. Both independent and regime-controlled media in Belgrade had loyal audiences, and one question to be examined in determining why people are informed in the way they are is why they choose the information sources they choose. Although

---

3. One version of the story of Yutel's brief existence is told through the voice of its former general director, Goran Milić, in Thompson (1995), 38–507.

the examination of news institutions shows that people did not make these choices without constraint, the investigation of motivations and orientations among audience members demonstrates that the types of choices people made both reflected and deepened the social divisions in Serbia on which the regime relied.

Media Portrait of Belgrade, 1994–1995

In Belgrade, various print media, both regime controlled and independent, were generally available during the period of my research. Those instances in which independent media were not available in the city are discussed later in this chapter. With regard to the principal broadcast media, radio and television, the selection of independent sources was somewhat more restricted, although two independent radio stations and one independent television station functioned during the period of research. The independent television station was taken over by the Belgrade city government shortly after the period of research had ended.

The fact that independent media outlets were generally available should not be taken to mean that they were as available as regime-controlled media outlets. Both independent broadcast media, and to a somewhat lesser extent independent print media, were limited in their extent to the city of Belgrade and its immediate environs. Hence although a visitor to the city might be persuaded that the rudiments of a free and open press exist in Serbia, a visit to the interior of the country would quickly debunk that notion. The only media source available throughout Serbia is the state-run television and radio network, and independent newspapers and magazines are infrequently and irregularly found outside major cities. In the city of Belgrade as well, technical and economic difficulties, as well as occasional regime attacks on independent media, have prevented them from occupying much more than a marginal role.

During the period of research in Belgrade, in 1994 and 1995, the following newspapers were generally available:[4]

1. *Politika* (Politics). The government-controlled daily is the oldest and most respected newspaper in Belgrade. As the "respectable" regime paper, its content is usually light on propaganda. It generally addresses

---

4. Two new dailies appeared in 1996 and are not discussed here. These are *Blic* (Flash) and *Dnevni telegraf* (Daily telegraph).

controversial local issues by ignoring them, by reporting vaguely, or by restricting its coverage to reprints of bulletins from the federal Tanjug news agency or direct reproductions of statements from government officials. Other than this, its content is principally characterized by world news from international agencies (UPI, Reuters, Agence France-Presse, ANSA), generally noncontroversial domestic coverage, and strong coverage of culture. Some of *Politika's* cultural correspondents, like the rock and roll critic Petar Janjatović, the television reporter Branka Otašević, the cultural chronicler Velimir Ćurguz-Kazimir, and the wry cultural columnist Bogdan Tirnanić, are well respected and popular. Because the "propagandistic" side of *Politika* operates more by exclusion than by repetition of messages, any strong statements appearing in the paper are given special attention by readers.[5] The press run of *Politika* averaged around 200,000 copies during the period of observation.

2. *Večernje novosti* (Evening news). According to its self-description, it is the newspaper "in the readers' party," which informs them "quickly, briefly, and clearly" (*brzo, kratko, i jasno*).[6] Detractors regard it as the most openly propagandistic pro-regime paper. The tabloid, with its sensational coverage and emphasis on scandals, turbofolk celebrities, and sports, is the best-selling newspaper in Serbia. It is also the medium of choice for attacks on opposition parties, independent media outlets, and international political figures. These attacks are not limited to commentaries, but also appear in news articles and in the daily jokes and witticisms column, which has a markedly political flavor. In this regard, it is widely considered to be the newspaper closest to the regime and the one that follows regime policy most closely. The press run of *Večernje novosti* averaged between 200,000 and 250,000 copies during the period of observation, with some special holiday issues printed in runs of over 400,000 copies.

3. *Politika ekspres* (Politics express). A publication of the *Politika* company, *Ekspres* is directed toward the same readership as *Večernje novosti*. Its content is more sensationalistic, and its orientation more openly pro-regime, than its parent paper. I do not have figures for the average press

5. This characterization of *Politika* applies to the period of observation. The paper took on a more openly propagandistic character during the period of war and the time leading up to it. For descriptions of these periods, see Thompson (1995), and Latinka Perović, "Beg od modernizacije," *Republika*, 16–31 March 1995.

6. Svetozar Đonović, "41. godišnjica 'Večernjih novosti': U partiji čitalaca," *Večernje novosti*, 16 October 1994, pp. 1–2.

run of *Politika ekspres*, but it may fairly be characterized as much smaller than that of *Politika* or of *Večernje novosti*.

4. *Borba* (Struggle), later *Naša borba* (Our struggle). The only independent newspaper in Serbia, *Borba* carried the reports of its own reporters and correspondents throughout the former Yugoslavia and in several other countries, as well as the reports of the independent news agencies AIM (*Alternativna informativna mreža*—Alternative information network), FoNet, and Beta. In addition to this everyday information, *Borba* published in its weekend edition a wide range of commentaries from domestic and international writers across the political spectrum. *Borba* was taken over by the government and transformed into a little-read pro-regime paper resembling *Večernje novosti* in December 1994. By February 1995, the editors and journalists of the independent paper reorganized under the title *Naša borba*. The story of the takeover is told in this chapter. Although the usual press run of *Borba/Naša borba* averaged between 30,000 and 40,000 copies during the period of observation, it was subject to fluctuation because of limited paper supply and other obstacles. (See Fig. 4.)

A survey of readership of newspapers in Serbia (excluding Kosovo) was undertaken by the Mark-plan agency in September 1996. The survey includes readership data for one paper, *Dnevni telegraf* (Daily telegraph), which began publishing after the period of observation had ended. Among the respondents of the Mark-plan survey, 25.3 percent reported reading *Politika*, 17.1 percent read *Večernje novosti*, 7.4 percent read *Dnevni telegraf*, 6.4 percent read *Naša borba*, and 5.9 percent reported reading *Politika ekspres*.[7] The most frequent answer on the survey, however, was that the individual read no daily newspaper at all, which accounted for 30.1 percent of all responses.

For people in the majority of the population who do not rely on newspapers as their principal source of daily information, television is the primary source. Research cited by Mark Thompson indicates that television is by far the most frequently used source of information in Serbia.[8] Mikloš Biro offered a more dramatic assessment, estimating that "over 60 percent of the population watches TV Dnevnik II [the main news program on RTS], compared with 2 percent who read newspapers."[9] According to

7. Unsigned, " 'Politika' najčitaniji list u SRJ," *Odraz B-92 vesti* (Internet izdanje), 14 October 1996.
8. Thompson (1995), 84 and n. 68.
9. Biro (1994), 84.

Fig. 4. When the newspaper *Borba* was taken over by the regime in December 1994, the "special edition" put out by the journalists could not be sold at newsstands. Volunteers appeared to sell the paper on foot. Photo courtesy of *Vreme*.

Sreten Vujović, television constitutes the primary source of information for 69 percent of the population.[10]

The only television station with a signal that reaches the entire territory of Serbia is the first program of the state television RTS (*Radio-televizija Srbije*), which has studios in Belgrade, Novi Sad, and Priština. The second and third programs of RTS reach a somewhat smaller audience. Several state-owned and "mixed-property" local stations broadcast entertainment-only programs, most of them for fewer than twenty-four hours, in smaller towns.[11] In Belgrade, six stations had programs, aside from the three programs of RTS, during the period of research. Of these, three (Art TV, TV Pink, and TV Palma) broadcast only films, music

10. Sreten Vujović, "Promene u materijalnom standardu i načinu života društvenih slojeva," in Mladen Lazić, ed., *Razaranje društva: Jugoslovensko društvo u krizi 90-ih* (Belgrade: Filip Višnjić, 1994), 87.

11. For a listing of all the television stations in Serbia and Montenegro as of October 1994, see "Lokalne TV stanice u Jugoslaviji," *Mala lokalna televizija*, special edition of *Novinarstvo*, 28:2–3 (Belgrade: Institut za novinarstvo i CLIO, 1994), 108.

videos, and other entertainment programs. Two stations broadcast news—TV Politika, operated by the company that publishes the newspaper *Politika*, broadcast a news program that drew principally on the bulletins of the Tanjug news agency; BK Telekom, operated by the Braća Karić bank, carried satellite broadcasts of international news programs and presented a nightly news program of its own production, which was technically strong, but differed little in content from the broadcasts of RTS and TV Politika.[12] Belgrade was also home to Serbia's only independent television station, NTV Studio B,[13] which broadcast the only independent nightly news program in the country. The station could be seen only in Belgrade and the immediate surrounding area, however.[14] In 1996, the city government of Belgrade took over NTV Studio B, leaving the country without any independent television program.

In December 1994, the Partner polling agency asked residents of the city of Belgrade which television station offered the best daily news program. The results of the survey are presented in Table 12.

Of the many radio programs in Belgrade, only Studio B and Radio B-92 offered independent news programs during the period of observation. Other stations, especially the three radio stations operated by RTS and the stations Radio Politika and Radio Novosti, offered news programs based on their television and newspaper equivalents. Most other

12. The journalist Aleksandar Tijanić became director of BK Telekom shortly after being dismissed as director of TV Politika. He retained the television post when he became federal Minister of Information in 1996 and returned to work at BK full-time after resigning from the ministry in December 1996.

13. Studio B was founded by the newspaper *Borba* in 1970 and became the first private broadcasting company in Yugoslavia in 1972. It expanded from radio to television in 1990. In 1995, 86 percent of the stock in the station was owned by its employees. For details, see Thompson (1995), 111–15.

14. As reported by Mark Thompson, an effort to broaden Studio B's signal capacity was dramatically thwarted: "On 29 December 1992, two trucks with equipment intended for Studio B, with a value of $236,000, which was acquired by the International Fund for Media, were robbed soon after crossing the border from Hungary. The government denies that the equipment ever entered the country, and therefore refuses to investigate the case. A month later, in January 1993, three employees of Studio B, among them the director of the station, were assaulted and threatened at the same border by four armed persons, who later opened fire on the journalists' truck which carried equipment for the station" (Thompson, 1995, 113). The final destination of the stolen broadcast equipment is not known, and the most popular rumor in Belgrade is that it was sent to Pale, where it was used for the broadcast of the Bosnian Serb television station.

Table 12. Popularity of TV news programs
Belgrade, December 1994

NTV Studio B	36.0%
RTS 1	26.4
Does not watch news programs	24.0
TV Politika	10.8
Other stations	2.8

SOURCE: Unsigned, "Program," *Vreme*, no. 229,
13 March 1995, p. 28.

publicly and privately owned stations in Belgrade offered principally music and entertainment programs.[15] When the city government of Belgrade took over Studio B in 1996, the company's radio station suffered the same fate as its television station. In the interior of the country, a few private radio stations maintained independent news programs, of which Radio Pančevo, Radio Smederevo, and Radio Bajina Bašta came to be the most highly regarded. In December 1996, the Serbian government had banned the operation of Radio B-92 after jamming its signal for several days. After two days, the station began broadcasting again, but its legal status remained undefined. Radio B-92 has undertaken several other ventures, such as distribution of daily news over the Internet, publication of an ad hoc daily bulletin, publication of books and records, and the operation of a cultural and artistic center in a former movie theater. In response to the efforts of the regime to suppress independent radio stations during the 1996–97 protests, Radio B-92 organized local independent stations into an Association of Independent Electronic Media (*Asocijacija nezavisnih elektronskih medija—ANEM*), distributing news and programming to stations that cover most of the territory of Serbia.

Of Belgrade's four principal newsmagazines, only one is strongly under the influence of the regime. This magazine is *Duga* (Rainbow), published biweekly. Its regular columnists run the gamut of pro-regime orientations, from the openly fascist and anti-Semitic Dragoš Kalajić to the self-declared leftist Mirjana Marković, whose husband is Slobodan Milošević. *Duga's* war correspondent, Nebojša Jevrić, wrote bulletins from the point of view of the Bosnian Serb military force, which he ac-

---

15. See the highly opinionated tour of Belgrade's FM dial prepared by Teofil Pančić, "What's the Frequency, Kenneth?" *Vreme zabave* (January 1995), 2–73.

tively supported.[16] From 1993 onward, *Duga* began publishing occasional articles moderately critical of the regime, as well as occasional interviews with opposition-party politicians.

The weekly magazine *NIN* (the name is an abbreviation for *Nedeljne informativne novine*, or "Weekly informative newspaper") attained its independence from the *Politika* publishing house in 1994. Generally anti-regime in orientation, the magazine is principally oriented toward the political right and toward some nationalist parties and intellectuals. The principal personality characterizing this orientation is *NIN*'s political diarist Milivoje Glišić. Another weekly, *Telegraf*, shares *NIN*'s political orientation but prints in a tabloid format with texts directed toward a less-educated readership. *Telegraf* is rich in articles presented as being "Exclusive!" "Sensational!" and "Scandalous!"

Vreme (Time) was set into motion as a private company in 1990, with most of its original personnel dissatisfied journalists from *Politika* and *NIN*, which were increasingly coming under regime control at the time. The choice of title was not coincidental: the journalists sought to emulate, in independence and breadth, as well as in appearance, the popular American weekly *Time* and the German weekly *Die Zeit*. The magazine characterizes itself as "a magazine without lies, hatred, or prejudice"[17] and has consistently opposed nationalist mobilization and the wars in Croatia and Bosnia-Hercegovina. Although *Vreme*'s broad-based group of correspondents has probably made it the most-cited magazine from former Yugoslavia among international journalists, it does not hold to an ideology of "objective" reporting. Rather, its highly opinionated and widely researched articles are often characterized by irony, sarcasm, and bitterness and a generally consistent antinationalist and pro-European orientation. This orientation is epitomized in the columns by political diarist Stojan Cerović, social-political correspondents Milan Milošević and Dragoslav Grujić, and media and music critic Petar Luković.[18] Like Radio B-92, *Vreme* has branched out into other publishing ventures as well, including an international edition (until 1996), a music and enter-

---

16. For a sampling of Jevrić's reporting, see Vladimir Đerić, "Duga: Izazovi ratne reportaže," in Branko Milinković, ed., *Govor mržnje: Analiza sadržaja domaćih medija u prvoj polovini 1993. godine* (Belgrade: Centar za antiratnu akciju, 1994), 51–58.

17. Thompson (1995), 122.

18. In 1996, Petar Luković left *Vreme* and began publishing a music and entertainment magazine, *X-Zabave*. He had previously been editor of *Vreme*'s music and entertainment supplement, *Vreme zabave*.

Table 13. Products and services on which respondents completely ceased spending money (in percentages)

Class of Respondent	Daily Papers	Weeklies and Magazines	Films, Theater, Concerts	Visits to Cafes
Directors/executives	47	26	64	66
Professionals	37	22	50	56
Clerks, technicians	44	64	63	63
Skilled workers	57	72	80	76
Unskilled workers	74	81	86	74
Agricultural workers	53	57	85	55
Retired	68	85	87	82
Unemployed	45	54	61	46

SOURCE: Sreten Vujović, "Promene u materijalnom standardu i načinu života društvenih slojeva," in Mladen Lazić, Danilo Mrkšič, Sreten Vujović, Bora Kuzmanović, Stjepan Gredelj, Slobodan Cvejić, and Vladimir Vuletić, *Razaranje društva: Jugoslovensko društvo u krizi 90-ih* (Belgrade: Filip Višnjić, 1994), 117.

NOTE: The categories of respondents are typical of the distinctions made between "classes" in survey research in Yugoslavia. The original-language designations are as follows, respectively: *rukovodioci, stručnjaci, službenici i tehničari, KV radnici, NKV radnici, poljoprivrednici, penzioneri,* and *nezaposleni.*

tainment magazine, and a book publisher. In 1996, the book publisher and music magazine separated from the magazine and established themselves as independent enterprises.

In general, although some independent media outlets do operate in Serbia—in particular, the daily newspaper *Naša borba,* the weekly magazine *Vreme,* and the radio station B-92—these reach a limited audience. To the extent that they are available, independent broadcast media are available for the most part only in Belgrade; print media are available in some other larger cities. Television, however, remains the dominant medium and is completely and directly controlled by the regime. Other factors have contributed to increasing the dominance of television, especially economic factors. Sreten Vujović, in research conducted during the 1993 economic breakdown, asked respondents to identify products and services that they had ceased purchasing altogether. His findings for media and entertainment activities are presented in Table 13. Undoubtedly many (although probably not all) the people who swore off nontelevision sources of information in 1993 have resumed using them since. Nonetheless, access to independent media, already restricted, narrowed further as a result of economic pressure on individuals.

Regime-Controlled Media: Messages and Strategies

The media under the control of the regime accomplished many of the basic tasks associated with establishing and entrenching SPS in power. When state-controlled media were not engaged in active efforts to discredit domestic opposition, they enhanced the sense that SPS was the inevitably dominant party by systematically excluding domestic opponents from coverage. In the period leading up to the wars of succession, the media monopoly was indispensable in catalyzing support for the Serbian regime through its efforts to promote fear of the regimes in other republics, a campaign reciprocated—and hence in good measure validated—by the media monopolies in other republics. Many observers have noted the sowing of nationalist panic by state-controlled media as one of the most important factors causing the wars of succession in the former Yugoslavia.[19]

Leading the charge toward war was the state radio and television network RTS, the only media outlet generally available throughout the country. From 1988 onward, while a series of "truth meetings" organized throughout Serbia by the Serbian Resistance Movement (*Srpski pokret otpora*) promoted Milošević's consolidation of power, Belgrade television journalists received instructions to publicize these meetings favorably.[20] When opposition parties began to form in 1990, journalists who refused to cover them critically were fired. After the March 1991 demonstrations in Belgrade, called in response to biased and selective information on RTS, television news programs emphasized threats of "a new genocide" against Serbs in Croatia. Within weeks after the huge demonstrations, battles between Croatian and Serb forces in Croatia had begun and offered more material for the rhetoric of threat that RTS had made its principal recurring theme. As nearly one-half of RTS journalists joined an independent union with the goal of "free and objective information

19. See Lalić (1995), Milinković (1994), and Mark Thompson, *Forging War: The Media in Serbia, Croatia, and Bosnia-Hercegovina* (London: Article 19, 1994).

20. According to Branka Mihajlović, former news director at RTS, instructions included according the meetings "special status" on the evening news program, inflating the number of attendees, emphasizing the "heroic status" and popularity of Slobodan Milošević, and removing from the scene "nationalist symbols (which were) unacceptable to the majority of viewers," such as Četnik symbols and old Serbian flags (Thompson, 1995, 88).

and professional rights of employees,"[21] political pressure grew. Union members were fired, sent on "forced vacation" (*prinudni odmor*), or removed from programs, a campaign of pressure culminating in the firing of nearly one-third of RTS journalists, some 1,300 people, in January 1993.

The role of RTS and the publications of the *Politika* company in leading the path to war in Serbia has been widely examined and documented by a number of researchers, from Veljko Vujačić[22] and Latinka Perović[23] in the period of nationalist mobilization, to Lazar Lalić[24] and Mark Thompson[25] in the early period of the war, and Ivan Čolović[26] as the war developed and continued. Although coverage of the developments in the wars in Bosnia-Hercegovina and Croatia changed to some degree after the regime altered its ostensible position on the war in August 1994, only some of this change was marked by a change in orientation of coverage. For the most part, the regime's change of position was indicated in state-controlled media by either silencing information about the war (which had previously dominated news programs) or by reporting events as if they did not involve Serbia at all. This strategy was easiest to follow for RTS, which had only to stop rebroadcasting the productions of TV Pale and cancel its multihour war reports, as it was easy to follow for *Politika*, which had long experience of ignoring and downplaying inconvenient stories.

The sensationalist *Večernje novosti*, however, had built a strong reputation for one-sided war reporting, which evolved into the viewpoint for the reporting of most stories. *Novosti* faithfully followed the new regime line in regularly running articles praising the "peacemaking policies" of Slobodan Milošević, but the war metaphor continued to define its news coverage generally.[27] One sensational, but transparently false, human-

---

21. Quoted in Thompson (1995), 88.
22. Vujačić (1995).
23. Perović (1995).
24. Lalić (1995).
25. Thompson (1995).
26. Čolović (1994a) and *Pucanje od zdravlja* (Belgrade: Beogradski krug, 1994b).
27. The metaphor also defined *Novosti*'s presentation of its own role. In an article marking the newspaper's forty-first anniversary, the following recollection was offered of its first days:

Novosti was born on a foggy October evening in 1953, in the time when the country was shaken by the famous Trieste crisis, when demonstrators in the

interest item featured an image of a young boy crying on a grave, with the accompanying text reading:

> The greatest victims of wars are children. That is the case in this newest war, in which the Serbian people are defending their bare existence. The picture which made its way around the world a year and a half ago, from the graveyard near Skelane, in which this boy—an orphan grieving over the grave of his father, mother, and other relatives who were killed by Muslims in their offensive, continues to disturb all those who know the suffering of children. In the meantime, the child in the photo has been adopted by a family in Zvornik, and he is now a first-year student at a military academy.[28]

The image printed in the paper was not, however, a photograph of the boy described in the text. Any person who had visited the National Museum in Belgrade would recognize the image as a photograph of the painting *Na majčinom grobu* (On his mother's grave), painted in 1879 by Uroš Predić, which hangs in the museum.[29]

Večernje novosti also distinguished itself from the remaining papers in its war reporting in the period in which "peace had no alternative." In May 1995, when Croatia reconquered the portion of Western Slavonia that had been under the control of the self-declared Republika Srpske Krajine, RTS and *Politika* limited their coverage to the protests lodged by SRJ's foreign ministry and to the flood of refugees who attempted to enter Serbia from the region. *Novosti* sprang to the defense of the Krajina Serb parastate, particularly when news broke that the Krajina army had fired missiles into the city of Zagreb. In an article claiming that the event

---

streets of Belgrade proudly and excitedly shouted the slogans: "Trieste is ours" and "Trieste, Gorica, and Rijeka—will always be ours" [*Trst, Gorica, i Rijeka—biće naša dovijeka*]. . . .
A great wave of patriotism rolled through the streets.

Svetozar Đonović, "41. godišnjica *Večernjih novosti*," *Večernje novosti*, 16 October 1994, p. 2. The revival of an old territorial claim against Italy, as well as the reprinting of a slogan laying claim to one city in Slovenia and another in Croatia, neither of which was the subject of dispute at the time, adds a quizzical dimension to *Novosti*'s generally nationalist profile.

28. Unsigned, "Bolno podsećanje," *Večernje novosti*, 19 November 1994.

29. The article and painting are discussed by Nenad Lj. Stefanović, "Siroče od 115 godina," *Vreme*, no. 214, 28 November 1994, pp. 29–30.

was staged, *Novosti* wrote: " '[T]he bombing' of Zagreb is yet another move by the profascist Tuđman regime to satanize Serbs, and once again, before the eyes of global public opinion and with the help of the so-called international community, frame them for the destruction of the peace process. That this is the case is evidenced by the suspicions of some western observers that Zagreb placed explosives in its own city and set fire to automobiles and tires, only to, as so many times before in this war, place anathema on the Serbs."[30] The effort to excuse the Krajina Serb military was unappreciated by its commander Milan Martić, who declared the next day that he had indeed ordered missiles to be fired at Zagreb and would do so again.

The above interpretations offered by *Novosti* are interesting in the sense that although they reflect neither the facts of the cases being reported nor the state policy of the moment (which was to distance the Serbian regime from the Serb parastates in Croatia and Bosnia-Hercegovina), they consistently reflected the organizing myths of nationalist authoritarianism—victimization, cultural threat, and a disapproving fear of Serbia's neighboring states. The dominance of this viewpoint is apparent in a report on pornography and prostitution in Slovenia, titled "Slovenians like to pay."[31] Similarly, a report on the activity of international religious sects in Serbia is titled "The Devil comes from the West."[32] The paranoid frame also informs reports on cultural events in other places: an article on the objections of the municipal government of Rome to the expanding number of Chinese restaurants in the city sympathetically reported the complaints of Romans:

If the "yellows" are permitted to expand through the city of Rome, the Peking duck will swallow the pizza, lasagna, and ravioli, and Italians cannot permit that to happen in their own land. . . .

30. D. Glušičević, "Markale u Zagrebu?" *Večernje novosti*, 3 May 1995, p. 7. The title of the article is a reference to the bombing of the Markale public market in Sarajevo, another incident for which regime-controlled media in Serbia presented the thesis that their opponents had "bombed themselves" for the purpose of publicity. *Novosti* was joined in its denial by *Borba*, which had been taken over by the regime five months earlier.

31. Igor Šaranović, "Slovenci vole da plate," *Večernje novosti*, 7 March 1995. An interesting comparison can be made to the admiring essay published in *Politika* the following month, after a forum with Slovenian publishers in Belgrade. Velimir Ćurguz, "O časopisima i izdavačima: Kako to rade Slovenci," *Politika*, 11 April 1995.

32. E. V., "Đavo stiže sa zapada," *Večernje novosti*, 5 April 1995, p. 11.

This fact [that Chinese businesspeople succeed in purchasing and maintaining businesses] has raised the question in the city: how is it that Chinese people have so much money, if they do not receive it through an invasion of the Mediterranean by the Chinese mafia? "I have seen how they pay for their business spaces. It was enough money to fill a truck," added one prominent Roman restaurateur to the complaints of city officials. There immediately followed assessments that in the "yellow" restaurants the service was poor, the cleanliness was at the lowest level, and that the food was such that it "turned the stomach." "I don't know whether they cook dogs or cats," declared . . . , the person responsible for sanitation in public places in the city center.[33]

Through promoting stereotypes of neighboring states, of the "decadent West," and even of Chinese cuisine, *Novosti* elevates the national-paranoia frame to the global level and provides a normalizing context for the local national paranoia that defines most of its reporting and interpretation.

The same frame elevated to the global level is also translated to the local level in portraits of the Serbian opposition. For the most part, opposition parties and their activities receive minimal attention in regime-controlled media, except as objects of attack or in instances in which their leaders attack one another. In this regard, the role of Vojislav Šešelj and his Radical party as "counteropposition," mentioned in the previous chapter, outlasted the regime's romance with the party. Even outside official favor, Šešelj could still be relied on for the occasional quote characterizing the leaders of other parties as traitors. Consistent with this approach was *Novosti*'s article reporting on the formation of a coalition by the Democratic Party (DS), Democratic Party of Serbia (DSS), and Serbian Radical Party (SRS). The article focused on the fact that Vuk Drašković's Serbian Renewal Movement (SPO) did not join the coalition, with the simple headline "Vuk did not come."[34]

When opposition leaders did not criticize one another sufficiently to supply regime-controlled media with quotes, other sources had to be relied on. Both *Novosti* and *Politika*, as well as the regime version of *Borba*,

33. Mirjana Radetić, "Patka guta picu," *Večernje novosti*, 23 February 1995, p. 13.
34. Unsigned (attributed to Tanjug), "Vuk nijo došao," *Večernje novosti*, 14 February 1995, p. 5. The coalition was inactive and short lived.

accused the opposition parties of obstructing the work of the Serbian parliament when, in March and April 1995, the parties extended the debate over the prime minister's annual report over several weeks. At other times, more direct methods were used, as in one of the rare letters printed in *Novosti* from the president of a Salzburg group named Fatherland Serbian Action (*Otadžbinska srpska akcija*):

> Listening to the statements of Mr. Drašković, we had the feeling that we were listening to Ms. ALBRIGHT, or Mr. SOROS, [Austrian Foreign Minister Alois] MOCK, IZETBEGOVIĆ, or TUĐMAN. . . .
>
> We appeal to and demand of the responsible state agencies that by their action or by taking certain measures they protect the Serbian people and citizens of Serbia from people like VUK DRAŠKOVIĆ and [Kosovo "shadow president"] IBRAHIM RUGOVA.
>
> We believe that the state has the power and the means to defend its own honor and that of its citizens from the appearances and statements of people who are—NATIONAL PARASITES.
>
> This should be done in the name of the future of our people and our state. (capitals in original)[35]

In another instance, *Novosti* took on the role of state security and published two uncredited photographs of DS leader Zoran Đinđić at a restaurant with Ljubodrag Stojadinović, a Yugoslav Army colonel who had been dismissed the previous week for criticizing the regime. The quality of the photographs suggested that they had been secretly taken with a surveillance camera, indicating that *Novosti* was either flaunting or pretending to have close connections with services practicing espionage against domestic political opponents.[36]

On the other side of the coin, regime-controlled media reported on the activities of state institutions and politicians with a markedly positive attitude. The 1995 annual report of the prime minister, which provoked weeks of exchanges in the Serbian parliament, was reported in *Politika* under the headline, "Very successful work by the government of the Re-

35. Predsednik udruženja Srba Novica Ranđelović, Salzburg (letter), "Vuk nas obrukao," *Večernje novosti*, 22 February 1995, p. 12.

36. Unsigned, "Novi imidž," *Večernje novosti*, 23 March 1995, p. 19.

public of Serbia."[37] *Novosti* accompanied its story, titled "The government works wonderfully,"[38] with a man-in-the-street survey on the topic titled "Beyond expectations."[39]

Spokespersons for the regime expressed the same high regard for the media outlets they controlled as these media outlets expressed for the regime. In various statements of support and sympathy, they articulated a sense of what, in the view of the regime, the role of information media ought to be. Serbian Minister of Information Milivoje Pavlović saw RTS as a force of national unity in the face of global conspiracies: "Thanks to the advantages of electronic media, RTS ensures that there is a valuable degree of spiritual unity among all Serbs in the world in these times in which neither justice nor truth prevail, but are made to order, and poisoned by Serbophobia and other products from the creators of the new world order."[40] A more pragmatic view was taken by Slobodan Jovanović, director of the Tanjug news agency and president of the Belgrade SPS organization, who regarded the role of regime-controlled media as being the promotion of regime policy: "*Večernje novosti* has succeeded, in these stormy and dramatic times as in all of its rich and honorable decades of existence, in preserving its integrity and remaining a faithful and dependable foundation of this people and this country in their struggle for truth and survival. Today, when the world acknowledges ever more openly that we were in the right, it would not be an exaggeration to say that of all of our media outlets, *Večernje novosti* has been the most honest and most faithful."[41] Yet more pragmatic was the perspective offered by Dragan Tomić, chair of the Serbian parliament, who emphasized the size of the readership of regime-controlled newspapers: "*Večernje novosti* plays a very important role in this political moment. By their method of informing people, they have conquered the most numerous reading public. I consider *Novosti* and *Politika* to be vital institutions to the national interest."[42] In addition to frequent warm statements of support, regime officials also aided the media outlets they controlled by subsidizing their paper supply,

37. Unsigned, "Veoma uspešan rad Vlade Republike Srbije," *Politika*, 25 March 1995, p. 12.
38. Unsigned, "Vlada odlično radi," *Večernje novosti*, 25 March 1995, p. 7.
39. Unsigned, "Više od očekivanja," *Večernje novosti*, 25 March 1995, pp. 6–7.
40. Quoted in William Shawcross, "Predgovor," in Thompson (1995), xii.
41. Quoted in Unsigned, "Prvi i najtiražniji," *Večernje novosti*, 16 October 1994, p. 5.
42. Unsigned, "Rog za sveću," *Večernje novosti*, 1 December 1994.

providing fuel to ease distribution, and excluding independent media from many news events. Thereby the favorable treatment the regime received in these media was reciprocated through privileged treatment.

Instruments in the Marginalization of Independent Media

At the same time, independent media and independent-minded journalists working in state media were subject to various pressures from the regime. The instruments used against independent media outlets in Serbia included open use of police power. This included violence against reporters and photographers during the antigovernment demonstrations of 9 March 1991 and 1 June 1993 in Belgrade, the kidnapping of *Vreme*'s Dušan Reljić in 1993,[43] and the beating of *Srpska reč*'s Milovan Brkić in 1996.[44] The cases of journalists fired from the Tanjug news agency and RTS remain unresolved before the courts. These sensational cases, however dramatic, are not typical of the everyday means engaged to marginalize independent media. Principally, the regime acts against these outlets by attempts to disqualify them in the media under the control of the regime, by the selective application of law, and by the control of resources and distribution necessary for production and publicity.

The regime's most-frequent and common strategy against independent media outlets is its effort to disqualify them as irresponsible, controlled by foreign influences, and lacking in objectivity. Although, as observed above, regime officials regularly praise the involvement of media under their control, they as regularly criticize media that are not. Typical of this perspective is the statement of federal Minister of Information Dragutin Brčin, in which he sought to undermine the perception that any media are independent:

> Brčin commented that "voyeuristic peeking into private lives, interfering with people's privacy, lies, inventions, insulting the state and its institutions, are not [examples of] freedom of the press."

43. See Thompson (1995), 63. Reljić had earlier been dismissed as director of the federal Tanjug news agency and replaced by Slobodan Jovanović, who was also the editor of the regime-controlled *Politika ekspres* and president of the Belgrade SPS organization. Jovanović lost these positions in the purge of SPS "hawks" after the signing of the Dayton peace accords.

44. The case was reported in *Naša Borba* (Internet izdanje), 21 October 1996, and in *Odraz B-92 vesti* (Internet izdanje), 20 and 21 October 1996.

The federal Minister of Information said that he does not accept the division between "independent" and "dependent" media. "Stories about the independence of the media lead to (*nameću*) dependent media," he said.[45]

In this view, "dependent" regime-controlled media act "independently" as the organic voice of the people,[46] whereas "independent" media disguise their dependence on the enemies of the state.

Sometimes these enemies are specified, and one favorite target of regime-controlled media is the American financier George Soros.[47] In March 1995, regime-controlled media launched an aggressive campaign against Soros, which culminated in a court decision closing the offices of his Open Society Foundation in Belgrade. In addition to accusing him of making "Janissaries out of children" through educational programs[48] and of promoting an unelaborated but implicitly threatening "Coca-Cola democracy" and "hot-dog democracy,"[49] regime media described his foundation's program of assistance to independent media as an effort to take over the country: "The aid which George Soros sends through his foundations and subsidiaries presents a perfidious attempt to easily break into all pores of our system. He found a point of entry in Montenegrin 'independent' media and in shrewd separatists who went blind before a fistful of dollars."[50] Through the attempt to discredit Soros and other international organizations that assist independent media, regime-controlled media hope to cast a shadow of doubt over the information independent media provide.

The media monopolies in other republics provide rhetorical ammunition for the media monopoly in Serbia. Provocative antiregime essays in the Croatian independent weekly *Feral tribune* are occasionally publicized

45. Unsigned (attributed to Tanjug), "Dragutin Brčin, Savezni ministar za informisanje: Slobodno i neodgovorno," *Večernje novosti*, 18 October 1994, p. 7.

46. In this regard, see Brčin's comments with regard to the newspaper *Borba* quoted here, as well as the comments of his colleague Ratomir Vico, for example in Lj. Bajagić and D. Dimitrovska, "Nezavisni neće mir," *Večernje novosti*, 14 April 1995, p. 4.

47. Soros has been an ideological target not only of the Serbian regime, but of the Croatian and Bosnian regimes as well. Each of these regimes accuses him and his foundation of sympathy with its "enemies" in the other regimes.

48. Unsigned, "Od dece janičari," *Večernje novosti*, 10 March 1995, p. 2.

49. Anđelka Popović, "Humanista ili bombarder," *Večernje novosti*, 11 March 1995, p. 2.

50. V. Kadić, "Podrška 'nezavisnim,' " *Večernje novosti*, 24 March 1995, p. 7.

in *Večernje novosti* and *Politika;* domestic independent media are occasionally showcased as examples of the "excessive" media freedom in SRJ. For example, a reader in Tivat wrote to *Večernje novosti*[51] to attack the independent Montenegrin weekly *Monitor:*

> The magazine *Monitor,* which is unfortunately published in Montenegro, has yet to write a single bad word about the bloody regime of Franjo Tuđman or the *džamaharija* of Izetbegović, but rather directs all of its attacks on everything which is Serbian and everything which is Yugoslav. Such foul work has not been recorded anywhere before. . . .
> Therefore it must be banned, because it writes violently, because it is credited and financed by the biggest Western scam. This has been recognized even by its editor-in-chief Esad Kočan.
> Imagine that somebody writes critically about the *ustaša* regime of Franjo Tuđman in Croatia, or that somebody negatively writes in any paper in Izetbegović's *džamaharija,* they know what consequences will follow.[52]

Ironically, the regimes described in the most insulting terms in the letter are, in the end, taken as models for the treatment of independent media.

In addition to attacks on the level of affiliation and content, independent media are subject to attacks claiming that, because they publicize political divisions in Serbia, their activity encourages the development of a civil war in Serbia. This perspective invites elaboration through conspiracy theory, as suggested in another letter to *Večernje novosti* addressed to two directors of the independent television station Studio B, presented in the form of a question the writer was unable to ask at a public forum:

> Gentlemen, everything you are propagating represents the fifth phase of the plan by Hitler's admiral Canaris for the destruction of the Serbs, which is carried out by [former German Foreign Minister] Hans Dietrich Genscher by way of [German Chancellor Helmut] Kohl, [Foreign Minister Klaus] Kinkel, the two of you, and

51. *Večernje novosti* publishes readers' letters very rarely and has no regular letters section. The letters that it publishes are generally of the type cited below.

52. Milutin Novaković (letter), "Zabrinuti 'Monitor,' " *Večernje novosti,* 25 February 1995, p. 11.

others who support it consciously or unconsciously. The first phase is the secession of Slovenia, the second the secession of Croatia, the third the secession of Macedonia, and the fourth is the secession of Bosnia and Hercegovina. The fifth, which you plan and propagate in the carrying out of Canaris's plan, is civil war in Serbia, which will begin as [Studio B director Dragan] Kojadinović says, with the meeting of support for Studio B and with the settling of accounts among Serbs, who is a *četnik* and who is a Partisan, as it is written on the flyer which you passed out at the entry to this meeting.

Tell us, how many Serbian lives do you plan to be lost in this civil war?[53]

As extreme and perhaps laughable as the conspiracy presented in the letter may seem, the basic message is consistent with statements by regime spokespersons accusing independent media of acting against and destabilizing the country.

For a view of the regime's use of its control of material resources and legal strategies, the case of the takeover of the independent newspaper *Borba* in 1994 and 1995 provides an illustration of these themes.

One Attack on Independent Media: The Borba Case

A repeated target of the regime's activity against independent media was the daily newspaper *Borba*. *Borba* had begun its life in 1922 as the organ of the Communist party and continued in this role during and after World War II, but it had, like *Politika*, started to take on a more independent profile and to move toward a more professional and objective model of journalism in the middle and late 1980s. *Politika* did not last long in this effort: one of Milošević's first moves after taking power in 1987 was to replace the director of the *Politika* publishing house and to bring its journalists and editors under his influence.[54] During this period, *Borba*

53. Slavko Đukić (letter), "Monopoli na istinu: Skinuta nezavisna maska," *Večernje novosti*, 15 March 1995.

54. The oldest and most respected newspaper in Serbia, *Politika*, was formally independently owned—as "social property" (*društvena svojina*), it was legally defined as being the property of its workers, represented by the Socialist Union of Working People (*Socijalistički savez radnog naroda—SSRN*), which in practice meant the League of Communists. The League of Communists had the power to name the director of the publishing house and the editors of its publications. In the current period, SPS exercises the same power.

remained close to the federal government and became a strong supporter in its editorial policy of the reformist federal prime minister, Ante Marković.

The paper built a strong reputation for providing independent information, for remaining open to opposing points of view, and for opposing the nationalist rhetoric that media controlled by the Serbian regime adopted as a principal theme. When Slobodan Milošević's unsuccessful attempt to gain control over the federal League of Communists of Yugoslavia (*Savez komunista Jugoslavije—SKJ*) ended with the walkout of the Slovenian, then the Croatian parties, *Borba's* banner headline read "The SKJ no longer exists."[55] Whereas state media either ignored or provided heavily one-sided information about the protests of 9 March 1991 and the following days, *Borba* reported on the parallel meetings of the "Terazije Parliament" and the pro-Milošević meeting at Ušće with the headline, "Parents at Ušće, children on Terazije."[56] The paper came to be considered as the only source for news about the activities of opposition political parties and other groups, as well as for an account of the writing about the former Yugoslavia by international news agencies. As the wars began in Croatia and Bosnia-Hercegovina, *Borba* distinguished itself by providing accurate on-the-spot reports and garnered severe condemnation from the Serbian government and from the warring parties. *Borba* published these condemnations as indications of its objectivity.

The paper's independence from the government became stronger in 1991, when it was privatized and transformed from "social property" to a stockholding company (*deoničarsko društvo*, indicated by the suffix "d. d."). The federal government bought 17 percent of the shares, banks purchased 15 percent, and employees 12 percent. When the paper appealed to readers to buy stock to prevent businesses close to the regime from acquiring a controlling interest in the company,[57] some three thousand of them bought 7 percent of the stock. Another 14 percent of the stock was purchased by various business interests in Serbia; the largest portion of shares, 35 percent, was purchased by a businessman, Dušan

55. Quoted in Ivan Mrđen, "Osvetoljubivost uvređenih," *Dosije Borba*, 22 November 1994, p. 1.

56. Quoted in Nada Kovačević, "Tako je pisala 'Borba,' " *Dosije Borba*, 22 November 1994, p. 11.

57. This was the fate of *Večernje novosti*, the paper closest to the Serbian regime. Although the company is, formally speaking, a private one, its stock is owned by non-privatized businesses under the control of the regime.

Mijić. As the largest shareholder, Mijić became the director of the company "Borba, d. d.," and journalists elected longtime correspondent Gordana Logar as editor-in-chief. On 5 September 1991, Judge Mirjana Trninić registered the new stockholding company "Borba, d. d." in the name of the Belgrade civil court.[58]

Borba's business prospects were hindered by a variety of means, including an insecure supply of newsprint, lack of access to distribution through some chains of newsstands, and regime pressure on advertisers not to place ads in the paper. As a consequence, it did not reach as wide a readership as the papers controlled by the regime. Its availability outside Belgrade was sparse and irregular, and its price was higher than that of the other newspapers.[59] In addition, *Borba* became the target of frequent attacks from positions of political power, which made it appear unattractive to people inclined to believe such statements and insecure to people for whom such statements play a role in planning (such as potential advertisers). Nonetheless, the paper managed to gain a loyal following. Former company director Ivan Mrđen estimates the average readership of *Borba* to have been around 40,000 in 1990, and its sales climbed to near 140,000 at the time of the March 1991 demonstrations.[60] Economic crisis and a lack of newsprint reduced its press run to around 7,500 copies in 1993.[61] By November 1994, Ivan Mrđen estimated the paper's readership at about 35,000.[62] Although the modest size of *Borba's* readership did not seriously threaten the position of state-controlled media, which were larger, cheaper, and more easily available, the regime did have some reasons to worry. *Borba's* readers were an influential group—they were more likely to be urban and more highly educated, and they expressed greater confidence in the reliability of the information they received than did

58. A facsimile of the registration document is reproduced in *Borba*, 19–20 November 1994, p. 2. A period of eight days was given for appeal of the registration, during which time no appeals were recorded.

59. Among the reasons for *Borba's* higher price, in addition to the lack of income from advertising, was that Matroz, the only factory that produced newsprint in SRJ, charged double the amount for newsprint that regime-controlled papers paid.

60. Ivan Mrđen, "Osvetoljubivost uvređenih," *Dosije Borba*, 22 November 1994, pp. 1–2.

61. Thompson (1995), 37.

62. Ivan Mrđen, "Osvetoljubivost uvređenih," *Dosije Borba*, 22 November 1994, pp. 1–2. The figures noted above refer to the press run of the paper. These figures are not, therefore, identical to the number of people who read the paper, as one copy may be read by several individuals.

readers of the state-controlled *Politika, Politika ekspres,* and *Večernje novosti* or audiences of the state television news program.

Attacks remained strategic and verbal until 1994, when the regime decided to move directly against *Borba.* On 22 July 1994, federal prosecutors demanded to the courts that the registration of "Borba, d. d." be removed from the judicial register, which effectively would have made the existence of the company illegal.[63] The government did not pursue the case, however, but petitioned the court with a request that it be put off "for an indefinite period of time."[64] A hearing was scheduled for 23 January 1995, but this hearing never took place.[65] In the meantime, the federal prosecutors approached the court with a successful request: to find that "Borba, d. d." was never registered. On 8 November 1994, civil court judge Goran Kljajević granted the petition, finding that the company had not been legally registered, hence reversing the decision made by his colleague Mirjana Trninić three years earlier. *Borba* reported the news of its disappearance sardonically: "*Borba,* therefore, does not exist. The thing you are holding in your hands is indeed *Borba,* but from the point of view of the state it is advisable that you not draw too many conclusions from that evidence. Just as a few days ago in the civil court it was decided that the stockholding company 'Borba' does not exist, it could be decided that the paper does not exist either, and after that, we surmise, the readers are next in line."[66] *Borba* also began organizing its own defense. In the following month, the pages of the paper contained facsimiles of documents relating to the case, messages of support from political parties, unions, organizations, and individuals, and reports on the situation from international media. The paper's appeal to attorneys to join their defense team received 165 responses from lawyers throughout Serbia and Montenegro by 21 November.[67]

63. In his capacity as director of "Borba, d. d.," Dušan Mijić wrote to federal Prime Minister Radoje Kontić on 8 September 1994, requesting a meeting so that, as the two largest stockholders, they could discuss the situation. A facsimile of Mijić's letter is reproduced in *Borba,* 16 November 1994, p. 2.

64. Quoted in the article collectively signed by Uređivački kolegijum i Kolegijum direktora (Editorial committee and Board of directors), "Državni udar na nezavisnu 'Borbu,' " *Borba,* 14 November 1994, p. 1.

65. B. O. Ilić, "Država SRJ protiv 'Borbe, d. d.': Još jedno odlaganje procesa," *Borba,* 8 December 1994, p. 20.

66. Uređivački kolegijum i Kolegijum direktora, "Državni udar na nezavisnu 'Borbu,' " *Borba,* 14 November 1994, p. 1.

67. Unsigned, "Za odbranu 'Borbe': Dosad 165 branilaca," *Borba,* 21 November 1994, p. 2.

Although it was clear to most observers that the use of the civil court to determine that "Borba, d. d." did not exist represented an attack on independent media, regime spokespersons were generally careful to present the case as a dispute over property and claimed that the transformation of *Borba* into a private company had been illegally carried out. Federal President Zoran Lilić put the argument as follows: "The civil court has to find now whether the transaction was carried out according to law. This action has nothing to do with editorial policy. It seems normal to me that a person cannot acquire stock in a newspaper for nothing (*badava*). The state has invested in *Borba* for fifty years and now it has only seventeen percent of the stock. Something is not right about that."[68] A similar position was taken in *Večernje novosti*'s report on the conflict:

Federal Minister of Information Dragutin Brčin told [the federal news agency] Tanjug yesterday that the case before the civil court, the nature of which is the regulation and protection of the right of ownership, that is social and state property, is the object of an attempt by the editors of the newspaper *Borba*, by means of classic changing of the topic about the subject of the case, to present it as an attack on the freedom of the press, even as an attack by the state against *Borba*.

"The editors of the paper have reduced themselves to political agitation, slandering their state not only before domestic, but also before global public opinion," said Brčin.[69]

These careful public statements reflected an awareness on the part of the state that open attacks against independent media would not be spared international criticism, but also reflected the hope that veiled attacks might.[70]

The intentions of the regime became clearer in other instances. Dragutin Brčin, quoted immediately above, offered more insight into the case when he named names: "Who can give away to the Panićes, Mijićes,

---

68. M. K., "Ako Sud utvrdi da je sve po zakonu, status 'Borbe' ostaće nepromenjen," *Borba*, 19 December 1994, p. 4.

69. Unsigned, "Ko trguje 'Borbom,' " *Večernje novosti*, 22 November 1994, p. 10.

70. The selective application of law became a general strategy defining regime takeovers of independent media. The regime-controlled newspaper *Politika* offered a foreshadowing of events to come in a headline on 11 February 1995, promising to go "By law for Studio B as well" (Unsigned, "Po zakonu i za Studio B," *Politika*, 11 February 1995). Studio B was in fact taken over by Belgrade's municipal government in 1996.

and Soroses our newspapers, their traditions, and the tradition of Serbian journalism, including *Borba* which is older and richer than they are?"[71] Other regime spokespeople were less careful. Serbian Minister of Information Ratomir Vico allowed himself to stray from the subject in a letter to the editor of the weekly magazine *NIN*, which was also under pressure at the time:

> The insistence of the judicial and state organs on stopping the theft of social property in all fields, including media, can in no case be considered as attacks on the free press. On the contrary, that insistence can only benefit the freedom of journalists from manipulation. Maybe there are grounds to speak of synchronized pressures on the media. But these pressures do not come from the state, that is the ruling power, but rather from those who would like to replace that power and to establish their own or a foreign one. They calculate that they would then control some very important media in Serbia, and could have decisive influence in the conquest of power. The deafening campaign in some media against the state is consistent with these types of pressures.[72]

In a similar statement, Dragan Tomić, director of the state-owned petroleum company Jugopetrol and chair of the Serbian parliament, asserted that he had developed a functional definition of independent media:

> On the pages of *Borba*, for example, you can find more attacks against this state, against the social structure (*društveno uređenje*), against order (*poredak*), than in the newspapers of the countries that are openly against us. . . .
> It is easy, meanwhile, to demonstrate that a great correlation exists between the so-called independence of these media and their man-

71. Unsigned, "Ko trguje 'Borbom,'" *Večernje novosti*, 22 November 1994, p. 10. The individuals named in the comment are: American businessman Milan Panić, who briefly acted as prime minister of SRJ in 1992 and became a key opponent of Slobodan Milošević; Dušan Mijić, director of "Borba, d. d."; and American investor George Soros, whose Open Society Foundation provides financial assistance to independent media in East European countries.
72. Unsigned, "Pritisak s druge strane," *Večernje novosti*, 2 December 1994, p. 2.

ner of writing. The more you throw mud on your own country, the more independent you are.[73]

Critical objections to the editorial policy of independent media eventually reached the point of open provocation. As Mirjana Marković expressed the view in her biweekly diary, independent editorial policy and political action amounted to treason and justified unspecified action against those who engage in them:

> Before long, it will be known who participated in the financing of some political parties and the financing of some sources of information in East European countries. But that identification will also show who was financed, that is, who was paid to act as a fifth column in their own country. That has long been and will always be the most shameful action an individual can take against his own country. . . .
>
> But, in taking money to work against their own country and for another one, these people should think about their descendants. Those mercenaries (*plaćenici*) and informers, who with foreign currency organize "democratic" parties and "independent" media, naively think that the truth about their activity will not see the light of day. And they naively hope that if trouble finds them, their financiers will protect them. But of course they will not.[74]

These types of statements, particularly from personalities whose closeness to the ruling party was undisputed and reproduced in media known for following the party line, did not enhance the credibility of the official claim that the takeover of *Borba* was exclusively a property dispute.

The regime's claim to be, in Ratomir Vico's words, "stopping the theft of social property" was not strongly founded. On the one hand, the transfer of "social property" to the hands of private owners who were regime supporters had not been questioned—as indicated by the use by SPS and

73. Unsigned, "Rog za sveću," *Večernje novosti*, 1 December 1994. The formula articulated by Tomić found an echo in the words of Dragan Radević, editor of the state-controlled Novi Sad daily *Dnevnik*. At the ceremony celebrating *Dnevnik's* fiftieth anniversary, Radević reformulated the thesis as "the more independent media are, the more anti-Serbian they are." Reported in Ž. S., "Viđenja kroz nacionalnu prizmu," *Borba*, 15 December 1994, p. 4.

74. Quoted in *Večernje novosti*, 6 January 1995, p. 2.

SK-PJ of the real estate owned by the defunct SKJ as private property. Nor had particular attention ever been directed to the valuation of "social property" in media, particularly when media outlets were purchased by state-owned corporations close to the regime. The regime had also never been bothered by the continuous operation of three television stations in Belgrade (Art TV, TV Palma, and TV Pink) without licensing. When the regime-sponsored Braća Karić bank set out to found its own BK Telekom television station, a frequency and a license were immediately obtained, whereas the independent television station Studio B never received permission to use a transmitter that would allow its program to reach beyond the city of Belgrade. Part of the explanation can be found in Bogoljub Karić's statement of his company's intentions, in which he referred to the position of *Večernje novosti:* "We will make a nationally-, patriotically-, and business-oriented (*narodsku, patriotsku, i tržišnu*) television station, like the newspaper you have made."[75]

The regime's most untenable position was its simultaneous prosecution of a legal suit requesting that the registration of *Borba* be removed and another asserting that *Borba* had never been registered. In this way, regime prosecutors held both that "Borba, d. d." did exist and that it did not. To the objection that the regime had waited three and one-half years from the time of the registration of "Borba, d. d." to the time it filed its suit, regime spokespeople claimed that they had not known about the existence of the company until federal prosecutors decided to take legal action.

As *Borba* repeatedly pointed out in its editorials during the course of the dispute, the regime not only knew of the existence of "Borba, d. d.," but sent representatives who actively participated in the company's board of directors as part owners of the company. The newspaper also ran facsimiles of documents indicating the regime's knowledge and participation. A document dated 26 February 1993, acknowledging receipt of stock in the company, was signed by Radomir Radulović in the name of the Federal Executive Council (*Savezno izvršno veće—SIV*), Veronika Đerić in the name of the Ministry of Justice, and Vera Dišić in the name of the Ministry of Finance.[76] A letter dated 14 December 1993, announc-

75. D. N., "Bogoljub Karić posetio 'Novosti': Na istom putu," *Večernje novosti*, 28 February 1995, p. 7. For another view, see V. Didanović, "Televizija velikih ambicija," *Borba*, 8 December 1994, p. 11.

76. Reproduced in *Borba*, 18 November 1994, p. 2.

ing the intention of the government to sell some of its stock in "Borba, d. d.," was signed by federal Minister of Information Slobodan Ignjatović.[77] In public statements as well, regime spokespersons left no doubt as to the knowledge they would later deny. Five days before Judge Goran Kljajević found that *Borba* did not exist, SPS deputy Ivica Dačić characterized *Borba* as state property: "Today we have *Borba*, which is 17 percent owned by the state, that is to say that it is the property of the federal government. This is the only example in the world in which a state newspaper writes against the state."[78] In the light of such documents and statements, the regime's explanation of its three-and-one-half year delay in taking legal action held little credibility.

The credibility of the state became an issue in the polemics *Borba* directed in its own defense. Writing in a special issue of the paper dedicated to the conflict, Branko Baletić pointed out that the regime was not recognized by other countries and was not a member of the United Nations:

> In this case I am most interested in the legitimacy of the plaintiff—d. d. SR Yugoslavia. The validity of the plaintiff will probably interest a serious court: should it believe on word of honor that d. d. SR Yugoslavia is properly and in a timely manner registered by the will of all of its founders and shareholders, in accordance with the positive rules of the global community. What would happen if, in the case of a countersuit (*Borba* vs. the state), the court were to investigate the matter, and carry out its duty by looking for information from the people in that tall building on the East River where all recognized firms are registered?[79]

The point had more than rhetorical significance. The regime's claim to any portion of *Borba* relied on its assertion of continuity with the previous state, SFRJ, under which the paper had been originally privatized. The continuity of SRJ with SFRJ, however, had not been established in international law or recognized by any international organization or by any other country.[80]

77. Reproduced in *Borba*, 18 November 1994, p. 2.
78. Unsigned, "Da li je 'Borba' državna novina?" *Borba*, 4 November 1994, p. 5.
79. Branko Baletić, "Borba u pomračini," *Dosije Borba*, 22 November 1994, p. 13.
80. The government of SRJ is explicitly not recognized as the successor-owner of *Borba* in international law. Division of the property of SFRJ among its former constituent republics remains an unresolved issue of negotiation, and the newspaper *Borba* and its property are on the list of objects to be divided in the negotiation process.

Uncertain of its legal standing but certain of its power, the federal government acted in a way that assured that the issue never appeared openly before a court of law. Having secured a higher court's confirmation[81] of the 8 November decision that held that "Borba, d. d." did not exist, the cabinet suddenly and unilaterally named an editor for the paper. The last issue of the independent *Borba*, on the weekend of 24–25 December 1994, featured the following announcement from the Tanjug news agency on the front page:

In yesterday's meeting, the federal government—Vice President Jovan Zebić presided—made the decision to name as director and editor-in-chief of NIP "Borba" Dragutin Brčin, the federal secretary of information. The naming was carried out in conformity with the decision on the taking over of directorial rights on public information agencies, which the federal Parliament adopted in May 1990.

By a decision of civil court on 19 December the decision of the lower court was affirmed, in which the petition for registration in the judicial register by "Borba, d. d." was rejected, as was the petition for the removal of NIP "Borba" from the judicial register.

As is known to public opinion, decisions about the transformation of "Borba" were taken in spite of (*mimo*) and in contradiction to (*suprotno*) applicable legal procedure and the authority of individuals, or organs, it is stated in the announcement of the federal Secretariat for Information.[82]

81. The higher court ruled for the government without the participation of "Borba, d. d." in the hearing. The reason for this is technical: As a previous court decision (on 8 November) held that the company did not exist, it was therefore not recognized by the higher court as a party to the proceeding.

82. Unsigned, "Odluka savezne vlade: Dragutin Brčin imenovan za VD direktora i VD glavnog urednika 'Borbe,' " *Borba*, 24–25 December 1994, p. 1. The abbreviation NIP (*Novinsko izdavačko preduzeće*) stands for "news and publishing business" and indicated the corporate name of Borba before its privatization. The abbreviation VD (*Vršilac dužnosti*) translates most easily as "acting," as in "acting director." As to the date of the announcement, 25 December coincides with the date of the Christmas holiday in most parts of the western world. In Serbia, however, where the majority of the population practices Orthodox Christianity, that holiday is commonly celebrated on 6 January. Hence if the timing of the takeover was directed toward limiting diffusion of the news, this gesture was directed more toward West European and American media than toward domestic media.

Rather than allowing its claim to *Borba* to go to appeal, the federal government acted unilaterally by naming one of its own members as director and editor.[83]

For the next three weeks, from 26 December 1994 to 16 January 1995, two editions of *Borba* appeared every day in Belgrade. At the federal Secretariat for Information, Dragutin Brčin and his team of mostly unidentified journalists produced the official *Borba*, which was available for purchase (although rarely purchased) at newsstands throughout the city. The overwhelming majority of *Borba*'s journalists remained with editor Gordana Logar and produced a paper that first emerged under the name *Borba: Vanredno izdanje* (Borba: Special edition) and later appeared for one week as a "special thematic issue" of the magazine *Nezavisnost* (Independence). Printed in small numbers and usually sold out before noon, the independent paper was available from street vendors at a few sites in the center of the city. People hoping to purchase the independent publication questioned street vendors, asking whether the paper they sold was "the real" (*prava*) *Borba*, or simply "our" (*naša*) *Borba*.

Brčin's *Borba* demonstrated the character the regime believed a newspaper ought to have from its first day of publication. In a front-page box titled, "One *Borba* by Law," Tanjug quotes federal Minister of Information Ratomir Vico to the effect that the only legally existing *Borba* is the one edited by Dragutin Brčin and that "anything else which is printed under that name, and which is edited by anybody else, is illegal."[84] The leading news article revealed a surprising finding about the progress of the war in Bosnia-Hercegovina, under the headline "Only the Muslims are fighting."[85] The headlines on the front page of the 29 December edition featured federal President Zoran Lilić characterizing the country as a "fortunate, peaceful and prosperous Yugoslavia"[86] and described the previous year, during which the rate of inflation had averaged over 100

83. The federal cabinet, in unilaterally naming an editor and director for the paper, also acted in contradiction with the court ruling it claimed as its authority. The ruling found that the parliament of SFRJ had ownership rights over the paper. The parliament of SRJ could plausibly claim succession to such rights, but the federal cabinet could not legally claim the right to act in its name.

84. Unsigned (attributed to Tanjug), "Ratomir Vico: Po zakonu jedna 'Borba,' " *Borba* (Brčin), 26 December 1994, p. 1.

85. Unsigned, "Ratuju samo—Muslimani," *Borba* (Brčin), 26 December 1994, p. 1.

86. Unsigned, "Predsednik SRJ Zoran Lilić u intervjuu Radio Beogradu: Srećna, mirna i bogata Jugoslavija," *Borba* (Brčin), 29 December 1994, p. 1.

percent, as "a year without inflation."[87] Not only news stories were subject to this type of political recasting. In the 23 March 1995 edition of Dragutin Brčin's *Borba*, the weather report is accompanied by the story "Federal Premier Radoje Kontić visits the meteorologists: Decisive peacemaking activity."[88]

In the first edition of Brčin's *Borba*, some pains were taken to state the intentions of the new-old publication. An unsigned center-page spread titled "Borba: Truth and lies" began with a fairly dramatic restatement of the regime's principal thesis about its property rights in the paper, with unmistakable political overtones added: "Two days of noisemaking about *Borba!* And, nothing else can or will happen except that this paper belongs once again to the one who was always its owner—to the state of Yugoslavia, and not to various merchants of venison (*preprodavci polutki*), Soroses, and other domestic and foreign adventurers and fishers in troubled waters (*lovci u mutnom*)."[89] These introductory sentences make clear what, in the minds of the ministry employees who were now producing *Borba*, a daily paper ought not to resemble. And what should a daily paper resemble? The answer comes only sentences later in the same article: "The editors of the paper produced a daily with a modest press run. At the same time, a team half as large, just a floor above them, made a paper with a press run ten times as large."[90] The reference was to the newspaper closest to the regime, the large-circulation tabloid *Večernje novosti*.

Brčin demonstrated his esteem for *Večernje novosti* in other ways as well. On 27 December, Brčin's *Borba* announced its own existence by reproducing in its entirety *Novosti's* coverage of the event. Other articles were run directly from *Novosti* as well, on the same or the following day. The underground *Borba: Vanredno izdanje* (edited by the displaced *Borba* editor Gordana Logar) ran on 30 December a statement from Dragan Savić, *Novosti's* correspondent in the town of Osečina, wondering how his articles ended up in Brčin's paper: "I do not work with *Borba*. In

---

87. Unsigned, "Godina bez inflacije," *Borba* (Brčin), 29 December 1994, p. 1.

88. Unsigned, "Savezni premijer Radoje Kontić u poseti meteorolozima: Odlučna mirotvornost," *Borba* (Brčin), 23 March 1995, p. 20.

89. Unsigned, "Borba: Istina i laži," *Borba* (Brčin), 26 December 1994, pp. 10–11. The "merchant of venison" in question is "Borba, d. d." director Dušan Mijić, whose previous business activity included the directorship of the state-owned agricultural export firm "Centroslavija," followed by the founding of a private agricultural-products firm, "Finagro," in 1989.

90. Unsigned, "Borba: Istina i laži," *Borba* (Brčin), 26 December 1994, pp. 10–11.

Osečina it does not even arrive to the kiosks. The only possibility is that 'Brčin and comrades,' without my knowledge, stole the text in question from *Večernje novosti*. I am really without any comment."[91] The directors of *Večernje novosti* returned the favor—on 29 December, *Borba*'s first and only advertiser was the radio station owned by the newspaper, Radio Novosti. The near-identity of the two papers had another explanation aside from ideological closeness. It was unclear who produced Brčin's *Borba*, as it had no legally established director and employees. Of 120 journalists who had worked on *Borba* before its takeover by the regime, only four accepted offers of employment from Brčin.[92]

The remaining journalists, led by editor Gordana Logar, produced the "illegal" paper *Borba: Vanredno izdanje* each day from the time that *Borba* was taken over on 24 December 1994 until their supply of paper for printing ran out on 17 January 1995. On two days during that period, *Borba: Vanredno izdanje* did not appear. Its absence was variously explained as attributable to technical problems at the private printing shop that produced the paper and less certainly as a result of government pressure on the printer. The press run of the paper was limited to about 10,000 copies by both the capacity of the printers and the limited supply of newsprint at hand.

Because *Borba: Vanredno izdanje* was not provided access to the four major chains of kiosks in Serbia,[93] it was sold exclusively by street dealers. Although some of these dealers sold papers and magazines by occupation, the journalists themselves often sold the paper. In the first few days after the government takeover, *Borba: Vanredno izdanje*'s street dealers also included journalists from other publications, opposition members of parliament, and well-known writers, film directors, intellectuals, and other public personalities. Because wide and systematic distribution and larger press runs were not available, copies of the paper were generally sold only in the center of Belgrade, and supplies generally ran out by noon. Dedicated readers shared copies.

In addition to the news of the day, *Borba: Vanredno izdanje* reported about its own case, carrying both condemnations and messages of support

91. B. Vicentijević, "Dragan Savić, dopisnik 'Večernjih novosti' iz Osečine: Otkud moj tekst u Brčinovoj čorbi?" *Borba: Vanredno izdanje*, 30 December 1994, p. 16.

92. Unsigned (attributed to Beta), "Gordana Logar: Nastavićemo sa izdavanjem lista," *Borba: Vanredno izdanje*, 27 December 1994, p. 3.

93. The four companies operating kiosks were "Duvan," "Štampa," "Politika," and "Borba-plasman."

it received, as well as offering translations of the articles about the case appearing in the international press. In addition to messages of support from political parties, trade unions, and other institutions, *Borba: Vanredno izdanje* received messages of support from individuals, some of whom expressed them in the form of letters to the editor. Reader Dragoljub Tasić expressed his feelings about the case in one such letter: *"Borba* is the only daily newspaper I can read without disgust. All the rest of the journalistic-political trash (*šund*) does not interest me in the least. What they are doing to you, and to us, your readers, is a scandal, shamelessness without precedent. I do not know what to do. This morning I bought the special edition. I like it. But, how will you go on? How will we go on?"[94] Other supporters of the paper also related its predicament to their own situation. At a meeting held to discuss the case, a participant articulated the general sense of threat awakened by the takeover of the newspaper: "We may have had some serious objections to *Borba*'s writing. But it also gave us hope. Whoever peacefully watches another being strangled cannot expect anything good for himself. Maybe there is no more hope for *Borba*. Is there any for its readers?"[95] Some readers expressed the feeling that in losing access to an independent source of information, they had also lost access to a sense of having some control over their own lives and of hoping that some aspect of their everyday experience would not be under the control of the regime.

The association between the regime's efforts to make independent media unavailable and other aspects of everyday life was drawn in the largest protest to occur in connection with the takeover of *Borba*. The Belgrade branch and the youth organization of the Democratic Party (*Demokratska stranka—DS*) combined the themes of the physical "darkness" caused by the irregular supply of electricity in Serbia that winter, the metaphorical "darkness" of war, corruption, and international isolation, and the "informative darkness" imposed by attacks against independent media to sponsor a "meeting against darkness" on the square in front of the building where *Borba* had its offices.[96] On 29 December 1994, participants held candles while they listened to speakers at the postsun-

94. Dragoljub Tasić, "Ima li spasa?" (letter), *Borba: Vanredno izdanje*, 26 December 1994, p. 10.

95. Aleksandar Nenadović, quoted in V. Didanović and B. Cani, "Odbrana 'Borbe'—odbrana slobode," *Borba: Vanredno izdanje*, 29 December 1994, p. 4.

96. J. Spasić, V. Didanović, and V. Simonović, "Beograd je u mraku, mrak je u Beogradu," *Borba: Vanredno izdanje*, 30 December 1994, p. 1.

down meeting. Two days later, several hundred protesters formed a human "ring of freedom," joining hands around the block on which *Borba*'s offices are located.[97] The opposition parties in the parliament set in motion an initiative to call a vote of no confidence in the federal government for its violation of the constitution in the takeover of the paper.[98]

Neither political initiatives nor the support of its readers, however, could make *Borba*'s temporary moral victory permanent or material. Having run out of newsprint, *Borba: Vanredno izdanje* published its last issue on 16 January 1995. For two weeks, no independent daily newspaper was printed in Serbia. The paper re-emerged as the product of a newly formed stockholding company on 1 February 1995. Granting the federal government its claim to an exclusive right to the name *Borba*, the new paper took its title from the name that readers gave the special edition, calling itself *Naša borba*.

The Emotional Function of Independent Media

The preceding discussion presents both an overview of the Serbian regime's efforts to establish and entrench a media monopoly and an examination of one case in which the regime moved against an important independent media source. Were the establishment of a media monopoly the only story about politics of information in Belgrade, the chapter could end here as a "classic" story of dictatorial control over information resources. However, conventional references to monopolies over information media do not tell the complete story of the politics of information in Serbia. At least in Belgrade, and to a somewhat lesser degree in other major cities, nonregime media did exist. The journalists who left *NIN* at the time that the regime took it over formed the core of the legendary independent weekly magazine *Vreme*. The journalists of *Borba* launched *Naša borba*, a new independent daily, after their paper was taken over by the government. Although the Belgrade television station Studio B ceased functioning as an independent station in 1996, Belgrade's independent

97. Unsigned, "Prsten slobode oko 'Borbe,' " *Borba: Vanredno izdanje*, 1 January 1995, p. 1.

98. J. Kesić and V. Vignjević, "Zajednička inicijativa četiri stranke u Saveznoj skupštini: Zbog 'Borbe' nepoverenje Kontićevom kabinetu," *Borba: Vanredno izdanje*, 29 December 1994, p. 1.

radio station B-92 has provided an independent source of news, as well as its own world-class musical and cultural program, since 1991.

To the extent that the regime's monopoly over media is felt, it is felt far less strongly in the city of Belgrade than elsewhere in Serbia. The limited and one-sided information provided by state-controlled media may explain the consumption habits and opinions of people in the provinces, but this explanation cannot be universally applied in Belgrade, where a choice of information sources, however precarious and limited, exists.

To summarize the problem, the story of the politics of information in Belgrade is complicated by two perhaps inconvenient facts: Despite pressures, constraints, and takeovers, independent media have survived, albeit as a result of continuous effort in the face of a stronger power; and even with a choice of information sources, a large enough portion of the population seems to prefer regime-controlled media to make the state television's news program the most-watched program and to make the two principal regime-controlled newspapers the most widely sold papers. The question of who follows which media sources and why can be only partly answered by looking at institutional and structural factors. The choices media users make must also be examined by looking at questions of meaning.

I held repeated discussions with people in Belgrade about information media and which ones they preferred throughout the period of research, but most intensively in the months when the survival of the independent *Borba* was in question. The findings indicate that motivation and orientation are crucial factors in determining media choice: the information sources a person prefers constitute a part of that person's self-perception and help to construct that person's image of his or her role in society.

The thesis that media choices derive from needs and perceptions of self is a well-established one in media studies and forms the core of the "uses and gratifications" approach to investigating media use, which dates from the 1940s and 1950s and continues to have some currency.[99] The

99. The foundational study in the "uses and gratifications" approach is the study of readers' responses to the 1949 New York City newspaper workers' strike by Bernard Berelson, "What Missing the Newspaper Means," in Lazarsfeld and Stanton, eds., *Communication Research, 1948–9* (New York: Duell, Sloane and Pierce, 1949), 111–29. Over the years, the approach has been elaborated by several researchers, notably Elihu Katz. A contemporary elaboration of the approach can be found in Alan Rubin, "Media Uses and Effects: A Uses-and-Gratifications Perspective," in Jennings Bryant and Dolf

media choices made in Belgrade, however, differ from the choices postulated in the "uses and gratifications" model in that they are not made free of constraint. Although a wider range of media sources is generally available in Belgrade than elsewhere in Serbia, not all media sources are equally available. The programs of the state television network are generally accessible, and the news programs are repeated with frequency. Similarly, the three principal regime-controlled newspapers all have relatively large circulations and are sold throughout the city. The independent television station Studio B, however, broadcast only one daily news program, which directly competed with the state television's principal news program. Similarly, the independent radio station B-92 broadcast only one daily news program. The situation with independent magazines was somewhat more equal, but these, as well as the independent daily newspaper *Borba* (after February 1995, *Naša borba*), could often be found only at kiosks in the center of the city, and then only before noon. Although the difference was minor, state-controlled newspapers were subsidized and sold for a price well below the cost of production, whereas the independent newspaper cost between two to four times as much.

These may be small distinctions—whether one develops the habit of turning on the radio or television at a particular hour or whether one develops the habit of going outside a residential neighborhood to buy a paper. Yet they turned out to be significant ones because a level of will was involved. The distinction between passive and active approaches to information—between the wish to be informed and the desire to inform oneself—became crucial. Those people inclined to be satisfied with the information readily available to them from regime-controlled sources do not have the motivation to seek other sources or to be bothered by questions of objectivity or balance. Such effort likely interferes with the comfort they achieve by trusting, or pretending to trust, that they are already adequately informed.

For those who felt the motivation to inform themselves, the pursuit of information became an important part of their lives. They attributed great value to the feeling of being informed (in spite of attempts to limit information), to having access to information resources that were not under the control of the regime, and to possessing information that al-

Zillman, eds., *Media Effects: Advances in Theory and Research* (Hillsdale, N.J.: Lawrence Erlbaum Associates, 1994), 417–36.

lowed them to refute the official lines of the state media. In addition to the obvious informational function of independent media, several emotional functions were also important among this audience.

First, independent media provided a sense of connection. Alternative information presented in professional style and read by a significant group allowed people who doubted the veracity of information presented in state media to feel that they were not alone in their doubts. The broadened range of information of independent media also allowed people to generate for themselves an empowering sense of selectivity among sources. As one Belgrader described to me his news reading habits: "I read *Novosti* to find out what the regime is thinking, *Politika* to find out what the limits of criticism are, and *Borba* to find out what is happening." This sense that meaningful alternatives exist allowed readers like the one quoted above to feel that they could inform themselves—and explains the sense of personal outrage they felt when *Borba* was taken away from them.

In addition to providing a sense of connection, independent media provided tools by which people were able to develop a strategy of self-presentation in relation to their social environment. By buying, reading, and displaying independent publications, a person could demonstrate his or her own sense of "independence." This probably explains the statement of the Belgrade woman who described to me her satisfaction and pride in asking her neighborhood news agent for *Naša borba* in the loudest possible voice.

Beyond these specific functions, independent media played a more crucial role in the lives of their followers, offering an element of a strategy for living in conditions of limitation. An analogous situation is analyzed by Erving Goffman in his landmark study *Asylums*,[100] in which he investigated the means by which patients in mental hospitals and other "total institutions" construct for themselves a life worth living under conditions that restrict their possibilities and their freedom. Their strategies were remarkably simple: breaking rules, keeping some possessions or items of clothing that indicate the individuality of the bearer, maintaining contacts with the "forbidden world" outside the institution. These small everyday strategies offered people the ability to feel that they exercised some control over their lives.

Independent media functioned similarly for the people in Belgrade

---

100. *Asylums: Essays on the Social Situation of Mental Patients and Other Inmates* (New York: Anchor Books, 1961).

who pursued and followed them. More than the information these media offered, members of the audience wanted the feeling of having access to a variety of sources and of having the ability to inform themselves. Hence the largest demonstration in defense of *Borba* protested not censorship but "darkness"—a condition of life rather than a political move. The feeling was summarized to me by a young Belgrader on the day after *Borba* was taken over: "I just feel like I've been cheated again. And for all the young people who can't get information, it's just one more reason to leave the country. Just one newspaper, which hardly anyone reads—and we can't even have that." From this point of view, independent sources of information provided more than daily news and opinion. They also provided the feeling that objective information was available, that it was possible to develop and present an orientation to the social environment, and that normal conditions of life were possible.

On the other side of the social divide, members of the audience for regime-controlled information media also developed and expressed orientations and fulfilled expectations by means of their media preferences. These orientations and expectations were of course quite different from those expressed by followers of independent media, and the differences offer a glimpse into the wide social divisions in Serbia.

First, regime-controlled media offered a sense of authoritarian comfort and security and gave their audience a sense that the interpretations and opinions they received through these media were shared by influential and powerful people. Because these media sources were the most widely diffused, they also offered a feeling that the perspectives presented in them were shared by a broad majority. In this sense, a formula existed by which certain perspectives were set forth as the ones a person needed to hold to "get by" and by which individuals were relieved of the obligation to seek out and construct their own perspectives. The state television news thus acts as the authority of last instance. One older Belgrade woman, a strong supporter of the regime, summarized a political discussion by telling me the following: "I understand why you think the way you do because you live in America and watch American television. But I live here and I watch Yugoslav television, so I think differently." The formulation not only assumes the model of "strong effects" from information media, but uses it to justify particular perspectives held by individuals.

Related to the first function, regime media also provide a sense of authoritarian certainty. One cynical woman described to me her experience of watching the news on the state television network by saying, "I love watching the news on state television. It's my instructions on what to think for the day." Some indications exist, however, to suggest that the remark is not merely cynical. Mark Thompson cited the surprising result of two surveys in Serbia:

> Research in public opinion can be cited in support of the assertion that mass media in Serbia have an improbable influence on public opinion and the level of information. In this sense two surveys by the Belgrade agency "Medium," carried out in April 1993, are widely cited. The first, carried out on 9 April 1993, showed that 70 percent of Serbs in Serbia opposed the Vance-Owen peace plan for Bosnia. The second, identical survey, carried out on 27 April (after the regime's reversal on that question, which was faithfully followed in the media it controlled), showed that only 20 percent of respondents opposed the plan, and 39 percent supported it.[101]

If, as Thompson suggested, the surveys demonstrate the influence of regime-controlled media on public opinion, then the results are genuinely "improbable." They seem instead to demonstrate the contention that regime-media audiences bring strong expectations to their reception of news and opinion and that among these expectations is the demand to be relieved of the responsibility of holding their own beliefs.

Finally, regime-controlled media offer their audiences the reassurance of authoritarian boundaries. This function derives from the cynicism directed not only toward regime-controlled media, but toward information media generally. The suspicion that all media are "controlled" by some force was used in the quotations from Dragutin Brčin and Ratomir Vico earlier in this chapter, in which they attacked independent media as "dependent" on dubious foreign sources. It also has some currency as a folk belief. When the contention that "all of them are controlled" is taken as a basic assumption, it justifies reliance on the media sources controlled by the regime. Because followers of regime-controlled media granted that manipulation took place on all sides, they made a choice to be manipulated by a source close to them, which could plausibly offer them some benefit.

The broad outlines of orientations and modes of reception listed here

101. Thompson (1995), 125.

account not only for the differences between the audiences for two opposed varieties of information media. They also appear to translate well to the other dimensions of everyday life examined in this research. As practical and value orientations, they broadly describe the wide social division in Serbia and correspond as well to the differences in geography, age, and education discussed in the previous chapter.

The story of the politics of information in the Milošević regime is paradoxical. Although the regime made many efforts to strengthen its control over information media and to weaken or destroy independent media, it did not succeed in establishing a complete monopoly over information—at least not in Belgrade. At the same time that regime-controlled media presented a decidedly one-sided and propagandistic view of local and international events, several independent media outlets also offered information and interpretations that constituted a real and consistent alternative to the official line.

These independent media operated under conditions of severe constraint, however. Often their legal and financial status left them insecure and open to attack. In almost no cases did they have access to resources that allowed them to reach an audience nearly as large as the audience reached by regime-controlled media. Their success in surviving and the influence they did have in places where they were available testify both to the regime's failure to fully control the information available to its citizens and to some citizens success in informing themselves in spite of the regime's efforts.

Only a certain measure of the advantages enjoyed by regime-controlled media can be attributed to the institutional facts that operated in their favor. Not all the people who had access to alternative sources of information chose to use them. The story of the politics of information in Belgrade is not only a story of the conflicts between regime-controlled and independent media, but also a story of diverging expectations, orientations, and motivations in media audiences. Just as a plurality of people who participated in elections cast their votes for SPS, a significant portion of people who had a range of information sources available to them chose sources controlled by SPS. Although the pressures to which both media institutions and audience members were subject may account for this fact to a certain degree, the crucial issues in explaining the informational landscape in Belgrade reside not only on the institutional level but on the level of everyday life as well.

4

The Destruction of
Musical Alternatives

I once loved this city because here my life was a great party.
There were days that I regretted that Belgrade wasn't Am-
sterdam, but there were many more when I was pleased that
it was not East Berlin. Today I understand that this was a
great place for life. And then darkness started to fall. At the
very beginning, seven, eight years ago, nobody knew what
it was all about. Nobody sensed that the devil himself was
coming to town. When it became clear, it was already too
late. The city was divided. They were on one side, and we
were on the other.[1]

The preceding chapters have explored the structure and means of control
over formal politics and public information and have demonstrated that
the regime's efforts to maintain its power relied extensively on making
alternatives unavailable in these fields. Many people with whom I spoke
expressed the view that short of leaving the country, their best option
was to withdraw into private life and pleasure and to act as though the
alternatives not available to them in the public sphere could somehow be
compensated for by free enjoyment in the private sphere. This realm of
taste, orientation, personal identity, and pleasure is generally considered
both a means of escape and a strategy of compensation for the restraint

1. Mladen Matičević, from the introduction to the film, *Geto* (Belgrade: Radio
B-92, 1996). Quoted in Izabela Kišić, "Inertnost je smrt," *Naša borba* (Internet izdanje),
6 May 1996.

people feel in other areas of everyday life. Conventional political philosophy in Western Europe and the United States codifies such a position and seeks guarantees against censorship by asserting a right to privacy and to all the activities assumed to fall under the categories of "life, liberty, and the pursuit of happiness." In contemporary research into the sociology of culture, varieties of subcultural pleasure are regarded as sites of counteridentity, resistance, or at least compensatory power over one's own life. Many Belgraders, disillusioned with the range of possibilities open to them in politics, information, and work, also believed that they could find a refuge in private life.

The realm of taste and enjoyment was not free from the involvement of the nationalist-authoritarian state against society, however. Many Belgraders with whom I spoke tell the story of the regime's battle against them through the lens of popular culture. In this chapter, several dimensions of that story are explored.

The same social divisions that, as shown earlier, determined to a large degree the political orientation of different social groups to the regime also determined to a large degree the cultural orientation of different social groups. As it became apparent that the young urban population was the least likely to cooperate in nationalist mobilization, the rock and roll culture that defined this group came under attack. At question was not only the distribution of political, social, and financial benefits to favored segments of the population; cultural and emotional benefits were at stake as well. With the diminution of cultural space available to the rock and roll culture, its members, already removed from influence, were made to feel more intensively isolated in an environment hostile to them culturally as well as politically. As the rock and roll culture moved from the center to the margins, however, it became more uncompromising and more conscious of itself as a lifeline to Belgrade's cosmopolitans and as a line of defense for urban culture.

The new nationalist elite began to search for a musical culture appropriate to the changed social order and appealing to its rural and semirural bases of support. State-controlled media outlets began to intensively promote neofolk music[2] and the transformation of neofolk into a dance-pop-

2. "Neofolk" refers to the genre of "newly composed folk music" (*novokomponovana narodna muzika*), defined by the use of styles and structures borrowed from various folk forms combined with pop instrumentation and arrangements. It is distinguished on the one hand from "authentic folk music" (*izvorna narodna muzika*), in which performers seek to reproduce music from folk traditions, and on the other from "turbofolk," in

folk commercial melange under the name of "turbofolk." With the resources of the state media monopoly available to it, neofolk quickly occupied the cultural spaces once dominated by rock and roll and even became established in the city of Belgrade, where folk and neofolk forms had long been marginalized. As widely publicized as they became, however, neofolk and especially the turbofolk variant became just as widely despised—both on the aesthetic level and because of their close association with the regime. Musical taste became an important signifier, not only of the distinction between urban and peasant culture, but also of orientation toward the regime, the war, and the environment created by the regime and the war.

When in August 1994, Slobodan Milošević turned against the nationalist client armies he had encouraged and financed, Serbia's new policy was promoted under the slogan "Peace has no alternative." At the same time, the Serbian Ministry of Culture turned against the neofolk music that was associated with the period of nationalist mobilization and declared a "struggle against kitsch" and a "campaign for true cultural values." Like peace, taste had no alternative either, and the government declared its intention to cut neofolk loose from the official favor it had enjoyed.

The story of Belgrade's changing musical environment in the war period, then, is one of the marginalization of popular cultures and of the popularization and instrumentalization of marginal cultures. It is not a story of the cultural tastes or preferences of the new nationalist-authoritarian elite. To the extent that taste can be seen as a quality of the group, its changing cultural preferences reflect its unchanging will to remain in power. Along the way, its effort was to destroy any existing or potential alternatives.

Belgrade Between Present and Past

Like most East European cities, Belgrade has a mixed urban and rural character, all the more so since its population has increased dramatically with the massive rural-to-urban migration that has rapidly taken place from 1945 onward. The city's population did not exceed 100,000 until

which instrumentation and arrangements borrowed from commercial dance and disco music dominate while a few folk elements remain.

1921. From a population of 385,000 in 1948, the city grew rapidly. By 1961, the population had grown to 843,209; by 1971, to 1,209,361; and by 1981, to 1,470,073.[3] Most of this urban growth was the result of migration from the provinces: for example, in 1971, only 38.84 percent of the city's population had been born in Belgrade.[4] The basic division of Belgrade's identity proceeds from two related facts: on the one hand, it has become home to a rapidly increasing urban population; on the other hand, much of that population is not, or is not yet, entirely urban in character.

During the period of tremendous growth, the culture of the city changed in two opposing respects. On the one hand, its increased population, growing industrial and service economies, and position as an international capital helped it to develop from a medium-sized provincial city into an increasingly cosmopolitan and urban cultural center. Although interwar Belgrade had been home to some important cultural and artistic movements, the city remained in an extended transitional phase between a peripheral provincial town and a modern city.[5] Only after World War II, during the period of its rapid and massive expansion, did Belgrade develop a mass urban popular culture. Miloš Nemanjić tracked the growth of Belgrade's film and theater audience in this period and showed that although availability of cultural productions was enhanced and the size of the audience increased, this increase did not match the pace of the increase in population, nor were cultural institutions used by all sectors of the population.[6]

Hence the second major axis of Belgrade's postwar cultural development: at the same time that a metropolitan culture was growing, another culture was also developing. Rural migrants, generally poor, came to the city to take jobs in the growing industrial and service sectors, and many did not entirely integrate into the culture of the city.[7] With the demand of new arrivals overstraining Belgrade's limited housing stock, many newcomers found their way to substandard housing of various types, whether

3. Nemanjić (1991), 11, 66, 92.
4. Nemanjić (1991), 67.
5. This transitional period is discussed in detail in Peđa J. Marković, *Beograd i Evropa, 1918–1941: Evropski uticaji na proces modernizacije u Beogradu* (Belgrade: Savremena administracija, dd., 1992).
6. Nemanjić (1991).
7. In the popular expression, these new arrivals made their way *trbuhom za kruhom*—led by their bellies in search of bread.

this meant crowding additional people into existing apartments and houses or a hurried construction job in one of the *"beogradske favele."*[8] Many newcomers continued to maintain close connections with their villages of origin as well, received food from relatives in the village, and took leave of their factory jobs to participate in the harvest. Andrei Simić defined this group as "the peasant urbanites,"[9] and their intermediate status has been commented on by many observers. Perhaps the classic definition comes from Đorđe Balašević's song decrying the dominance of "folkies" (*narodnjaci*): "a hybrid class halfway on the road from village to city."

The urbanites and peasant urbanites were publicly differentiated by taste, particularly musical taste. Whereas the urban residents of Belgrade, particularly the young ones among them, looked to the European and American West, developing a strong domestic jazz and rock and roll culture, the peasant urbanites developed a taste for neofolk, a hybrid form marrying the conventions of traditional folk songs with contemporary themes and also increasingly with contemporary instrumentation.[10]

Neofolk music achieved huge popularity among Yugoslav workers in other countries,[11] who brought a taste for the music back to the provincial towns from which they came. The private taxi companies and cafes that many returning *gastarbajteri* opened helped to diffuse the music, which with time came to define the tastes of "peasant urbanites" as well. Reaching an audience ranging from the domestic provinces and workers' colo-

8. The term *favele* derives from the name given to Brazil's urban slums and is borrowed from the Portuguese language. For a discussion of the environment in one of these settlements, see Branislava Saveljić, *Beogradeska favela: Nastanak i razvoj Kaluđerice kao posledica bespravne stambene izgradnje u Beogradu* (Belgrade: Istraživačko-izdavački centar SSO Srbije, 1988).

9. Andrei Simić, *The Peasant Urbanites: A Study of Rural-Urban Mobility in Serbia* (New York: Seminar Press, 1973).

10. Hence Andrei Simić's ("Commercial Folk Music in Yugoslavia: Idealization and Reality," *Journal of the Association of Graduate Dance Ethnologists, UCLA* 2 [Fall–Winter 1978]) characterization of neofolk as "Yugoslav Country-and-Western."

11. In many cases, the genre was known as *gastarbajterske pesme*, the German term for "guest worker" having been lifted directly into the Serbo-Croatian language (in Belgrade street slang, a term for job is also *arbajt*). Not all workers abroad went to Germany, of course. Some of the most lucrative international jobs were on construction and engineering projects in the Middle East and North Africa, where local popular music probably contributed some of what later critics of neofolk called the "Islamic melos" of the music. Another source of this is domestic folk music, which, especially in Serbia and Macedonia, had long been enriched by elements of Turkish music.

nies in other countries to the peripheries of large cities in Yugoslavia, neofolk became the best-selling and most widely diffused genre.

Beogradski rokeri: From Center to Margin

Neofolk was, however, marginalized in the cities, as was its audience, regarded as composed of "peasants" (*seljaci*) and "primitives" (*primitivci*). As Srđan Gojković-Gile, leader of the popular rock and roll group *Električni orgazam* (Electrical Orgasm), recalled his high school days, "[I]n my time, in my high school class there were maybe two unfortunate types who listened to folk, and they were completely written off (*prokazani*)."[12] Increasingly open to the West since the middle 1960s and still relatively prosperous, Belgrade youth generated a rock and roll culture that, at least in the minds of local fans, was on a par with the pop scenes of Western Europe. In 1981, the British music magazine *New Musical Express* listed the Belgrade art students' club *Akademija* as one of the finest music clubs in Europe. It also rated Belgrade's punk-pop group *Električni orgazam* as one of the finest bands in Europe. Srđan Gojković-Gile recalled the atmosphere of the period: "We weren't surprised at being called one of the best bands in Europe because we thought we were one of the best bands in Europe ourselves."[13] As late as 1995, Ljubljana's legendary Radio Student promoted its "You-Rock It" program with "Certain critics put ex-Yugoslav rock and roll bands in third place—after American and British bands."[14]

Električni orgazam's appearance on the scene illustrates the quick and definitive conquest of cultural space by Belgrade's rock and roll youth. The joint album released in 1981 by that band, *Idoli* (Idols) and *Šarlo akrobata* was meant to showcase the new musical scene in Belgrade and carried the simple title "Package Deal: Belgrade" (*Paket aranžman: Beograd*). To further underscore the close identification of the bands with the city itself, the album cover featured a black-and-white photo of another

12. Radovan Kupres, "Srpski režim i srpski rok: Od presije do kolaboracije (1)— Suvišna muzika u godinama raspleta," *Naša borba* (Internet izdanje), 23 May 1996.
    13. In his television interview in the series *Rockumenti—Gile: Misterija orgazma*, RTS Belgrade, 20 May 1995.
    14. "Enlistment of Radio Student's Broadcasts: The Present Weekly Program Scheme" (Ljubljana, 1995).

symbol of the city—the cultural and consumer center on Terazije in the center of town, with the logo of the "Beograd" department store above.

Among the songs by *Električni orgazam* on the album was *"Zlatni papagaj"* (The golden parrot), the song for which the group is still best known. Dedicated to the first fancy privately owned cafe in Belgrade, the song ridicules its customers and attitude[15] in a chorus that is still universally known among young people in Belgrade:

Zlatni papagaj—tata plati sve
  račune
	The golden parrot—Daddy pays
	  all the bills

Zlatni papagaj—jer mi smo
  snobovi
	The golden parrot—because
	  we're snobs

In the video promoting the song, Gile and the band members shout the lyrics and frolic in and around the cafe *Zlatni papagaj*, happily advertising both the song and the cafe that is the object of the song's ridicule. More than demonstrating that the owners of the cafe are good sports, the video announced the arrival of a new urban cultural order, with punk rock right in the center. Its place was in the center of the city, in the same place as the fancy cafes, as the cultural form that defines what life in the city is about.

"Yugo-rock's" place was not only in the city of Belgrade. Zagreb, Ljubljana, Sarajevo, and other urban centers—some of them regional centers, like the Istrian port town of Pula—all developed strong local musical scenes, in intensive contact with one another. As a rule, popular bands made their records, and often built their publics, more successfully in other republics than at home. This was true for *Električni orgazam*, a band that repeatedly took opportunities to publicly demonstrate its anti-war orientation in later years, that recorded principally for the Zagreb-

---

15. The well-off and well-dressed young crowd that congregated in these and similar venues was known at the time as *šminkeri* (makeup wearers), their values opposed to those of the *pankeri* (punks) and *hipici* (hippies). For a detailed analysis of these groups and their various styles of self-presentation, see Ines Prica, *Omladinska potkultura u Beogradu: Simbolička praksa* (Belgrade: Etnografski institut SANU, 1991). By the time I had arrived in Belgrade, the heirs to the *šminkeri* had become the "fancies"; the various elements of rock and roll culture were mostly grouped under the general category of *padevičari* (epileptics); and the neofolk youth were added to the mix either as *narodnjaci* (folkies, or in Marko Živković's felicitous translation, "folknjaks") or *dizelaši* (diesels).

based Jugoton (later Croatia Records).[16] It was no less true for *Riblja čorba* (Fish chowder), whose leader Bora Đorđević later became a vocal supporter of Arkan and who recorded principally for RTV-Ljubljana.[17]

The rock and roll culture did, however, remain an urban culture, and neofolk continued to dominate the taste of the provinces. Before provincial culture came to political dominance with the rise of nationalism, taste was already a marker of identity and orientation. As much as the rock and roll culture defined life in the cities, maintaining a *rokerski* identity was difficult in the provinces, with at best a weak social environment to support it. Toza Rabassa of the band *Zvoncekova bilježnica* (Zvoncek's notebook) described the trials of being a punk rocker in the Šumadija town of Aranđelovac:

In 1978, when I received the first Sex Pistols album from a friend in Kragujevac, the infection was complete. Then (the depressive-punk group) *Pekinška patka* (Peking duck) appeared, and general madness began. Now imagine being a punk in Aranđelovac in those years! I

16. Indeed, probably the finest live album in "Yugo-rock" is *Električni orgazam*'s "*Braćo i sestre*" (Brothers and sisters!) (1987), recorded in Zagreb's Kulušić auditorium. Possibly Gile's most poignant song is his remembrance "Zagreb," from his 1988 solo album "*Evo sad vidiš da može*" (Now you see it can be done).

17. Bora Đorđević achieved tremendous popularity with the band *Riblja čorba* (literally, Fish chowder, although the name also contains an implicit obscene connotation) in the first several years of the band's existence, mostly through his comic songs, which were principally about his own drunkenness and oafishness. At the same time, several of *Riblja čorba*'s early songs became anthems of anti-Communist rebelliousness, especially "*Pogledaj dom svoj, Anđele*" (Look homeward, angel), "*Na zapadu ništa novo*" (Nothing new in the west [also the Serbo-Croatian title of Remarque's *All Quiet on the Western Front*]), and "*Neću da budem član mafije*" (I don't want to be a member of the mafia). When his writing turned to politics, Đorđević combined his anti-Communism with hard Serbian nationalism, especially in his published collections of verse, particularly *Neću* (Belgrade: self-published, 1989) and *Hej sloveni!* (Belgrade: Glas, 1987). During the same period, the Union of Serbian Writers (*Udruženje književnika Srbije—UKS*) was crystallizing its nationalist positions and elected Đorđević a member, trying in Leninist fashion to legitimate itself by bringing on a "leader of youth." Losing the comic irony that had once characterized his songs, Đorđević took easily to the flattery, began signing his texts as "the writer (*književnik*) Bora Đorđević," and gave himself over to political agitation in the nationalist cause. Where the rock critic Petar Luković (in his *Bolja prošlost: Prilozi iz muzičkog života Jugoslavije, 1940–1989* [Belgrade: Mladost, 1989]) had once referred to him as "the first Serbian rock star," the weekly rubric that Luković directs of amusing and appalling quotations in the newsweekly *Vreme* would henceforth refer to him as "professional Serb."

was going to middle school then and they sent me to the school psychologist every day. My clothing provoked the kind of shock as if you were today to walk naked on Terazije. Whenever I would write "punk is not dead" on a wall, the cops (*murija*) would come right to my house because they knew it was me who wrote it and they would make me remove it.[18]

In addition to being a marker of difference between urban and rural cultural inclinations, music already indicated, to a certain degree, orientation toward the regime. In this regard, the individualism of the rock aesthetic played a defining role. Noise-rock pioneer Dušan Kojić-Koja, leader of the band *Disciplina kičme* (Discipline of the spine), staked out a cultural position opposed to the conformity of mainstream popular culture, singing:

Mnogo ljudi ne zna	Many people don't know how
Mnogo ljudi ne sme	Many people cannot
Doživeti tu radost	Experience the pleasure
Moje lepe pesme	Of my beautiful song

His followers in the band *Boye* (Colors, but also a pun involving the addition of a feminine plural suffix to the English "boy") asked in one song:

Da li želiš da znaš?	Do you desire to know?
Da li umeš da želiš?	Are you able to desire?

Other approaches were more pointed in their relation to the organized and joyless character of the regime. When the garage-rock pioneers of Belgrade chose the name *Partibrejkers* (phonetically, Party breakers) for their band, there was no doubt as to what "party" they had in mind.

By the end of the 1980s, Yugoslav rock culture had reached the point that one longtime foreign observer of its development called it "mature."[19] Its dominant cultural position had developed to the point that, as the music journalist Petar Janjatović described it: "The most popular

18. Petar Janjatović, "Zvoncek i druge seksualne devijacije" (interview), *Vreme zabavo* (February 1995), 52.

19. Sabrina Ramet, *Balkan Babel: Politics, Culture, and Religion in Yugoslavia* (Boulder, Colo.: Westview Press, 1992).

bands—Fish Chowder (*Riblja čorba*) and Bajaga and the Instructors (*[Momčilo Bajagić-] Bajaga i instruktori*) from Belgrade, for example, and White Button (*Bijelo dugme*) and Blue Orchestra (*Plavi orkestar*) from Sarajevo—regularly did two-month tours of Yugoslavia covering around 60 towns, and some of their albums sold as many as 500,000 copies. On the eve of the war, private record labels were gaining ground, working with unknown but promising bands."[20] The market fell apart, however, as wars divided the audience and sent many of its most enthusiastic members to other countries in search of a better future or from fear of being forced into military service.

Although the demise of SFRJ physically isolated the urban audiences of Yugoslavia's republics from one another, music continued to make its way through borders. A brisk bootleg trade assured that recordings remained available, if only to a limited public. In Belgrade, that public was limited to those who could check the stock at the sidewalk stands in front of the Student Cultural Center (SKC), which always had a far wider selection than the "official" PGP-RTS (*Produkcija gramofonskih ploča— Radio televizija Srbije*) and *Jugodisk* stores, if consumers were willing to risk dubious recording quality. A handful of private shops also existed in Serbia's smaller cities. The sidewalk stands carried the products of the small independent labels that grew up with the demise of domestic rock and roll production by the official publishing houses and some products by independent labels in other republics—from the Slovenian "Primitiv-C" label, which produced Pula's *KUD Idijoti*, for example.[21]

Most artists at least tolerated, if they did not quite appreciate, distribution through the pirate market. Darko Rundek of the Zagreb band *Haustor* (Lobby), expressed (from his residence in Paris) sympathetic reaction to the Belgrade street dealer who made a pirate "Greatest Hits" compact

20. Petar Janjatović, "Yugoslav Civil War Halts Growth of Local Music Biz," *Billboard* 104, no. 28, 11 July 1992.

21. The first part of the band's name comes from the official abbreviation for amateur singing and musical groups: "Cultural-Artistic Society" (*Kulturno-umjetničko društvo*). Among all the bands whose music was distributed "informally" during the war period, *KUD Idijoti* was the only one to object openly to bootleg and pirate recordings. The warning on one of its albums reads: "It is forbidden to lend or rerecord this CD for money. Whoever does that anyway is a criminal and a donkey. And should go to fucking hell [a loose translation: *I neka ide u pizdu materinu*]. Whoever asks that this CD be recorded onto cassette and pays for it—criminal and donkey. And should fuck off [another loose translation: *I neka ide u kurac*]. So be it. Amen." KUD Idijoti, *Tako je govorio Zaratustra*, Koper: Primitiv-C (PRIM-1021), 1994.

disk of his band—the first CD to be released "by" the band in its career.[22] Other bands openly discussed the results of the loss of markets that had suddenly become "foreign," like the members of *KUD Idijoti* in an interview:

> Ptica: We still live from concerts, we are forced to because we can only sell our CDs and cassettes in Croatia and Slovenia.
> Fritz: We are a band who had a market in all of the former Yugoslavia. Although today a lot of people like to be silent about it, the truth is that we sold very well over there. Considering what the market is like now and how [little] we are present in the media, we still sell well today because we have an audience that buys everything. It's a bit like [the Zagreb band] *Azra*, since people would buy even a fifty-sided album by [*Azra*'s notoriously self-indulgent leader] Johnny Štulić.
> Ptica: Our first album, "We're Only Here for the Money" [*Mi smo ovdje samo zbog para*] sold eleven thousand copies in all of Yugoslavia. Now our sales are ten times smaller.[23]

Accompanying the desire to maintain access to music from the rest of the former Yugoslav "cultural space" is a desire to know what is generally happening in culture. Probably exaggerating, *KUD Idijoti*'s Fritz told a Belgrade journalist, "700 people in Pula read one copy of [the Belgrade music magazine] *Vreme zabave*."[24] *Vreme zabave*, for its part, an offshoot of the legendary independent news magazine *Vreme*, does its best to keep its principally Serbian readership informed on the new music in Croatia, Slovenia, Bosnia-Hercegovina, and Macedonia. Sometimes the desire for contact is expressed openly as nostalgia, as in the concert in Kragujevac

---

22. Petar Luković, "Bolero u tajnom gradu" (interview with Darko Rundek), *Vreme zabave* (December 1994), 45–48. The producer of the pirate CD, identifying himself only by the nickname Šumi, sent a letter explaining his actions and expressing his love for the band's music, in care of the interviewer Petar Luković. With regard to the financial side of the pirate production, Rundek was less enthusiastic: "[A friend] mentioned to me the bizarre case that I might get some money for this. You know, fuck it, it is after all my work" (46).

23. "Mi smo Jugo nostalgičari," *Yu rock magazin* (October 1994), 9.

24. Petar Janjatović, "Mačke oko vruće kaše" (interview), *Vreme zabave* (December 1994), 56.

in which local bands played a repertoire exclusively made up of the songs of Zagreb bands.[25]

The improbable tolerance on the part of artists for people pirating their recordings and the continuing desire for information and other contact from the far side of new borders were symbols of a dramatic change in the culture of Belgrade, which came with the onset of war. On the one hand, the breakdown of contact between urban centers caused the rock and roll market, which was always interurban, to virtually disappear. What the establishment of new borders did not achieve in this regard, the exodus of the younger generation across the borders did. At the same time, changes at the level of political structure had cultural consequences. With a rural- and regional-oriented nationalist elite taking the place of an urban-oriented communist elite, peasants and "urban-peasants" colonized the cultural space that rock and roll youth once dominated. The cultural consequences of this shift are apparent in every aspect of everyday life, but perhaps nowhere so clearly as in the field of music. The rock and roll music that had once defined the youth culture of the city was shunted to the margins, its public presence replaced first by the "newly composed folk music" (*novokomponovana narodna muzika*) popular in the provinces and later by an eclectic dance-folk melange known as "turbofolk."[26]

Rokeri at the Margins

With the collapse of the interurban rock and roll market, the confidence of Belgrade *rokeri* withered quickly. A sizable urban audience continued to buy such records as were produced, although these became progressively fewer, and continued to fill to capacity and beyond the few rock and roll clubs that continued to operate in Belgrade. However, Serbia, a country with a population roughly equal in size to the population of the city of New York, could not commercially support a cultural market

25. Unsigned (attributed to Beta), "Zagrebačka rok scena u Kragujevcu," *Borba*, 17 November 1994, p. 24.

26. The term "turbofolk" was coined by *roker* Rambo Amadeus (about whom see more below) to describe his satiric co-optation of neofolk forms and imagery. However, commercial neofolk performers who lacked Rambo's irony adopted the term for themselves, and it came to refer less critically to an amplified and synthesized dance kitsch form, which received tremendous commercial promotion.

mostly confined to an urban minority. As the mainstream center of the rock and roll market shrank, the culture came to be dominated by avant-garde and exotic musicians. In an earlier paper, I described this phenome-non as "hermetic rock and roll."[27] Radovan Kupres went further in a newspaper series chronicling Serbian rock and roll in the nineties, with the title of the final installment reading: "Harmless, depressive, minority-oriented."[28]

A paradoxical increase in importance—at least for members of its rela-tively small audience—accompanied the decline in public presence of rock and roll. Research by Thomas Cushman[29] and Anna Szemere[30] chronicles crises of identity experienced by Russian and Hungarian rock-ers, respectively, as they emerged from undergrounds where their cul-tural importance was secure to commercial markets where their position was precarious (and where their former "oppositional" roles seemed sud-denly anachronistic). The order of events seems to have gone in the re-verse direction in Belgrade, however. Rock and roll's possession of popular cultural space in the days when Yugoslavia was the most liberal, open, and prosperous of East European states seemed trivial in retro-spect; now their fight for a voice in the culture of Europe's poorest and most-isolated dictatorship seemed a more important matter.

Where the rock and roll culture of the relatively open late-Communist period of the 1980s had been a successful cultural and commercial opera-tion, the marginal rock and roll of the 1990s earned less, reached a smaller audience, and stood for more. In particular, by standing as the strongest representation of urban and international culture against the nationalist domination of the "peasant urbanites" and rural bosses, Bel-grade *rokeri* during the war period acted as an antidote to the isolation imposed on young people in Serbia both from without—in the form of sanctions including cultural and artistic exchange—and from within—in

27. Eric D. Gordy, "The Struggles Against Popular Music in Serbia" (unpublished paper presented at the conference of the International Association for the Study of Popular Music, Glasgow, 1995).

28. Radovan Kupres, "Srpski režim i srpski rok: Od presije do kolaboracije (3)— Bezopasno, depresivno, minorno," *Naša borba* (Internet izdanje), 23 May 1996.

29. Thomas Cushman, *Notes from Underground: Rock Music Counterculture in Russia* (Albany: SUNY Press, 1995).

30. Anna Szemere, "Subcultural Politics and Social Change: Alternative Rock Music in Postcommunist Hungary" (unpublished paper presented at the conference of the International Association for the Study of Popular Music—USA, Nashville, 1995).

Fig. 5. Under the stage name Rambo Amadeus, rocker Antonije Pušić fused together rap, folk, rock, and Communist nostalgia into a complex lampoon of the regime and the culture it promoted. Rambo coined the term *turbofolk,* but the form quickly grew away from his control. Photo courtesy of *Vreme.*

the form of dominating nativism and the exodus of a good portion of the young urban population. In their stand against neofolk kitsch, *rokeri* also constantly reminded the urban population that war and nationalism are associated with the new dominance of semirural culture—its nativism, lack of interest in global culture, and xenophobia were epitomized by the explosion of neofolk and directly associated, in the minds of Belgrade *rokeri,* with the regime and with the war it brought on.

The new position of rock and roll is best represented in the change of figures who personified it. If the Belgrade scene of the 1980s is personified by Gile and *Električni orgazam,* who in the course of their long career translated West European and American pop forms into domestic hits, then the face of rock and roll culture in the nineties is almost certainly Antonije Pušić, the music-composition graduate who made his popular career as the idiot-savant peasant rapper Rambo Amadeus (later Ranko Amadeus, and still later Rajko Amadeus). (See Fig. 5.) The critic Petar Janjatović identified Rambo in 1992 as "the most interesting figure on the Belgrade music scene";[31] the critic Petar Luković greeted Rambo's 1995 greatest hits collection—saddled with the faux-literary title "Selected Works" (*Izabrana dela*)—with high praise:

> [W]hoever spent the last five–six years under a blanket in this Serbia/ex-Yugoslavia/SR Yugoslavia knows very well what Mr. Rambo Amadeus has meant for the mental health of this people. . . . [His songs in the collection] are not only the tip of the iceberg of something called "R. A. creativity" [*stvaralaštvo*] but also the apex of a musical-political position which has been consistently maintained all these years, in spite of the social-Serbian-political paranoia which Pušić has perfectly incorporated with extraordinary irony which is not difficult to read in between the lines and above them. . . . ['I']his CD is crowning evidence that we have somehow survived and that some of us have remained normal.[32]

If the rock and roll scene of the 1980s can be seen as an effort to create and define an urban culture, Rambo Amadeus epitomizes the orientation of rock and roll in the following period as a response to the threatened position of that urban culture.

Although Rambo famously declared that "rock and roll in Serbia died the moment Slobodan Milošević appeared,"[33] his improbable success in the Milošević period proved him wrong at least in his own case. His music radically combined elements of rap, rock, funk, and neofolk with his own idiosyncratic, ironic, and often obscene portrayals of life in the contemporary Balkans, as well as with his vitriolic opposition to the regime. Where Antonije Pušić the intellectual could comment only from the margins, the overblown character of the arrogant and foolish Rambo enjoyed broad satiric license. He borrowed from a cultural type already familiar in Yugoslav theater and cinema, which, akin to Shakespeare's "divine fool," was the confused and ignorant simple man, who inadvertently or with a special comic license reveals the truth. The figure is recognizable to Balkan audiences—in the nervous and scheming true believers played

31. Petar Janjatović, "Yugoslav Civil War Halts Growth of Local Music Biz," *Billboard* 104, no. 28, 11 July 1992.

32. Petar Luković, "Rambo Amadeus: Izabrana dela 1989–1994" (review), *Vreme zabave* (April 1995), 45.

33. Janjatović, "Yugoslav Civil War Halts Growth of Local Music Biz," *Billboard* 104, no. 28, 11 July 1992.

by the actor Danilo Stojković in the films *Balkanski špijun* (Balkan spy) and *Maratonci trče počasni krug* (The marathon runners run the winners' circle) and also in the naive and bombastic provincial immortalized by the actor Zoran Radmilović in the mostly extemporaneous theater performance *Radovan III.* Turning this figure into a celebrity cut two ways for Rambo Amadeus: On the one hand, he provided a living travesty of Serbia's extravagant neofolk stars (personified in Rambo's folksinger character "Halid Invalid-Hari"), while on the other hand he acted out a role that was, however absurdly exaggerated, familiar enough by local show-business standards to maintain access to the media.

His music was often received as comical or enjoyed for its ostensibly foolish content, but the erudition of Antonije Pušić moderated, at least in part, the public reception of Rambo Amadeus. As Rambo described the motivation of his songs: "I began with my turbofolk thing (*fazon*) when I came to Belgrade, bought a radio, and found to my delight that there were ten radio stations. But then I saw that on all ten they played nothing but folk (*narodnjake*). Since I did not have a cassette player I listened to the radio and the texts of the songs were endlessly ridiculous (*smiješni*) and stupid to me. So I tried to radicalize them, to create even stupider and more ridiculous texts, until the stupidity reached the point of genius."[34] In addition to his own compositions, he played in his concerts the "Ode to Joy" from Beethoven's Ninth Symphony, arranged as a Gypsy *kolo*, and turned to his rough translation of the rock standard "Hey Joe," aided by neofolk monument Mica Trofrtaljka. Whereas the musical references and samples he employed borrowed from popular film, Communist children's groups, and Yugoslav and American popular music, the figure to which Rambo always returned was the neofolk peasant of the Balkans. In a rare moment of apparent sincerity, he told an interviewer:

> I want to isolate that gold Mercedes with diamond wheels and to observe it as a work of art. . . . The same as I want to observe the man who has a gold necktie, who listens to [neofolk star] Šemsa Šuljaković and knows which *kafana* has good food and how to make easy money. But other than that, he understands nothing and knows nothing, he doesn't know whose body his head is on [*ne zna ko mu*

34. In his interview on the television documentary *Rockumenti: Rambo Amadeus, Crnogorac*, RTS 1, May 1995.

glavu nosi] and is as happy as a sheep. That man interests me as an artist. . . . I want to break into [*prodrem*] his consciousness and make civic culture out of it.[35]

Incorporating the madness, paranoia, kitsch, and inauthenticity of the neofolk ascendancy into his antimusic, Rambo Amadeus presented a detailed ironic reading of the cultural moment, with the capacity of reaching broad audiences. In doing so, he also occasionally provided space for Antonije Pušić to break through the character of Rambo, as in the encyclopedic antiregime song "Karamba karambita."

Rambo's lampoon of neofolk culture had more than simply comical resonance. In making a travesty of the conventions and conceits of neofolk, he gave ironic voice to the members of the urban rock and roll audience who felt that their access to the culture in which they lived was slipping out of their hands. *Rokeri* saw the decline of rock and roll in Serbia as emblematic of the defeat of urban culture generally, and the *primitivci* who came to prominence were directly associated in their minds with the war and the cultural decline and new criminality that came with it. When Belgrade's three most popular rock and roll groups, *Električni orgazam*, *Partibrejkers*, and *Ekaterina velika* (Catherine the Great), came together as the group *Rimtutituki*[36] to record the antiwar song *"Slušaj 'vamo (Mir, brate, mir)"* (Listen here [peace, brother, peace]), they made the association directly:

Nećemo da pobedi	We don't want
Narodna muzika	Folk music to win
Više volim tebe mladu	I love the young you more
Nego pušku da mi dadu	Than that they give me a rifle

Vocalist Zoran Kostić-Cane, who together with guitarist Nebojša Anton-ijević-Anton leads the Belgrade garage-rock group *Partibrejkers*, put the association of elements of neofolk culture with war clearly: "Three key components of this war are: alcohol, greasy food, and folk music. Those

35. Quoted in Vladimir Stakić, "Dvanaest crtica o kulturi i turbofolku: Davorike dajke," *Vreme zabave* (April 1995), 65.

36. The name of the ad hoc band is a complicated play on words with an obscene connotation. The band was joined in performances in Belgrade by Rambo Amadeus and again at an antiwar concert in Prague by the Zagreb band *Vještice* (Witches). Jasna Sarčević, "Muzika za nostalgičare," *Borba*, 24 October 1994, p. 15.

Fig. 6. Three Belgrade rock and roll bands combined to form the antiwar band *Rimtutituki* in 1992. Here the band performs at an antiwar demonstration in Belgrade. In the foreground is Zoran Kostić-Cane, lead vocalist of the *Partibrejkers*. Photo courtesy of *Vreme*.

are three points (*tačke*), three basic ingredients, which lead to somebody falling under the table and shouting from under there: 'I'll fuck you up, you'll see.' "[37] (See Fig. 6.) Both in their antiwar political engagement and their defense of urban culture, Belgrade *rokeri* combined the (innate?) rebelliousness of rock and roll with a high-culture opposition to neofolk vulgarity, associating the architects of war with the culture of their political supporters.

Visibly staking out a cultural position that carries clear political implications—for urban culture, for the decadence of the West, against folk nostalgia and nationalism—Belgrade rock and roll narrowed its own cultural space. As the scene took its cultural importance and cultural mission seriously, the borders of the rock and roll genre hardened. With production and distribution of recordings nearly impossible and press runs down

37. Vladimir Stakić, "Monoview: Zoran Kostić-Cane, Partibrejkers," *Vreme zabave* (May 1994).

to a minimum,[38] media access also minimal,[39] and only a few performance venues, most of them small,[40] commercial success in rock and roll was out of the question. Many musicians have stories of the difficulty of recording and releasing music; perhaps the most dramatic came from Vlada Jerić of *Darkwood dub*, a band that succeeded in releasing in 1995 an album they had recorded in 1991:

> Whoever touched *Darkwood dub* was destroyed utterly (*načisto*). We can start from the beginning, when we rehearsed in Zemun. It was awful and ended with a horrible event that I don't care to mention. Then we went over to SKC (*Studentski kulturni centar*), which after our long and productive stay began completely to fall apart. First it was supposed to be a Kentucky Fried Chicken, and now it is an SPS showplace and a market for expensive goods. One compilation on the *Nova Aleksandrija* label, in which we took part, was printed by *Jugoton*. The moment the printing was finished the war began and Yugoslavia fell apart. Nikola Medić became the publisher, a very dear fellow and a great friend, but he became mentally unstable, emigrated to London, and he is still there today. Our second publisher, Miloš Grozdanović from Sorabia Disc, when the time came to put out and pay off our recordings from the studio, decided to declare himself mentally incompetent, which he did. So we tried to

38. In early 1995, *Električni orgazam*, one of Yugoslavia's most popular rock and roll bands, released an ambitious double album, "*Zašto da ne?*" (Why not?), which marked its return to recording after a three-year hiatus as well as the band's fifteenth anniversary. The album was initially released with a press run of 500 copies.

39. To take television appearances as a key example, whereas two stations (TV Pink and TV Palma) that were oriented exclusively to promotion of neofolk videos and neofolk records received heavy promotion on the three state-owned television stations, programs showcasing domestic rock and roll were sparse. The "semi-independent" TV Politika had one Sunday program, *Paket aranžman;* the third channel of the state television included a "domestic top ten" on its Sunday-afternoon top ten countdown but canceled its regular domestic rock and roll program *Klati se i valjaj* (a literal translation of "rock and roll"); and the independent Studio B (taken over by the government in 1996) had intermittent programming.

40. The largest rock and roll venue was Prostor, in the premises of a former movie theater. Remaining clubs were generally basement rooms, like Akademija until it was closed in winter of 1995. The city's principal rock and roll venue, the Technical Students' Club (*Klub studenata tehnike—KST*) could hold around 500 people in its "summer garden." Otherwise, its main room could hold slightly more than 200 people, if they held their arms closely at their sides.

make contact and begin work with many publishing houses, which all went under one by one. I don't know whether to mention the recordings from the "Akademija" studio. . . . When I agreed with *Vreme zabave* about a group concert, that concert was supposed to be in December. However, because of technical problems . . . everything was put off until February. We scheduled a concert in Akademija, Akademija closed. We come for a concert in KST, the electricity goes out. . . . Whoever has tried to work with us hasn't lasted long, except Zlatko, and he is coughing suspiciously.[41]

In such a situation, the practice of rock and roll became more difficult, more rare, and more valued. A parallel situation was described by Thomas Cushman in his work on rock production in Leningrad in the Soviet era: "It was this very disorder that made music even more oppositional and resistant in the Soviet context. . . . [T]he fact that it was done under adversity made its practice all the more special to those who made it and those who consumed it."[42]

Belgrade *rokeri* responded to this difficulty, for the most part, by moving away from the mainstream rather than toward it. During the period of research, the most popular bands in Belgrade were a hard-edged garage rock group (*Partibrejkers*), an avant-garde poetic group modeled after Manchester's The Fall (*Obojeni program* [Color program]), a noise band (*Darkwood dub*), and the genre-bending Rambo Amadeus. One popular mainstream band, *Ekaterina velika*, had its career cut short by the death of its leader. Other bands playing in a pop style (*Eva Braun, Plejboj, Oružjem protivu otmičara* [With weapons against kidnappers]) did succeed in recording, but did not have access to the kind of publicity that allowed them to realize their pop ambitions. In general, pop style was regarded as an anomaly in the rock and roll scene. Reviewer Milivoje Čalija felt compelled to point out in describing the songs of the band *Kristali:* "So, we are talking about a band which tries to keep the verse-refrain-verse-bridge-refrain structure in every song. Yes, you read correctly: a refrain, a real rarity in recent domestically produced songs."[43] Aside from a few exceptions,

41. "Prokletstvo na delu," *Vreme zabave* (January 1995), 65. "Zlatko" is Zlatko Jošić, the director of KST, where the interview took place. He is universally known in Belgrade as "Zlatko KST."
42. Cushman (1995), 196.
43. Milivoje Čalija, "Kristali: Kristali" (review), *Vreme zabave* (November 1994), 51.

Belgrade *rokeri* in this period generally met the expectations of their hardest-core fans and detractors, making difficult music for a minority audience.

Dance and pop artists whose orientation was to the commercial mainstream had little to hope for in marketing themselves as rock and roll artists—on the one hand, the rock and roll audience seemed to be in a defensive mood, not receptive toward "inauthenticity" or "compromise"; and on the other hand, rock and roll was marginalized by the dominant media and produced and marketed so little that the publicity necessary for pop success was unavailable. Newer artists who, had they appeared a decade earlier, would have been marketed as pop-rock artists, were instead packaged together with neofolk's cultural offerings. The main neofolk outlets in Belgrade, TV Pink and TV Palma, had the reputation of offering round-the-clock neofolk, but in fact the situation was slightly different. In addition to the dominant neofolk offerings, these stations offered versions of dance pop and "light" rock that could not be considered threatening, along with a highly selective measure of nostalgia music from the 1980s (the proto-neofolk *Bijelo dugme*, but of the new wave and punk of that decade, nothing more challenging than the teen-heartthrob band *Piloti*).

The old commercial mainstream of the rock and roll market split. Pop singer Momčilo Bajagić-Bajaga, seeking a formula to compensate for the lost audience in the former republics, moved increasingly closer to the showbiz market dominated by neofolk. Some former rock and roll stars, like Oliver Mandić and Bora Đorđević, who supported nationalist mobilization, moved into full-time political agitation in the service of the regime and its clients—preserving their access to publicity in state-controlled media, but being for the most part written off by their audiences who came to see them as "fake rockers."[44] Favor was available from above for rockers who were inclined to throw their lot in with the regime. Critic Branimir Lokner detailed some of these favors in his review of a double album by the mythopoetic band *Galija*:

> The band's open flirtation (*koketiranje*) with the Serbian national syndrome, as well as the treatment of their career by the show-

44. Mandić and Đorđević were declared followers of the organized-crime boss and war criminal Željko Ražnatović-Arkan, whose political party received sponsorship from the ruling party after Milošević broke with Vojislav Šešelj. Ražnatović's extreme right-wing orientation allowed Đorđević to resolve, ostensibly, the conflict between his declared anti-Communism and his ideological service to the regime.

business and also the political establishment, have established an image of them with many observers as a privileged state pop-rock group. . . . The manner in which the production was realized furthers the story, in good measure, about [*Galija* being] a privileged state band. The album was recorded on Cyprus, considerable resources were given for its production, and as donors and sponsors there appear several state-owned companies. The album is a joint production of PGP-RTS and the Belgrade SKC, institutions which are directed by the party in power. The grandiose advertising campaign in the state media, and its expensive promotion as well, demonstrate in another way the "investment" of the state in the band.[45]

However, favor from above was no guarantee of a sympathetic reception from below. As heavily promoted and publicized as it was, *Galija* could not escape dismissal from the *rokeri* of Belgrade as an "SPS band."

The absence of a commercial mainstream was noticed and regretted by Belgrade *rokeri;* some attempts were made to address it. The band *Ekaterina velika* had ambitions to maintain a pop-mainstream center until its effort was cut short by the death of the band's leader Milan Mladenović in 1994. Zlatko Jošić, director of Belgrade's principal rock and roll club KST, described how the absence of a mainstream sound limits the audience he can attract:

The soft (*pitka*) rock scene remained on the other side of the border, groups like [the Sarajevo pop bands] *Crvena jabuka* or *Plavi orkestar.* So it was logical that people here would start to listen to some *novokomponovana* stars and that kind of foolishness. . . . Because of the empty space that was left, some bands came to the fore who should have remained in the underground. By 1992 a change occurred, and people who were oriented toward rock escaped into the underground, and the audience which couldn't listen to that kind of music stopped listening to music at all. A part of them who weren't

45. Branimir Lokner, *Kritičko pakovanje* (Belgrade: Vizija 011, 1994), 206. *Galija*'s access to publicity in state media was not hindered by the fact that its principal lyricist, Radoman Kanjevac, was a musical director on the state-owned Radio Belgrade's Second Program. Nor, during the period of nationalist mobilization, was it hurt (except from the aesthetic point of view) by lyrics like the ones celebrating the dominant religion of Serbia: *Pravoslavlje dolazi s juga / Pravoslavlje ispunjava želje* ("Orthodoxy comes from the south / Orthodoxy fulfills wishes").

strongly culturally inclined (*koji su bili neopredeljeni*), who basically listen to whatever appeals to them, began to listen to folk (*narodn-jake*). . . . Right now in rock and roll we haven't got an answer for the people who can't listen to the harder stuff, but would like to listen to something. That is a problem. There simply isn't a complete scene.[46]

Self-conscious efforts to enhance the presence of a mainstream did go on. A series of group concerts under the name *Groovanje* was promoted not as a series of concerts, but as "an action for the return of r 'n r onto the domestic scene."[47]

Such a return is likely only if there are changes in the structure of power and cultural orientation in Serbia. Although the disappearance of the commercial mainstream of rock and roll in Serbia is certainly in part the result of aesthetic choices, those choices were made under constraint. The disappearance of the commercial center of rock and roll can be explained by looking at the cultural orientation of the new nationalist regime to the provinces, at the influence of this cultural orientation on the media outlets that the regime controlled, and at the availability of publicity for rock and roll music—even mainstream rock and roll music. In addition, the most crucial factors that supported the autonomous rock and roll cultures of Yugoslavia's cities before the war disappeared with the war: open communication and contact between urban centers and a sizable audience of young people. Without these factors and a significantly greater presence of independent media, the second coming of rock and roll to the center of Belgrade's culture is unlikely. More probably, the music will remain the cultural outlet of an urban minority whose cultural dominance died, to paraphrase Rambo Amadeus, when Slobodan Milošević appeared.

The Neofolk Ascendance

Whether the regime turned intentionally against the domestic rock and roll culture, as part of a program to push culture in a direction consistent

46. Krofna i Vesna, "Ličnosti: Profesionalac," *Yu rock magazin* (October 1994), 27.
47. Maša Matijašević, "Groovanje: Decembar 1994," *Vreme zabave* (January 1995), 62.

with war, is certainly a matter to be debated, and the debate can probably not be resolved here. Certainly people in the rock and roll culture saw the association and drew the connection, as Rambo Amadeus argued: "You cannot force people in the trenches to listen to *Disciplina kičme*, Wagner, or Schnittke. Those atavisms in a person, those primitive impulses for tribal war, can only be awakened with primitive music. That is why, when it was necessary, meatheads under the big tops (*papci ispod šatri*) were moved directly to [Belgrade's elite performance hall] Sava Centar."[48] Purely aesthetic reasons were probably not at stake, however. Nonetheless it was impossible for regime supporters not to notice that their support was weakest by far among the young urban population—a fact repeatedly made clear to them in the political protests of 1991 and the student protests of 1992 and in the massive refusal of calls to military service.[49] It was also easy enough to observe that the young urbanites' refusal to follow along on the path of war was encouraged by the rock and roll culture that characterized them. Particularly active in this regard was the unlicensed "youth radio" station B-92, which combined its rock and roll-centered programming with the only independent radio news program in Belgrade, as well as with a number of performance-like public "actions" against the war and the conditions associated with it.

Whether the regime had any reason or desire to act against rock and roll, it had every reason to want to discourage the attitudes and activity of the rock and roll public. Regime ideologists were never unclear as to their opinion of the culture of Serbia's urban youth. Dobrica Ćosić, the novelist to whom the inspiration for Milošević's national program is generally attributed,[50] grouped together among the spiritual enemies of the

48. Quoted in Radovan Kupres, "Srpski režim i srpski rok: Od presije do kolaboracije (1)—suvišna muzika u godinama raspleta," *Naša borba* (Internet izdanje), 23 May 1996.

49. According to Mirjana Prošić-Dvornić, "There are various estimates of the success, or lack of success, of [military] mobilization, but all of them fall below 50 percent. For Belgrade, where, along with multiethnic Vojvodina, resistance was strongest, it is estimated that as many as 80 percent of reservists did not appear for mobilization." In Mirjana Prošić-Dvornić, ed., *Kulture u tranziciji* (Belgrade: Plato, 1994), 196 n. 17.

50. Ćosić is generally assumed to have been the principal author of the 1986 *Memorandum* of SANU, which laid out the grievances of Serbia against other republics and the Albanian minority in Yugoslavia. He lent legitimacy to Milošević during the period of his ascent to power by offering "neutral support" to the new dictator and continued to lend it by becoming the first president of the Federal Republic of Yugoslavia (*Savezna Republika Jugoslavija—SRJ*), which was constituted by Serbia and Montenegro.

nation a variety of exponents of modernity: "[Yugoslavism in its 'evil in-carnation' is] an expression of a political parvenu mentality; of the snob-bery of a part of the rock-and-roll generation; of the cosmopolitanism of liberal intellectuals; of a legitimate and 'progressivist' and 'democratic' mask for anationality and anti-Serbianism."[51] The culture of pleasure as-sociated with this variety of modernity was also associated in the minds of regime ideologists with the rock and roll audience, and they regarded it, probably correctly, as interfering with nationalist mobilization for war. Ex-humanist Mihailo Marković, in his role as vice president and chief ideologist of SPS, made his complaint against the popular culture of urban youth in martial terms: "Our youth was not psychologically pre-pared for war. Young people lived comfortably, dreaming of a future like in 'Dynasty,' and now they are shocked by the fact that they have no choice but to put on a uniform, take up weapons, and go to fight."[52] Whether it was carried out consciously or not, the destruction of the rock and roll market met two goals of the regime in the period of nationalist mobilization: It helped to demoralize and isolate members of the young generations of urbanites who were more inclined than any other group to resist the regime's rhetoric and plans, and it weakened a popular chan-nel of cultural expression, which was largely inclined and willing to stand in the way.

The regime, however, was not so certain of the attractiveness of its program that it believed that culture as entertainment and diversion was not required. Some form of popular entertainment had to be promoted, and several factors offered neofolk as the most opportune candidate. First, except in the cities, neofolk was already widely publicized and widely popular; a basis had been laid, and no great investment was re-quired to promote the music. Second, neofolk musicians had been, since at least the early 1960s,[53] eagerly bringing electric and amplified sounds,

51. Quoted in Vujačić (1995), 249. The translation is also by Vujačić.
52. Quoted in Prošić-Dvornić (1994), 191.
53. Ivan Čolović (*Divlja književnost* [Belgrade: Nolit, 1985], 142–43), dates the be-ginning of the "new folk songs" movement to 1962, contemporaneous with the expan-sion of local radio stations in Yugoslavia. However, he points out that more "traditional" folk songs are often also relatively recently authored compositions in the folk style: "Few people know that the well-known songs *Jesen prođe, ja se ne oženih* (Spring is passing, and I have not married) *Jesi l'čuo mili rode* (Have you heard, dear relative) or *Lepo ti je biti čobanica* (It is nice for you to be a shepherdess), which seem to come from ancient pastoral days, were written around 1950 by Dragiša Nedović of Kragujevac, and the music composed by Miodrag Krnjevac" (141).

as well as rhythms and styles from western popular music, into their own repertoire. Third, although rock and roll had been generally identified, and more so in Yugoslavia, as a music of rebellion, individualism, and resistant postures, folk forms had not had such an image since the waning days of the Ottoman Empire. Ivan Čolović described the principal forum for neofolk music on local radio, in dedication programs with titles like "greetings and wishes":

> They follow and confirm the exchange of signs of care and love occasioned by important events in the lives of individuals and families, such as birthdays, entry into school, enrollment in the university, graduation, entry into the army, return from the army, affiancement, marriage, receiving employment, the birth of a child, setting off to work in other countries, return from other countries, moving into a new house, receiving electricity, buying a car, receiving a driver's license, retirement, returning from the hospital, etc. These are happy occasions and successes which merit congratulations and good wishes and which should be made general knowledge, and so the sending of appropriate messages by the radio, with the dedication of songs, forms a part of the system of neofolkloric symbolic communication.[54]

Whereas rock and roll sought to express an orientation outside the general social order, neofolk had a place in it, as a part of the system of mainstream communication, especially in the small towns and villages.[55]

Most important, however, neofolk artists willingly offered musical forms for use as nationalist agitprop.[56] The most recognizable nationalist

54. Čolović (1985), 149.
55. There were, of course, neofolk listeners in cities as well. A hint as to the origins of part of this audience can be found in the idyllic-rustic themes of many neofolk songs, as well as in specific nostalgic themes (i.e., *U gradu sam sada, al' se selu divim* [I am in the city now, but I envy the village]). An anticosmopolitan orientation can be found to complement the antiurban inclination, as in Miroslav Ilić's lyric: *Ameriko, zemlja velika / Ali metar moga sela, Amerika cela* (America, a big country / But one meter of my village is all of America). A part of this anticosmopolitanism can perhaps be attributed to the fact that for many Yugoslavs, especially from rural areas, the only contact they were likely to have with other countries was the unpleasant experience of being a "guest worker."
56. The emphasis here is on neofolk, and not on the assortment of traditional styles usually called *izvorni*, or "authentic" folk. The cultural conflict between the *izvornis*

"folk" songs, *"Marš na Drinu"* (March to the Drina [river]) and *"Tamo daleko"* (Over there) in Serbia date from the First World War, and in the Second World War all the fighting groups composed songs in the folk style to promote their armies and causes. Consistent with its mainstream cultural orientation, the neofolk genre produced many a patriotic song in the Communist era, "sung in honor of Tito, the Party, and Yugoslavia."[57] Some historical basis exists for associating neofolk music with the cultural glorification of groups in power. The association applies particularly in regard to national movements,[58] as Čolović observed: "That folklore and politics, at least when the question is about [Serbia], are connected with one another from the very beginning, is clear from Vuk [Karadžić]'s reve-

---

and the "neos" in folk reaches, in many cases, the same pitch as did the cultural conflict between *rokeri* and *narodnjaci* in the war years. See Čolović (1985), 148, or for that matter the letters column of any of Serbia's folk-fan magazines such as *Sabor* or *Huper*. "Authentic" folk, however, is a minority music on a level with symphonic music, its performance most often restricted to professional ensembles of trained musicians; "neofolk," like most other commercial forms, is performed principally by self-educated performers. Andrei Simić (1978, 27) describes the distinction as follows: "[D]etractors [of neofolk] employ a variety of derogatory expressions such as 'clippity-clop national music' and the like. In this negative framework the implied comparison is with so-called 'authentic national music' (*izvorna narodna muzika*) an expression limited to an increasingly rare, orally transmitted village tradition, and to performances by professional and amateur folklore groups often composed of educated elites who in other contexts reject popular folk culture, especially when it is associated with their contemporary social inferiors." Simić goes on to claim of "authentic national songs" that "perhaps their major audience consists of foreign folk-song and dance enthusiasts."

57. Čolović (1985), 158.

58. The emphasis here is on artists willingly offering their services for nationalist publicity. Ivan Čolović cites two cases in which a rock and roll band, *Električni orgazam*, was involuntarily used for a similar purpose, in the chants of football fans, which often took a nationalist character. The chorus of one of their songs:

Igra rokenrol cela Jugoslavija	Dance to rock and roll, all of Yugoslavia
Sve se ispred tebe ispravlja i savija	Everything before you folds and unfolds

was rendered by patriotic football fans to include the lines (in the version of fans of Belgrade's team Partizan):

Samo pravi Srbin za Partizan navija	Only real Serbs root for Partizan

And alternatively (in the version of fans of Split's team Hajduk):

Samo pravi Dalmatinac za Hajduk navija	Only real Dalmatians root for Hajduk.

See Ivan Čolović, "Fudbal, huligani, i rat," *Republika*, no. 117 (1–15 June 1995).

lation (more precisely: representation) of folklore as the framework of the life of the nation."[59]

Slobodan Milošević tied his rise as a political figure to cultural projects of "national revival" as well as to political projects of emphasizing national grievances, as in Kosovo. Popular response was expressed both in slogans composed in the folkloric key and in neofolk songs dedicated to presenting the new leader in the light of a national hero. Čolović cited many of these songs, both from his observations of political meetings and from agitprop cassettes, among which is the song "*Čovek dvadesetog veka*" (Twentieth-century man):

| Mila braćo, došlo novo doba | Dear brothers, the new era has come |
| Rodio se Milošević Sloba | Sloba Milošević is born[60] |

In this regard too, the ground had been laid for neofolk to take the role of the regime's favorite genre, legitimating the projects of the regime by implicitly associating them with other national traditions.

The cultural ante was raised as war neared and then finally arrived. Folk performers took the lead in producing agitprop cassettes of "patriotic" and militaristic songs on all sides of new and future borders. The cheap production and poor quality of performance on most of these cassettes indicate that they were produced hurriedly and with more of an eye toward agitprop among specific preselected groups than toward any potential commercial market.[61] One indication of how hurriedly com-

59. "Folklor i politika," *Bordel ratnika* (Belgrade: XX Vek, 1994), 23.

60. "Stan'te paše i ustaše," *Bordel ratnika* (Belgrade: XX Vek, 1994a), 103. Any association between the title of this song and the King Crimson classic "Twenty-First-Century Schizoid Man" is probably coincidental, as the two do not resemble each other musically. The King Crimson song was covered by the Rijeka band *Let 3* on its 1994 album, *Peace*. Several examples of the music with which Radovan Karadžić promoted himself and his parastate can be observed in the film *Serbian Epics* (London: BBC, 1993). Consistent with his representation of himself as an heir to the nineteenth-century folklorist and language reformer Vuk Stefanović Karadžić (Radovan's evidence that they are related: they both appear to have dimples on their chins), Radovan claimed to prefer epic poetry to the more commercial variants of neofolk.

61. To these aesthetic qualifiers one might also add that the lyrical content of the songs seems to fall into three general categories: insults directed toward political leaders on the opposing sides, threats, often of sexualized violence, toward the same, and claims about the historical ownership of particular areas of land. See the selection of songs offered by Petar Luković, "Šta pevaju Srbi i Hrvati," *Vreme*, no. 110, 30 November 1992, pp. 29–32.

posed the selections were: Serbian and Croatian nationalist folk performers often used the same songs, many of them borrowed not only from the
World War II–era songs of the *Četnici* and *Ustaše*, but also from the old
Communist catalog of pro-regime folk songs, with only a few alterations
in the lyrics distinguishing the versions on either side of the border from
one another.[62] Together with the music came cultural claims about the
"naturalness" of folk forms both for the purpose to which they were put
and for the people for whom they were intended. Čolović cited a nationalist reporter's response to a performance of an epic poem in the
traditional *deseterac* metric scheme[63] by Krajina schoolchildren: "They
probably do not even know what *deseterac* is, nor did they consciously use
it in writing the song. It is born into them, it is found inscribed in their
genetic code."[64]

A brief period of promotion of agitprop neofolk coincided with the
period of nationalist mobilization. In Belgrade, an all-agitprop radio station, Radio Ponos (Radio pride), offered a program of "only Serbian folk
songs, of those only the 'really Serbian' ones."[65] The station promoted
the only singer of contemporary nationalist songs to become, however
briefly, a commercial success. Baja "Mali Knindža" (the stage name is
derived from a play on words involving Ninja warriors and the city of
Knin) was called by Zoran Đokić, the director of the station, "the Serbian
Dylan,"[66] however much the lyrics and style of his songs argue against
such a comparison. To offer an example of Baja's verse:

62. For several examples, see Milena Dragićević-Šešić, *Neofolk kultura: Publika i
njene zvezde* (Novi Sad: Biblioteka elementi, 1994). There were distinctions between
Serbia and Croatia, however. Reflective of the fact that neofolk had always been more
popular in the "eastern" republics (Serbia, Montenegro, Bosnia-Hercegovina, Macedonia) than in the "western" ones (Croatia, Slovenia), nationalist agitprop in Croatia
inclined toward the pop end of the scale as much as to the folk end. Hence saccharine
nationalist compositions like *"Danke Deutschland"* and the songs by Tomislav Ivčić encouraging Croatian expatriates to "come home."

63. *Deseterac*, a ten-syllable line with a break after the fourth, is the meter in which
all Serbian epic poetry is written, as well as contemporary variations on the epic theme.
The song quoted above, "Twentieth-Century Man," is a contemporary example of this
metric structure.

64. Unidentified news reporter quoted by Ivan Čolović, "Vreme i prostor u sa-
vremenoj političkoj mitologiji," in Prošić-Dvornić (1994), 124.

65. Srboljub Bogdanović, "Philips Višnjić," *NIN*, 5 March 1993.

66. Quoted in Bogdanović, "Philips Višnjić," *NIN*, 5 March 1993. The motivation
of the promoters of neofolk to displace the pop and rock market may be suggested by

Mogu da nas mrze	They can hate us
da nas ne vole	or not love us
al' Srbinu niko	but nobody
ništa ne može.	can do anything to a Serb.
Živeće ovaj narod	This nation will live
i posle ustaša	even after the ustaše
jer i Bog i Srbi	because God and the Serbs
nebesa su naša.	the heavens are ours.
Mogu da nas mrze	They can hate us
dušmani od reda	all our series of enemies
al' Srbi su najjači	but Serbs are the strongest
rekao mi deda.	my grandfather told me.[67]

Radio Ponos, however, was *not* the strongest. Its operations were suddenly shut down in 1994, when the regime made its political move away from public support for its client parastates in Croatia and Bosnia-Hercegovina. The nationalist folk movement survived "as a phantom radio movement which occasionally organizes benefit concerts (with singers from the second and third folk-leagues)."[68] As for Baja "Mali Knindža," during the period of observation the only video spot of his that I saw broadcast was for the appropriately titled song *"Hteo bih negde da odem"* (I'd like to go away somewhere).

Neofolk survived the cutting off of its agitprop branch, however, and developed in a new direction. The tremendous publicity that folk celebrities received in state media as the rock and roll market vanished and the perceived need for some material to fill the void left by the evaporation of the rock and roll mainstream created an opportunity for the neofolk market to speed up and exponentially deepen a transformation that had been going on for a long time. From the first moment that neofolk composers and writers began addressing contemporary themes,[69] and from the first moment that neofolk performers switched from peasant garb and formal suits to fashionable clothing, neofolk had been on a long trek, to extend an analogy heard many times in the course of research and noted

---

Đokić's insistence, in spite of his narrow nationalist orientation, on promoting his radio station's biggest star by reference to an American musician.

67. Quoted in Bogdanović, "Philips Višnjić," *NIN*, 5 March 1993.
68. Dragan Ilić, "Keba i Stonsi," *Imperium of Trivia* (fanzine, 1994), 13–14.
69. For some examples, several of them comical, see Simić (1978).

frequently by scholarly observers,[70] from Nashville to Broadway. The ag-itprop revival of *Četnik* tunes was a brief and state-pleasing step backward on that journey, but when that ended the adaptation of commercial forms, values, and techniques by the most successful neofolk performers became complete.

The new direction combined neofolk, with varying degrees of success, with images of the consumer high life, synthesized and amplified sounds, beats borrowed from western commercial dance music, and styles of pre-sentation borrowed from MTV. Its promoters called the music, borrow-ing a phrase from Rambo Amadeus but leaving out the irony this time, "turbofolk." Turbofolk became the house style of new and expensive ven-ues like the *Folkoteka* in New Belgrade and new television stations like TV Pink and TV Palma, and it became the soundtrack music of the new urban subculture of *"dizelaši,"* young toughs so called in recognition of their favorite clothing manufacturer (Diesel) and also because many of them seemed to be employed in various illegal activities epitomized by the street trade in smuggled motor fuels. Although the music continued to be identified by its performers, promoters, and fans as "folk," folk elements fell quickly out of the mix, to be replaced by the accoutrements of MTV dance culture as understood by Serbia's peasants and peasant urbanites.

Although turbofolk's radical extension of the influence of western commercial pop styles did represent a continuation of a process of change that had been occurring in the neofolk genre for at least two decades, it can hardly be thought of as an "organic" development. Most products of the genre can be traced to a few specific sources: the dance school oper-ated by Hamid Đogani of the band *Đogani fantastico*, the songwriting and composition team of Marina Tucaković and her husband Aleksandar Radulović-Futa, the composers and arrangers Zlatko Timotić-Zlaja and Zoran Starčević-Stari, and the record label ZAM (*Zabava miliona—* Entertainment of the millions) owned by former folk-pop sensation Fah-reta Jahić-Lepa Brena and distributed by PGP-RTS.

An archetypal turbofolk video is perhaps Ivan Gavrilović's song *"200 na sat"* (200 [kilometers] an hour), a paean to the joys of fast driving filmed in what appears to be a showroom for Renault automobiles. The song begins with the chant, "Folk! Folk! Techno-folk!"; then Ivan sings the lyrics while behind him dance four members of the Funky House

70. For example, Šimić (1978), Dragićević-Šešić (1994).

Band, led by dancer Gagi Đogani-Funky G, in colorful mechanics' jump-suits. In its musical and lyrical, as well as visual, aspects, the song is indistinguishable from any of a number of instant synthesized dance hits, that is, until the song reaches a bridge, which consists of a few seconds of folk-style accordion playing—just the suggestion of reference to a folk tradition. The trend continued as turbofolk developed, with more folk elements falling out of the mix. Finally, only two musical elements identified with "folk" remained in the music: the sound of accordions (often only suggested by a similar sound from a synthesizer, as in the rhythmic riff around which Svetlana Veličković-Ceca's and Mira Škorić's duet *"Ne računaj na mene"* [Don't count on me] is constructed), and the tremor in the voice characteristic of some types of traditional duophonic singing, generally described by the derogatory term *zavijanje* (howling). Even these remained in the music inconsistently, with the accordion sound absent or confined to a single phrase, or with the *zavijanje* appearing only, for example, at the end of a line in the chorus.[71]

Another aspect of the turbofolk ascendancy appears in the video spot mentioned and came to largely characterize its domination. As opposed to the briefly publicized wave of nationalist agitprop, turbofolk was rarely engaged with national or any other political questions in a self-conscious way. Nor was it particularly well favored by the proponents of nationalist songs, who regarded the music's heavy production and rhythmic orientation as falling outside their preferred range, as Radio Ponos director Zoran Đokić explained: "Now, that Branka (Sovrlić) isn't a Muslim but her songs sound very Islamic and we don't play her. We play Dragana Mirković because she is very popular, although to me her songs sound like pop music and don't sound very Serbian."[72] Lyrically, the dominant orientation of turbofolk, as with most popular commercial musical forms, was toward songs about relationships, romance, and love. Visually, there was a strong orientation to images of glamour, luxury, and the "good life" as imagined by the peasant urbanites—a world populated by young women in miniskirts who drive luxury automobiles, live in fantastically

71. I am indebted to Dragan Ilić for making this evolution of form clear to me in his descriptions of the history of neofolk style and the neofolk constellation of references.
72. Quoted in Bogdanović, "Philips Višnjić," *NIN*, 5 March 1993. The term "Islamic" is meant to refer to rhythms that some detractors of turbofolk trace to Turkish folk and to Mideastern and North African pop music. In fact, the singer Branka Sovrlić had her greatest hit with a cover of *"Bilo bi dobro"* (It would be good), a song originally recorded by the Croatian pop singer Cassandra.

spacious homes, and spend their time in fashionable hotel bars. In contrast to the older neofolk, which had as a repeated theme the sadness of the migrant to the city and the image of the rustic idyll of the past,[73] turbofolk presented the good life as a feature of the Serbian present—something that, given the conditions of general poverty and international isolation, was available to only a small group generally considered to constitute a new criminal elite. Occasionally these images found their way into turbofolk lyrics:

Coca-Cola, Marlboro, Suzuki	Coca-Cola, Marlboro, Suzuki
Diskoteke, gitare, buzuki	Discotheques, guitars, and bouzouki
To je život, to nije reklama	That's life, that's not an ad
Nikom nije lepše nego nama	Nobody has it better than us.

and:

Lepo mi je sve	Everything is fine for me
Samo tako neka ostane	Just let it stay that way.

Two ideological purposes, it seems, are filled by this style of presentation. First, the representation of glamour and luxury, with a generous helping of images of beautiful young women often wearing scanty clothing, offered strong escapist diversion from the actual situation in which most members of the audience lived. More than this, the emphasis on various types of pleasure (whether musical, visual, or emotional) complemented the official lines about international sanctions against Serbia and the fighting in Croatia and Bosnia-Hercegovina—that these faraway events cannot affect people at home. Second, by presenting the lifestyle of the new criminal elite in a glamorous and romantic light, the ascendance of this group was made to appear normal and acceptable.

The preceding discussion points out several distinctions between turbofolk and earlier neofolk, many of them musical. Given the paucity of folkloric elements in the music, then, the question ought to be asked: What is "folk" about "turbofolk"? An answer grounded in musicological

73. These themes are explored in detail in Simić (1978) and Čolović (1985).

distinctions cannot be given.[74] Sociological elements—the fact that the music is marketed as folk and that its principal audience shares demographic characteristics with earlier neofolk audiences—define it as folk. The category of "folk" can be regarded not as a descriptive aesthetic category, but as a construction derived from other basic social oppositions: the urban against the rural and semiurban publics, and as a parallel, rock and roll against folk. From the aesthetic point of view, neofolk has never been highly valued for its musical qualities, neither by its listeners[75] nor by its critics, and to the extent that political power structures have addressed such issues at all they have had little positive to say either. Mythological views of totalitarian regimes excepted, states and governments generally have little to say about music. However, they do have a stake in the distribution of benefits—including cultural and broadly emotional ones—to different sectors of the population. In the war period, the interests of the party in power in Serbia found its greatest resonance among the social groups that broadly constituted the neofolk audience and the least among those that broadly constituted the rock and roll audience. In this sense, important political and social divisions came to be expressed in differential access to media and publicity, which were widely interpreted as representing the cultural orientation of the regime.

As turbofolk consolidated its dominance over the musical soundscape of cities as well, employing more elaborate and expensive production and promotion techniques, several of its products could be viewed as taking its position of official favor as its theme. One of the genre's major stars, Svetlana Veličković-Ceca, produced videos promoting her songs, which were indistinguishable in style and in production values from the MTV videos *turbaši* took as their gold standard, drawing attention not only to the star and the music, but also to the high production budget she had at her disposal, a rarity given both cultural and economic conditions in Serbia. (See Fig. 7.) Her ostentatious marriage to the state-sponsored para-

74. To draw further on the analogy presented by Simić and Dragićević-Šešić between neofolk and American "country-and-western," the increasingly technologized and commercialized mainstream country coming out of present-day Nashville has led one old-time country singer (a parallel to the "authentic" folk musicians of Serbia?) to respond to a recording, "I don't know what country that music is from." Philip Tagg (unpublished address at the conference of the International Association for the Study of Popular Music, Glasgow, 1995).

75. For a general description of the value and aesthetic orientation of the neofolk public, see Dragićević-Šešić (1994), part 1.

Fig. 7. Turbofolk singer Svetlana Veličković-Ceca in performance. In 1995, she married organized-crime boss Željko Ražnatović Arkan in a wedding that regime media made into a massive public spectacle. Photo courtesy of *Vreme*.

militarist and organized-crime king Željko Ražnatović-Arkan in February 1995 was a public spectacle of the first order. The ceremonies and celebrations surrounding the event, taking place both in Belgrade and in the singer's native village of Žitorađe, were televised live and marketed as a videotape in the production of PGP-RTS. The wedding merited both a full-page photo on the front of the regime-run newspaper *Večernje novosti* and a two-page photo layout in the center of the paper. To many local observers, the huge publicity given the event labeled as "the wedding of the decade" symbolized the relation among turbofolk, the state-controlled media, and the new criminal elite, much as the marriage itself seemed to represent the consummation of this complex relationship.

Another major statement of the arrival of a new urban-peasant class to power came in the song by Dragan Kojić-Keba, "*U crno obojeno*" (Colored black). (See Fig. 8.) Backed by turbofolk guitar wizard Zoran Starčević-Stari, Keba sported a new Clark Gable–style mustache as he sang his translation/cover/transformation of the Rolling Stones' iconic "Paint It, Black." The stylistic differences between Keba and Jagger and Richards, however, could not be clearer. Stari's guitar hook was not Keith Richards's famous wiggly sound but an aggressive, rhythmic reduction of it. Mick Jagger's original lyrics to the song stand as a classic representation of the dark and desperate worldview the Stones refined in the late 1960s and early 1970s, but Keba set his own song of the pathos of spurned love to Jagger's meter. Compare Jagger's desperate:

> I see the girls walk by
> dressed in their summer clothes.
> I have to hold my head
> Until the darkness goes.

with Keba's rendition of the verse:

> Bog mi je dao sve   God gave me everything
> dao i uzeo.   gave and took away.
> Kao tebe nikoga   I've never loved anybody
> nisam voleo.   as much as you.

Keba claimed that the inspiration for the cover came from a desire to show respect for the music that he and Stari enjoyed in their youth, in the long-ago days when rock and roll was contemporary music:

Fig. 8. Folksinger Dragan Kojić-Keba made a career of reproducing urban culture with a peasant twist, as in his controversial cover of a Rolling Stones song. Here he embodies the mixture of urban and peasant motifs. He is wearing the jersey of the *Obilić* football team, which is owned by Arkan. Photo courtesy of *Vreme*.

To make myself clear, the Stones' songs have been sung in Romanian, German, Italian, so why shouldn't a Serb like me be able to sing them? Zoran Starčević and I got the idea of covering that song because we listened to that kind of music as kids. That song has a lot of elements of our folklore although maybe that might sound astonishing. Its harmonic resolutions are very close to ours. So, you could say that the Stones ripped us off. Why not? . . . Nobody has said that I sing the song badly, but a lot of people wonder what right I have to sing it. It simply bothers them that a folkie (*narodnjak*) did the cover.[76]

For many Belgraders who heard the song, it was a historic document epitomizing the new dominance of turbofolk. Turbofolk owned the television, the large concert venues, the *kafane*, and the radio. Now, apparently, turbofolk owned the back catalog of the Rolling Stones as well, laying claim to the rock and roll culture's holiest of holies.[77]

Self-Perception in the Cities: Popular Resistance to Neofolk

If an otherwise minor and amusing cultural artifact—a cover of a Rolling Stones song by a neofolk celebrity—generated such strong feelings on both sides of the cultural divide, that is because the song stood as a representation of a situation that Belgrade *rokeri* viscerally resented. The structure of control of urban cultural space had dramatically shifted in a short period of time, and neofolk and turbofolk were the most visible, audible, and recognizable symbols of this transformation. My own research

76. Lj. G., "Novokomponovani rok," *NIN*, 9 December 1994, p. 35.
77. Interestingly, if cosmopolitans objected to appropriation of another type of international culture by *turbaši*—the kind represented by "Coca-Cola, Marlboro, Suzuki"—it was not on the same ground. The consumption of imported luxury objects is more generally associated with the conformist *šminkeri* and carries with it a connotation of inauthenticity. Hence it could be argued that both *rokeri* and *narodnjaci* cultivated some kind of relation with the (outside) consumer world, but that a significant distinction was made between relations bounded by culture and those defined by other than cultural consumption. For a discussion of the style of *šminkeri* and various responses to them, see Prica (1991), and Snežana Joksimović, Ratka Marić, Anđelka Milić, Dragan Popadić, and Mirjana Vasović, *Mladi i neformalne grupe: U traganju za alternativom* (Belgrade: Istraživačko-izdavački centar SSO Srbije and Centar za idejni rad SSO Beograda, 1988).

involvement in the rock and roll culture of Belgrade met with surprise among some people with whom I spoke there, with one denizen of KST telling me: "There aren't any places to go now for people like us. You should have been in this city ten years ago. It was really something then, the whole night life, young people. Now the scene is basically dead. There's just KST for me." The *rokeri* of Belgrade experienced this loss of cultural space as a life-defining absence and viewed the decline of the city through the lens of the neofolk ascendance, which was associated in their thinking with the war, isolation, the decline in living standards, and the domination of cultural as well as political life by a new class—not the "new class" first described by Milovan Đilas,[78] but a newer assortment of regime politicians, nationalists, criminals, and war profiteers. One Belgrader drew together the elements of nationalism, low-culture pop, and the *Četnik* revival in his appraisal of the turbofolk culture, defining the music disparagingly as "ethno-techno-chetno."

The term *novokomponovana*, originally used to refer to "newly composed" folk music, took on a variety of derisive uses in this new environment. A tasteless and garish piece of clothing would be called *novokomponovano*. The rare examples of new construction in Belgrade, like the high-end retail mall on Ćumićevo Sokače or the massive heavy-on-the-reflective-glass showcase of the Ktitor furniture company, would be called *novokomponovana arhitektura*. A variety of social actors had the adjective attached to them as well. The pyramid-scheme "bankers" Jezdimir Vasiljević-Gazda Jezda[79] and Dafina Milanović became the *novokomponovana elita*. Rural political bosses epitomized by the all-powerful mayor of Niš, Mile Ilić, or by the ostentatiously uneducated provincial SPS parliamentary deputies Radovan Radović-Raka and Dobrivoje Budimirović-Bidža, became *novokomponovani političari*.[80] If anybody doubted that the linguistic association between the servants of the regime and the carriers of regime-sponsored culture described a real situation, these doubts were firmly dispelled by the huge publicity accorded the wedding of Ceca and Arkan, the faces on either side of the equation.

78. Milovan Djilas, *The New Class* (New York: Praeger, 1957).

79. Although best known in Serbia for his gargantuan "take the money and run" maneuver, "Gazda Jezda" also briefly achieved fame in the rest of the world for enticing former chess champion Bobby Fischer out of retirement in 1992.

80. By no means did SPS hold a monopoly over ridiculous grandstanding in the parliament. It had close competition from its sometime allies, sometime bitter enemies in SRS.

With the association between the rejected sounds of turbofolk and the real conditions of life in mind, Belgrade *rokeri* responded to the dominance of turbofolk on a deep emotional level—they hated the music. One young Belgrade man, explaining that he and his friends listen only to rock and roll and never to turbofolk, told me that "it hurts my soul to hear that kind of music." In the course of a discussion on how we might respond as parents if our daughter were to begin dating a turbofolk enthusiast, a young father told me that his feelings ran strongly against turbofolk because it is "the symbol of all the evil in this society." The mother of a twelve-year-old girl expressed similar concern from a high-culture perspective: "My daughter constantly watches the videos on Palma, just to see what the singers are wearing. I am trying to play some good rock music for her, just so she won't think that is all there is. All these stupid songs! She has to find out that there is more to sing about than just tragic love!" The highly publicized neofolk was generally regarded as kitsch and "garbage" (*šund*) and openly contrasted, as in the young mother's comment above, with rock and roll and other international forms regarded as higher and more artistically accomplished culture. At the same time, rock and roll was regarded as emblematic of both the cosmopolitanism and personal autonomy that a generation that lived in and enjoyed pre-Milošević Belgrade saw as eroding. Contrasts were made between the older-younger generation, which enjoyed some prosperity and traveled widely, and the younger-younger generation, which, coming of age in a time of isolation and war, did not have these advantages: "I don't see much [of the current popular culture]—now that we have a child we don't go out that often. But I see it for example when I go to funerals, when a friend's parent dies or something. The people of our generation who lived the city life, who traveled to other countries, who brought back records, books, ideas—they still have that, they still think for themselves. They haven't lost that culture. But younger people, who haven't had that chance, who can only get what's on television or radio—I worry about that generation." In this view, a generation growing up without rock and roll grows up without the kind of breadth and cultural support seen as vital if they are to "think for themselves."

Of course, Belgrade *rokeri* saw the neofolk ascendancy not only as symbolizing a new equation of power and as narrowing the horizons of a younger generation. They saw it as affecting them directly, restricting the cultural space available to them and making their city less familiar and accessible to them. The same KST denizen who told me that I should have come to Belgrade ten years earlier stayed in the club after the band had finished playing, at around 3:00 in the morning. When I asked him whether he would be able to catch a bus to go home, he answered: "I just want to stay a little longer, to take in the *rokerski* atmosphere here. This is the only place in the city that really suits me." Another Belgrader, an artist long active in the rock and roll culture, described his feelings about the loss of cultural space: "Now the culture is gone, there is nothing but this garbage (*šund*). But our generation, we listened to rock and roll. That was the normal music then, it was what you heard in the *kafane*, over the radio. It was our music—not because it was American music but because it was international music." With the rise of nationalism and the ascendance of neofolk, the normal delineation of the "normal" shifted dramatically. Whereas participating in and enjoying international consumer culture had been normal for a generation, suddenly it was not. The new normalcy of narrow national identity, local kitsch, and closed access to the world was felt as constraining. More than this, it was a constant reminder of the changed terms of life in the war regime.

The connection between the neofolk ascendance and the character of the regime was made frequently in my conversations with Belgrade *rokeri*. Sometimes coincidence was taken to be sufficient to draw the association—most people observed that neofolk had not been so predominant before the war period, and most observed that state-controlled media were the most involved in promoting the genre.[81] In some cases, the association was made in general terms, as by the high school student who told me "We get the culture we deserve." Some people with whom I spoke were more precise in discussing the role of state-provided publicity for the promotion of neofolk: "Look at the ads on RTS. If the publishers had to pay for all the advertising time their albums get, they would have to sell hundreds of thousands of albums. But they don't, it's the same company [RTS, which includes both the state television network and the music publishing company PGP-RTS] promoting its own products." Others looked for connections in the amorous lives of performers, real or imagined: "All the starlets have some connection. Ceca is with Arkan,

81. In addition to heavy advertising and program promotion on the state RTS network, the state-controlled newspaper *Večernje novosti* promoted neofolk celebrities both in its paper and on the radio station it owned, Radio Novosti. The two neofolk television stations in Belgrade, both of them set into motion without the inconvenience of applying for a frequency, had their offices in the headquarters of Milošović's SPS (TV Palma) and Mirjana Marković's SK-PJ (TV Pink).

Vesna Zmijanac is with [RTS director and SPS parliamentary deputy Mi-lorad] Vučelić, so it's no problem for their spots to be played. The rock musicians haven't got that kind of access, so they aren't as visible. But it's not that people aren't listening. They just aren't listening that loudly." At the same time, some did their best to deny that the music was as popular as it seemed to be—a potentially credible claim, considering that I encountered very few people who claimed to like neofolk and a consid-erable number who despised it:[82] "The turbofolk stars constantly sell out halls in Austria, Germany, where people from here are living and work-ing. It's not so popular here, even though it gets a lot of advertising. Ceca managed to fill *Hala pionira*, but not many people know that Vesna Zmijanac sold only thirty tickets in Kragujevac. You can get a totally mistaken picture of what people listen to by looking at what they play on television." For all these respondents, the impressive public presence of neofolk and its turbofolk derivative could be traced directly to institutions controlled by the regime, the cultural and political orientation of the regime, and the demographic base of regime support. Rather than an "organic" manifestation of public taste, the neofolk ascendancy was viewed as an imposition from above—as was the increasingly limited cul-tural space accorded the rock and roll culture.

In this atmosphere of shrinking cultural space and material constraint, rock and roll acquired the power of counteridentity in two respects. On the one hand, in contrast to its ascribed cultural value in most parts of Western Europe and America, rock and roll is perceived by Belgraders as high art and implicitly opposed to neofolk, which is regarded as "Balkan" and "primitive." In the nationalist-authoritarian environment of Bel-grade, the epithet of "primitivism" also applied to nationalist ideology and to the party in power.[83] On the other hand, its increasingly limited

82. These self-reports, however, should not be taken at face value. Many people who claimed to never listen to turbofolk, when I prompted them with the first lines of a verse, would happily complete the verse for me. At the same time, nearly everybody with whom I spoke, whether lovers or haters of turbofolk or not strongly inclined either way, knew the products of the genre well enough to joke extensively about songs, celebrities, and video images.

83. Hence the references enumerated by Živković (1995) associating the Milošević regime with the Ottoman Empire. Hence also the introductory line of Rambo Ama-deus's antiregime song *"Prijatelju, prijatelju . . ."* (My friend, my friend), which precedes a string of obscenities with *"Kada primitivci dođu na vlast"* (When primitives come to power). In concert, Rambo dedicates the song to *doktor Buldog Sloba* and *doktor Pingvin Franjo*, that is, to presidents Milošević and Tuđman.

audience and more limited range of venues qualified it as a minority urban cultural formation in opposition to the semirural and omnipresent variations of neofolk. *Rokeri* came more and more to see themselves as the last line of defense of urban culture. At the presentation of Milan Mladenović's posthumous album, one presenter hailed "the Belgrade that defends itself against the savages who attack it." More picturesquely, the presentation took place underground, albeit in a lavishly restored Roman catacomb in Belgrade's Kalemegdan fortress. The image is nonetheless apt: nearly all of Belgrade's rock and roll venues are housed in basements, adding a geographic and spatial dimension to the image *rokeri* have of themselves as constituting an underground culture.

As an underground culture, rock and roll adopted a defensive posture, emphasizing its difference from all that was mainstream, popular, and promoted in state media. One fan praised an album by the band *Instant karma* from Zrenjanin in boundary-defining terms: "This is pure (*čist*) rock and roll, it doesn't have any folk in it." The ideology of rock and roll authenticity made for some shifts in the "Yugo-rock" canon, so that the once-adored *Bijelo dugme*, who had been producing rock covers of folk tunes since the mid-seventies, came to be regarded less as domestic pioneers of cultural fusion and more as the precursors of turbofolk.[84] Similarly, *rokeri* who abandoned the rebellious postures of rock and roll, like Bajaga and Bora Đorđević, came to be increasingly regarded as outside the rock and roll culture. Conversely, otherwise mainstream figures who maintained a strong antiregime and antiwar posture approached the status of underground heroes.

This was certainly the case with *Ekaterina velika's* leader Milan Mladenović, whose death in November 1994 led to a competition over the valuation of his role and his work. As a figure in the early days of Belgrade's new wave—the band *Šarlo akrobata* included him and Koja, later of *Disciplina kičme*—and as one of the exponents of the ad hoc antiwar band *Rimtutituki*, Mladenović could certainly lay claim to underground "credibility." As a pop figure and one of the key exponents of artsy synthesizer-based light rock in his later days, however, he was open to co-optation as, in the words of the regime's *Večernje novosti*, "the voice of the soul."[85]

84. People do not abandon things they love, or once loved, so easily, however. At one party in Belgrade, when the host put on a *Bijelo dugme* record, the assembled guests, all convinced *rokeri*, improvised a rough approximation of a *kolo* dance in the host's small room.
85. M. Aksić, "Glas iz duše," *Večernje novosti*, 7 November 1994, p. 29.

The city government of Belgrade arranged for a difficult-to-obtain grave site in the central cemetery, with the condition that the vice mayor Milenko Kašanin speak at the burial. Stories circulated around the municipal government about naming a street for "our great poet." Videos, including those of antiwar songs from *Ekaterina velika's* last album, suddenly began to appear on state television. Working against these efforts at cooptation were the memories of Mladenović's friends—who remembered, for example, his commitment, once the wars began, not to play concerts in any places where churches or mosques had been destroyed (excluding in practice the entire territory occupied by nationalist armies in Croatia and Bosnia-Hercegovina).[86] His lack of commercial success came to be seen as a virtue:

> Milan was one of only a few *rokeri* from here who stayed honest. And he paid a high price for it. I'm talking about a guy who didn't own a car, who didn't have his own apartment, who died with fifty marks in his pocket.
> [EDG: And who has sold out?]
> Bands who picked up on the political wave, who started producing shit, like Bajaga and *Riblja čorba*. And they got big money for it. Milan is like a father to them. Their music, their ideas, they got from him.

Although *Ekaterina velika's* music inclined strongly toward mainstream pop, the defensive position of the rock and roll culture led it to be valued more highly as rock and roll than it might otherwise have been—not because of the music's rock and roll form, but because of its creator's rock and roll attitude and structural position.

In a similar way, small successes in the field of rock and roll came to be perceived as victories in the ongoing cultural conflict. The winter of 1994 was a dark period for Belgrade rock and roll—Milan Mladenović had just died, the *Partibrejkers* were inactive, few new appearances were being made—and a literally dark period in Belgrade. During the month of December, according to the report of the Serbian electric utility Elek-

---

86. This antiwar gesture did not meet with universal praise. As one prominent musician, also involved in *Rimtutituki*, explained to me, he would gladly play in Banja Luka: "That is my work and my life. I make music and share it with people. And I think it is most needed exactly there."

trodistribucija, districts of the city were subject to scheduled "reductions" in electricity lasting from two to four hours on twenty-eight of thirty-one days of the month.[87] As it turned out, one of these "reductions" began as the band *Darkwood dub* (whose difficulties with music publishers are described above) was preparing to hold a long-awaited concert in KST. As a large crowd, larger than the capacity of the club,[88] gathered and waited outside, a fan approached me proudly: "Do you see all these people? And this concert had no advertising at all, no posters, no radio announcements. But all these people found out and came." After midnight had passed, electricity came, and the concert was able to begin. The hard-noise music of the band, combined with the musicians' being "obviously well revolted which means inspired,"[89] offered an appropriately angry and noisy counterpoint to the darkness and silence of the long wait that had preceded the show. Reviewing the performance in *Borba*, Nenad Jevtić brought together the band's bad-luck history, the cultural climate of the city, and the uncertain supply of electricity, into a description of a night against fate:

> Many things have conspired against *Darkwood dub*. Still more against the young people of this city who live on the edge of horror, devalued and abandoned to themselves. Maybe it has always been that way, maybe not. Once in a while that darkness releases from its bosom events like *Darkwood dub* which redefine things and to some degree classify them. We are here and now, things do not come easily for us, but that is the way it is. Belgrade is a dark forest with no end. You are in it. Pay attention to yourself and to those near you because all kinds of things happen in the dark. (*Darkwood dub*, for example).[90]

87. M. Perović, "Za otklanjanje kvarova do tri godine," *Politika*, 27 March 1995, p. 17. Scheduled "reductions" account for only a part of the darkness of that winter. Several "reductions" either occurred unscheduled or lasted considerably longer than scheduled. Some of the "unscheduled" reductions were in fact the result of technical failures, and their duration was of unpredictable length. For more on the uncertain electrical supply in the winter of 1994 and its social echoes, see Chapter 5.

88. *Borba's* reviewer estimated the crowd as being "something less than 900 people." Nenad Jevtić, "Posle mraka—'Mrak'!" *Borba*, 21 December 1994, p. 16.

89. Nenad Jevtić, "Posle mraka—'Mrak'!" *Borba*, 21 December 1994, p. 16.

90. Nenad Jevtić, "Posle mraka—'Mrak'!" *Borba*, 21 December 1994, p. 16.

Moments like these were of course few and may well not have been perceptible to all the people who participated in them.[91] There were enough, however, to give the rock and roll culture some power among the people who took part in it—enough to allow one Belgrader with whom I spoke, an underemployed engineer disappointed with all official actors and institutions, to tell me, "Everybody is supposed to believe in something. I believe in rock and roll. That's all."

Maintaining a *rokerski* identity in Belgrade's poverty, isolation, and new culture of hostility was not accomplished without unease and disjunctions, however. For one thing, *rokeri* were aware that the high seriousness with which many of them took their defense of urban culture cut into the enjoyment that had been among rock and roll's principal appeals: "Dance music is party music, for a good time. And the clubs are usually nice new places. I can see why somebody might like that better than going to some dark, crowded basement where some heavy rock and roll band plays songs about our depressing situation." In the same vein, many *rokeri* were aware that the dissolution of the commercial mainstream made the music more and more the exclusive property of an urban minority audience:

> Maybe the only rock and roll band that could fill a hall now is *Obojeni program.* An alternative band, and they are now probably the most popular band in Serbia.
> (EDG: Alternative to what?)
> Well, that's it—the mainstream they were alternative to is gone. And imagine the "alternative" to *Obojeni program*—nobody would be able to listen to it.

The more Belgrade *rokeri* were aware of their own radical difference from the culture by which they were surrounded, the less sanguine they were about the future of the rock and roll culture in Belgrade.

Similarly, the urban and international orientation of the Belgrade rock and roll culture was difficult to maintain in an environment in which the local and the national had become the defining principles, and isolation from other cultures nearly compulsory. Cosmopolitans were far more affected by international sanctions, especially in the fields of travel and

91. For example, the evening was probably less than sublime for one friend whose nose was broken by an overly spirited dancer at the concert.

cultural exchange, than the nationalists at whom the sanctions were supposedly targeted. Cosmopolitans had much to lose by the breakdown of international contact, whereas nationalists were never interested in it. Isolation played a psychological role as well, led some *rokeri* to wonder whether they were falling behind events in the commercial and cultural centers of other countries, and encouraged to some degree a tendency among local urbanites to think of themselves as backward Balkan versions of metropolitan models. A critic insulted a Belgrade hard-core band in terms that suggest that that musical genre has no place in a peripheral country: "Ha, ha, ha, a HC band that buys sausages at the farmers' market and gets salmonella poisoning. Now please, there is none of that in hard core."[92] In this case, the nostalgia for international cultural forms carries with it a rejection of the domestic, and of lived experience as somehow not measuring up to the cosmopolitan standard. This rejection encompasses not only such particularly nationalism-identified forms as turbofolk, but also such ordinary aspects of everyday experience as sausages, shared (with varying degrees of enthusiasm, no doubt) by members of widely differing taste cultures.

In this context of rejection of the local as an expression of resistance to nationalism, I was surprised to find in Belgrade a considerable degree of local patriotism directed toward my own native city of Seattle. The effort to remain contemporary naturally included a passion for the "grunge" movement, which was popular in the United States in the first half of the nineties. This taste was shown in the programs of disk jockey clubs and radio stations, as well as by the painted dialogue, in English, on a wall on the building opposite my apartment in Belgrade, keeping the Elvis myth alive for a new generation. The original graffitist had written, "Kurt Cobain, 1967–1994." A later (revisionist!) graffitist crossed out the "1994" and replaced it with "still alive!" A local high school student expressed bewildered fascination when I told her that I had been listening of late to the music of folk-pop diva Snežana Babić-Sneki, from her hometown of Pančevo:

You listen to Sneki? How can you listen to that?
(EDG: You don't like it?)

---

92. Quoted in Vesna Džogović, "Vodič kroz trendove: We're sick of it all," *Talas* (April 1995), 41.

My friends and I never listen to that folk. Some other people in my
school do.
(EDG: What do you listen to?)
I listen to music from Seattle.

To maintain their attachment to the international culture they like, many
local *rokeri* find it necessary to reject various aspects of their own lived
experience. The decision carries with it some tension, as indicated, for
example, by a subculture magazine's description of *Folkoteka* in its guide
to the city's clubs: "Is *Folkoteka* a place to avoid? Of course, but then
when you consider the question maybe it would not be so bad if you were
to drop by once, to see what kind of country you are living in."[93]

Clearly, many did not decide to educate themselves in that way, but
rather to choose some other experiences, whether they are theirs or not,
from other places. One young Belgrader explained to me that he would
not have been able to cope psychologically if local television stations did
not pirate the signal of MTV after hours. Another explained to me that
she maintained her sanity by "living like I'm on another planet," studi-
ously avoiding local cultural products and especially news, determined to
follow only foreign music and films. A frequent topic of conversation
among young Belgraders is the question of whether to move to another
country.

For these young people, the rock and roll culture offers a strategy to
live outside a culture that has turned against them while still offering a
means of creative activity and expression. Whether they see themselves
as defending urban culture or simply seeking outlets for urban culture,
the identity that supports them is defined principally by opposition to
the new dominance of rural and semirural cultural forms, including their
expression in politics and other facets of everyday life. Every bit as isolated from the rest of the world as their anticosmopolitan counterparts,
their international identity is narrowly based in a small and probably
shrinking urban minority culture and receives little support or encour-
agement from outside. Sometimes its moments of strength can be felt, as
in those rare sublime moments when the feeling of the city, the crowd,
and its noise come together to create a momentary triumph of urban
culture. To the extent that the remnant of Belgrade's rock and roll culture

93. Unsigned, "Tema broja: Noć u Beogradu," *Talas* (April 1995), 28.

is united, however, it is brought together by its hostility to the neofolk form, its public, and everything that is represented by it.

Taste Has No Alternative: The Regime Joins In

Rokeri were not the only group that came to despise the explosion of turbofolk. Significant criticism also came from intellectuals and people who thought of themselves as intellectuals, who had developed a taste for high-culture products and instinctively rejected all that seemed to them to be "Balkan" and "primitive." Identifying themselves with Belgrade's pre-Communist elite, they objected particularly to the erotic display and simply written texts of the songs, which they regarded as typical of the rejected peasant culture. One older woman, who made certain to point out that her family had been wealthy before the Second World War, elaborately described to me the dress and dance conventions of turbofolk videos and argued: "That is not the culture of the city. The city resists that culture—it is some kind of kitsch, garbage (*šund*). It is called folk, but it has nothing to do with our real folk music, our old-city songs (*starogradske pesme*). There is also a lot of pornography in that—maybe these people come from the village, where they see animals doing it in the street. So they think they can do that here. I don't watch their videos. When it is on television, I feel like washing the screen. Do you know what I mean?"[94] The high-culture distaste expressed here indicates a transitional objection to turbofolk. On the one hand, some elements of the critique are shared by the *rokeri*, who are certainly not immune to some snobbish sentiment of their own and who hold the ideal of "authenticity" in as high esteem as any antiquarian folk enthusiast. On the other hand, the reference to and comparison with other folk forms bring up a new category of critique—those who disliked neo- and turbofolk because

94. The statement about not watching videos was not particularly credible, first because she had apparently watched enough of them to be able to describe them to me, and second because a television tuned to TV Palma was playing in the background in the woman's apartment throughout our entire conversation. The reference to *starogradske pesme* is of particular interest. In addition to *izvorni folk*, two urban folk forms were generally considered to be "acceptable" among urban audiences in the former Yugoslavia. These were the *starogradske* ("old city") songs mostly written and composed in nineteenth-century Belgrade, and the older folk songs native to Dubrovnik.

it competed with folk genres they regarded as more authentic or more typically Serbian.

Earlier, I indicated that the promoters of nationalist agitprop folk drew a distinction between the folk they considered to be "really Serbian" and other forms they considered to be impure. Radio Ponos's Zoran Đokić criticized one turbofolk starlet for sounding "Islamic"; another detractor of the music with whom I spoke referred to it as "turban-folk." Performers of more traditional styles of neofolk strained to distinguish themselves from the music, like the singer Miroslav Ilić: "I am still the same folk singer who has never got mixed up in foreign waters, Islamic ones least of all. Nothing is more lovely than the Morava and Šumadija."[95] More traditional performers cast their opposition to turbofolk in terms of alarm and emergency and pictured the principally Turkish influences on Serbian folk—hardly a new development—as a cultural crisis calling for immediate intervention: "*Novokomponovano* pollution has been suffocating us for a long time. This festival [of traditional Serbian music] is a proper step to put an end to our musical misfortune and evil. That means that the sounds of the Tigris and Euphrates need to be urgently replaced by the flute and accordion of the Šumadija hills and the Morava-Ibar valley."[96] Among these nationalistically minded folk fans, the turbo-newcomers represented a threat to the music and form they held dear. More significantly, they represented a threat from the East, harmonizing the cultural interest of the old-time *narodnjaci* with the political paranoia of the nationalists.

At times, the concern of the *izvornici* and the nationalists about the "Islamic" sound of turbofolk reached the proportions of conspiracy theory. As Milošević's SPS shifted its position overnight from wholehearted support to bitter criticism[97] of the Bosnian Serbs in August 1994, they came to be included in the conspiracy. Marko Živković described the arrival of turbofolk into the political conflict over "national questions":

Pavle Aksentijević, otherwise a respected singer of medieval Serbian spiritual [religious] music, acting as a member of the largest opposi-

95. Unsigned, "Miroslav Ilić: Rusija pa—Amerika," *Večernje novosti*, 22 January 1994, p. 21.

96. A. M., "Jordan Nikolić, pevač: Mi nismo novokomponovani," *Večernje novosti*, 6 May 1995, p. 23, and 8 May 1995, p. 21 (the article was printed twice).

97. This overt criticism was accompanied by covert continuation of material and financial support.

tion bloc (DEPOS), brought a tape recorder to the podium [of the Serbian parliament] and played a tape of a contemporary Iranian popular song. Then he played another tape—this time a song by Dragana Mirković, one of the most popular singers of the so-called "turbofolk" genre. The tunes were practically identical. He finished the performance with one sentence: "We Serbs sometimes behave as if we were made ('begotten') by drunken Turks."

Among the "intellectual" circles, a vague conspiracy theory was circulating at the time that the flood of "turbofolk" . . . was a cunning plot devised by "Them" (Milošević, the Socialist party, the authorities) intended to reduce the population to utter idiocy. Aksentijević's performance, however, added the theme of Oriental, or more specifically, Turkish taintedness. He was accusing the establishment . . . of deliberately polluting "Serbdom" with Oriental tunes, and simultaneously positioning himself and his party as defenders of some pristine Serbian purity.[98]

The conspiracy theory fit together neatly: It combined cultural disgust with frustration over state control of media and added an element missing in the *rokerski* critique of turbofolk: the essentialist categories of the "nation" and its purity.

With the detractors of turbofolk extending into broader social groups, the ruling party had reason to be concerned. As controllers of a broad monopoly over media, they were already subject to criticism from all sides. If this monopoly could be generally and successfully accused of poisoning the cultural atmosphere, it was that much more open to attack from those who had accused it all along of poisoning the political atmosphere. Disgust with turbofolk seemed to be expanding. If *rokeri*, snobs, "authentic" folkies, and nationalists all agreed on the point, this could constitute a powerful alliance of the rebellious, the influential, and the conformist.

In addition, and probably most crucially, by late 1994 the regime had strong motivation to undermine its own previous cultural interventions.

---

98. Živković (1995), 4–5. Parentheses in original. Živković goes on to point out that Turkish elements in all facets of Serbian culture—from music to language, dress, and food—are neither recent nor incidental. Čolović offers a conclusion that contrasts nicely with Aksentijević's, in his essay on nationalist attempts to "purify" the language: "[W]e are all a little bit Turkish. But I am not sure that that is the worst thing about us" (1994b), 56.

In August of that year, Milošević suddenly shifted his position, from opposition to support, on the so-called "Contact Group" peace plan for Bosnia-Hercegovina. When Karadžić's parastate did not go along with this shift, he publicly broke relations and support for the entity ruled from Pale. The regime-controlled media began promoting the slogan "Peace has no alternative" and presenting Milošević as "an unavoidable factor of peace" (*nezaobilazan faktor mira*) and "the key to peace in the Balkans." Karadžić and his followers began to be presented in the media as irresponsible gamblers and war profiteers, and suggestions that they might be responsible for crimes, including war crimes, began to be permitted in official media.

With this shift, the interest of the regime also shifted in two crucial ways. First, the neofolk and turbofolk performers they had promoted, in part to advance the nationalist cause and in part to glamorize the new nationalist elite, suddenly became embarrassing and perhaps even threatening to them. Few of the artists who had entertained paramilitary forces and put on benefit programs for them, if they did these things out of conviction, would be inclined to change their minds as suddenly as SPS did. Second, after publicly turning his back on his nationalist supporters, Milošević had once more to search for a political base for power. One strategy was to remobilize the old-line Communists who had been lying dormant in the unpopular political party headed by his wife; this was done, but with the awareness that, however much influence they enjoyed, the group in question was too small to constitute a strong base. Although larger, the group of people who had been antiwar from the beginning was unlikely to move toward Milošević simply because he altered his rhetoric—nor were memories so short that even a sincere change of position would be likely to bring much support.

Having run out of domestic options, Milošević turned to the "international community" as the last political sponsors of his regime. No longer would the neofolk song that boasted "We are Serbian supermen / We fight against the world" be heard on state-controlled airwaves. Instead, news media featured negotiators from the United Nations and European Union describing Milošević as essential to their work, as the "key to peace" or "guarantee of peace" in the region. Hope began to be extended that international sanctions against Serbia and Montenegro would be lifted or suspended, and these hopes were met in part in September 1994. The first international flight to leave Belgrade's Surčin airport since 1992 was greeted with official ecstasy,[99] as were the first international appearances of the Yugoslav national sports teams.[100] Having passed through the phases of Communist nostalgia and of nationalist demagoguery, Milošević now seemed to want to settle into the role of client of the West. With the end of state endorsement of international isolation, and with hope for real relief from international isolation, the turbofolk culture of isolation no longer met the regime's cultural needs. When Spain's Gipsy Kings, one of the first international musical groups to come to play a concert in Belgrade, appeared, the regime-controlled paper *Večernje novosti* wishfully titled its article on the event: "Once again a part of the musical Europe."[101]

Nada Popović-Perišić, the Minister of Culture, responded to the new cultural needs of the regime accordingly. In August 1994, she began to publicly attack the low-culture standards of neofolk and declared that her ministry would engage in a "struggle against kitsch," with the goal of affirming "true cultural values" (*prave kulturne vrednosti*). State-controlled media began to join in the fight—without abandoning their publicity for the now-disapproved genre—as *Večernje novosti* editorialized with uncharacteristic evenhandedness: "It happens that a person switches through several [television] channels, and on each one of them is pretty much the same face, or at least two or three easily recognizable ones, singing at the top of their lungs, followed by dancers in the 'Đogani' style. A true folk terror in turbo rhythm. That sort of thing should be around, but not to such a degree."[102] As the campaign progressed, more such critiques appeared, many of them coming, like the one above, from the very media outlets that had invested so much in promoting turbofolk in the preceding period.

The streets of Belgrade became a showplace for the "struggle against kitsch." As the place where the conflict between metropolitan and neofolk culture had been strongest, they were best suited for this kind of

---

99. See, for example, M. B., "Pilotirao direktor," *Večernje novosti*, 7 October 1994.

100. When the Yugoslav football representation played the national teams of Argentina and Brazil in December 1994, the government promised that the electric supply would not be interrupted during the broadcast of the games.

101. B. V., "Gipsy Kings na prijemu u Skupštini grada: Ponovo deo muzičke Evrope," *Večernje novosti*, 3 December 1994, p. 12.

102. M. K., "TV šeme: Folk teror u turbo ritmu," *Večernje novosti*, 27 April 1995, p. 19.

display, and the municipal government seemed to be taking the side of the metropolitans, albeit in its own authoritarian fashion. *Večernje novosti* introduced an interview on cultural politics with the vice mayor Milenko Kašanin with: "The streets of the capital city ring less with sounds of the East. Still, in the central part of the city there are still some cassette dealers who attack the hearing of passersby. Radio and TV stations endlessly run melodies which are below every criterion of value, but which bring great profit. Garbage (*šund*) and every type of tastelessness could be, however, cut off with large taxes."[103] Kašanin was more aggressive still, proposing in the interview: "Absolute order should be maintained here. Inspectors patrol the city every day not permitting that the streets of our metropolis be controlled by any kind of tastelessness."[104] As heady as the promises of punitive taxes and "taste police" sounded, little came of the project. The most publicized "defense" of the center of the city was the intervention by Belgrade's mayor, Nebojša Čović, to prevent the neofolk celebrity Džej Ramadanovski from opening a music club in a locale he had bought near the main location of Belgrade University: The mayor insisted that the locale be made into a bakery-cafe instead.[105]

The campaign for "true cultural values" deepened as the Ministry of Culture declared that 1995 would be "the year of culture" and promised funding for cultural projects and education. The funding did not materialize, unless an incident is taken into account in which the Minister of Culture attended a theater performance she liked so well that she gave 500 dinars (at the time, about 150 German marks) to each member of the cast. Most effort was instead directed to an advertising campaign, developed by the Belgrade affiliate of Saatchi and Saatchi, and designed, in the words of the agency director Dragan Sakan, to "make culture the most popular word of 1995."[106] The ads featured a fertility figure from the archaeological site at Lepenski Vir, with cartoonish colorful sunglasses and a smile added to the face and, in the television versions, an animated mouth with the voice of the actor Ljubomir Tadić[107] reciting the cam-

103. B. Nikolić, "Kulturom protiv šunda," *Večernje novosti*, 4 October 1994, p. 11.

104. Quoted in B. Nikolić, "Kulturom protiv šunda," *Večernje novosti*, 4 October 1994, p. 11.

105. *Novosti*, unsurprisingly, portrayed the intervention as a triumph of "true cultural values." See Z. Tomić, "Povratak dostojanstva," *Večernje novosti*, 22 October 1994, p. 10.

106. In an interview on TV Politika, February 1995.

107. The actor Ljubomir Tadić is not to be confused with the nationalist writer of the same name.

paign's slogan: "It's nicer with culture" (*Lepše je sa kulturom*). Alternative versions included a blank screen with the slogan "It's empty without culture" (*Prazno je bez kulture*) and the names of writers and artists in the shape of the Yugoslav flag over the slogan "We're stronger with culture" (*Jači smo sa kulturom*).

As clear as the purpose of the campaign may have been from the point of view of the advertising agency (to publicize the word "culture"), the purpose of the Ministry of Culture seemed tremendously unclear, beyond showing that a state ministry was capable of commissioning a slick and technically impressive advertising campaign and diffusing it widely. Not only were the practical policies to promote culture (policies that ought to have been publicized by the campaign) somewhere in the range between scant and nonexistent, but no effort seems to have gone into defining what was being promoted under the rubric of "culture." On the one hand, the advertisers argued for an anthropological definition including everything from good manners (in a television spot suggesting that a fatal gang conflict could have been avoided had the actors known that "it's nicer with the culture of discussion") to personal hygiene (in a poster showing a tube of toothpaste emblazoned with the logo *Kultura*). Public speakers promoting "the year of culture" more specifically called for promotion of high-culture products and condemned the "tastelessness" of neofolk.[108]

For the most part, the advertising campaign for "culture" was greeted with the hilarity appropriate to the imbalance between technical and conceptual thought it displayed. However, there was little substantive opposition to the campaign or to the assumption that "culture" could somehow be promoted or created by ministerial fiat. Coinciding with the inauguration of the Ministry of Culture's ambitious advertising campaign, in February 1995 the opposition Democratic Center sponsored a two-day conference on cultural politics, under the socialist-realist title "Culture as self-defense of society and personality" (*Kultura kao samoodbrana društva i ličnosti*). At this conference, neofolk culture was criticized in a manner that did not differ from the rhetoric of the Ministry of Culture, and proposals similar to those offered (but not implemented) by the ministry were made. To these proposals were added some frankly ridicu-

---

108. One set of ads became particularly controversial. This set featured barnyard animals saying "Don't look only at me. It's nicer with culture." The suggestion that peasants are void of culture did not go unnoticed.

lous ones, such as the suggestion that musical education could be advanced by playing Bach on municipal buses.[109] However, no debate was offered on the definition of "true cultural values" or on the general model that proposed that culture could be directed from above.

To the extent that there was criticism of the struggle "against kitsch"/ "for true cultural values," at least on the political level, it was largely limited to two themes. First, there was a general perception that the position of the ruling party was hypocritical in condemning *šund* (garbage) and promoting "culture" when it had been, through its control of the most important media outlets and through its heavy promotion of neofolk, directly responsible for much of the content of electronic media. Often critics added to this the point that by supporting nationalist movements in politics and culture, the ruling party was largely responsible for bringing a fair element of "kitsch" into politics and hence was poorly positioned to use politics against "kitsch" in culture. Second, there was a general perception that the ruling party's intentions were not serious and that it did not plan to involve itself in promoting "culture" either through constructive measures (such as finance and education) or through repressive measures (such as punitive taxes). To the extent that regime-controlled media altered their content at all, change was minimal. The state television network's "hit of the day" video was now more often a symphonic performance than a pop song, and a series of nostalgic documentaries on the Yugoslav rock and roll of the eighties was broadcast on RTV's first program—with the accent on nostalgia, presenting the music as that of an era past.[110] PGP-RTS, the only recording label with reliable countrywide distribution, began to sign contracts with local rock and roll bands after a long hiatus.

109. If the person who made this suggestion rode Belgrade municipal buses, she would have realized that Wagner would be a more appropriate suggestion.

110. The neofolk TV Pink added a rock and roll program to its schedule as well, under the title "We will return" (*Mi ćemo se vratiti*, also the slogan of Mirjana Marković's SK-PJ). In this case, however, the high-culture ambitions of some *rokeri* were taken overly seriously, as the ponderously poetic host of the program made it unbearably dull. As Bogdan Tirnanić, the cultural commentator in the "respectable" regime-controlled daily paper *Politika*, commented, "[I]t seems as if the program '*Mi ćemo se vratiti*' came at the right moment. But no! If something definitively buries rock in these parts, it will be just that program. The problem is not that the host is too well-fed for somebody who 'can't get no satisfaction.' The problem is that the program presents rock as if it were one of the most boring things in the world. You won't return that way." Bogdan Tirnanić, "Telefonski imenik," *Politika*, 25 February 1995, p. 20.

In fact, the ruling party was not serious, and the "campaign for culture" remained principally an advertising campaign. In addition to having motivations for undertaking the campaign, the regime also had motivations for not carrying it out substantively. On the political level, there were no guarantees that an end to international isolation, however much desired, would accompany the new official rejection of nationalism. If it did not, the regime would be well served to maintain turbofolk in reserve should it become necessary to use it again. On the cultural level, too, the ruling party was ill prepared to alienate the neofolk public by attacking its culture seriously, particularly as it had no substitutes to offer. The "year of culture" saw official Belgrade promoting, on the one hand, something it called "culture," while continuing to produce and distribute something it defined as "kitsch."

The campaign was greeted with little seriousness among people in Belgrade. Most expected little to change. One young Belgrader, a student of dramatic arts, expressed a cynical view, "They have destroyed the culture, and now they are trying to justify themselves." Others, in a newspaper survey in *Politika*, expressed the belief that little could be achieved through a publicity campaign:

I think all of this will, in the end, have a negative effect. Because we cannot become cultured just because the Ministry proclaims it. It is a long process which requires a lot of work. One year is not enough.

[A]s long as the most popular television program in the country is *"Folk metar,"* how can any progress be expected?[111]

Among the critiques offered was that the advertising campaign for "culture," however luxuriously carried out, still lacked the appeal that popular cultural forms had. Vladimir Stakić compared two advertisements:

In the advertising period before the RTS news program, on 6 March, a spot was shown in which a fishfaced idol from Lepenski Vir moves its mouth, while a voice from offscreen reads a text about how a person needs to spend time with books and similar cultural

111. M. Jovićević, "Reč gledalaca: Televizija u godini kulture," *Politika*, 19 March 1995. *Folk metar* is an entertainment program in which two "teams," led by folk singers, compete in singing folk songs for a panel of celebrity judges.

products. And then Snežana Babić-Sneki, in a mini skirt in the style of a children's pocket handkerchief, shakes her butt and sings "Davorike dajke," announcing concerts in obscure . . . out-of-the-way places on her Yugoslav tour.
My apologies to the cultured, but I do not believe that even the newest global research [on which Saatchi claimed to build its strategy] could show that a millennia-old sculpture which moves its mouth is a better carrier of advertising messages than a twenty-five-year-old blonde with legs three meters long who shakes her butt.[112]

Another distinction is also clear: those viewers who responded to advertising for Sneki's concert tour likely knew what to expect, whereas the Ministry of Culture never made clear what it was advertising.[113]

To a certain extent, the campaign can be said to have had an effect opposite to the one intended. Turbofolk had been widely despised before the Ministry of Culture turned against it, but defenses of it now came from unexpected quarters. On the elite side, *Politika*'s cultural commentator Bogdan Tirnanić associated the newest cultural campaign with Communist campaigns of years past and argued for the simple pleasures of the popular: "Our culture is not in lethal crisis because of the savage (*divljačka*) offensive of turbofolk. Rather, just the opposite, turbofolk is our fate as the end result of the final destruction of a false system of values which our elites have insisted on for decades. A culture which has produced so many 'new Tolstois' ought to be pleased that it has been, at the end, entertained at least by [the neofolk celebrities] Jami and Maja Marijana."[114] Arguments for the defense also came, surprisingly, from the rock and roll side, with critics like Teofil Pančić unwilling to reduce all the things the rock and roll culture opposed to just turbofolk:

There would probably be no turbofolk if there were not the destructive leadership of society of those who now anathematize turbofolk: TF began as one of the eminent signs of a (sub-) cultural blockade, but not as a sign of enjoying it. . . . [I]nstead it was an escape of

112. Vladimir Stakić, "Dvanaest crtica o kulturi i turbofolku: Davorike dajke," *Vreme zabave*, April 1995, p. 65.
113. To some degree, the advertising-industry truism quoted by Michael Schudson (*Advertising: The Uneasy Persuasion: Its Dubious Impact on American Society* [New York: Basic Books, 1984]) applies: "Nothing kills a bad product like good advertising."
114. Bogdan Tirnanić, "Vreme smrti i razonode," *Politika*, 18 March 1995, p. 20.

necessity for young people trapped in the Balkan provinces in the atmosphere of civil war, for those who wanted to feel the touch of the wider world but did not know how. . . .

All those who regard the turbofolk subculture as responsible for the dominant retrograde models and strategies of Serbian discourse should read again the last ten years of our respectable literary magazines and the cultural supplements of our most respected daily paper: in the endless poems of the "Kosovo cycle" and other "nationally grounded" creative works (*umotvorinama*) which will be found there, there is more simpleminded archaic kitsch (*arhikič*) and slimy (*sluzave*) pathetics than the turbofolk machinery could think up in the next two hundred years![115]

Most surprisingly, a defense of sorts came on aesthetic grounds from the rock and roll corner, with Vladimir Stakić naming globally recognized artists from other countries who mix genres as turbofolk does and meet with praise rather than disgust: "Are Rednex, Ofra Haza, and Youssou N'Dour turbofolk in their own countries? And if not, why not?"[116]

For the most part, however, neither *rokeri* nor other detractors of turbofolk had their sympathy awakened by the fact that this new form was now the target of political rhetoric. Many Belgraders with whom I spoke shared the "official" position of the Ministry of Culture toward the genre, however much they doubted that the ministry or any other official actor intended to do any constructive work in the field of culture. Such doubts proved well founded, as the "year of culture" changed little. Its main effect was that criticism of turbofolk culture, which was already widespread, became generalized. The ruling party, for its part, had now declared an affinity with high-culture classicists and "authentic" folkies, which remained entirely on the level of words. In the final analysis, Milošević's regime tried its hand at destroying an urban culture and replacing it with a semirural one, which it then, in turn, also destroyed.

The stories of the rise and fall of musical cultures in the Belgrade of the nineties seem clear enough, according to the nationalist side of the logic of nationalist authoritarianism, right up until the last part. Why did the

115. Teofil Pančić, "Slika Dorijana Džeja," *Vreme zabave* (February 1995), 56, 57.

116. Vladimir Stakić, "Dvanaest crtica o kulturi i turbofolku: Davorike dajko," *Vreme zabave* (April 1995), 65.

regime feel called on to marginalize the very genre it had a hand in creating? The answer lies on the authoritarian side of the logic of nationalist authoritarianism. As with the marginalization of rock and roll, the ruling party had in mind not aesthetic but political concerns. Its cultural policy, in all its variations, can be traced not to the taste of the regime, if regimes can be said to have taste, but to the changing orientations of the regime to various parts of the Serbian public. Rock and roll quickly fell out of official favor when it became clear that the rock and roll audience was willing to stand in the way of nationalist mobilization. Then much enthusiasm of this audience dissipated as the regime's control over the broadcast and diffusion of music served to make its members feel more isolated and helpless. Neofolk and turbofolk came to prominence partly by default and partly as a result of the willingness of some actors in these cultures to go along with nationalist mobilization. With the sudden political turn, "peace had no alternative," and the neofolk cultures threatened to interfere with the return to respectability that the regime expected to accompany its political move.

In both cases, whether it was mobilizing publicity against rock and roll or for "genuine cultural values," the regime was never against cultural production or artistic movements per se. Cultural manifestations have rather met with sympathy from a series of Communist and nationalist regimes in Yugoslavia as a useful answer to the image of the "primitive and backward" Balkans. These regimes would like cultural movements to flourish, but to be in their service. Rock and roll succeeded without much interference in the eighties[117] at least in part because it offered evidence of SFRJ's "liberality" in contrast with other Communist regimes. As liberality fell out of political fashion, its postures came into conflict with those of a new nationalist order, and its artists and audiences came under pressure. Neofolk and turbofolk, for their part, performed several ideological services to the regime that sponsored them, as detailed earlier in this chapter. The cultural conflict between the rock and roll and neofolk publics not only offered a means of looking into the larger urban-rural conflict that pervades Serbian society, but it also had some use. For a time, the conflict between the two cultures probably displaced, to a cer-

---

117. Several rock and roll artists did, however, come under regime pressure during that time for views expressed intentionally or unintentionally. For some examples, see Sabrina Ramet, ed., *Rocking the State: Rock Music and Politics in Eastern Europe and Russia* (San Francisco: Westview Press, 1994).

tain degree, at least temporarily, the real grievances that members of both publics had against the regime—instead they were concerned with one another.

As much as the ruling party was able, through its control of major media outlets, to control the production and distribution of neofolk, it could not control neofolk's potential. The control of institutions over culture weakens considerably once cultural products leave the site of production. At that point, elements of creativity and interpretation come into play, which do not lend themselves to control. The question then is: Did neofolk ever have the capacity to act as something other than regime culture?

To the extent that neofolk was genuinely popular—and it certainly was, at least among Serbia's large population of "peasant urbanites"—it had the potential to gain that capacity once the set of conditions it had been set up to glamorize ended. The music of nationalist mobilization passes easily into being the music of nostalgia for the time of nationalist mobilization—and of resentment toward the party that set it into motion only to cut it off. Similarly, although critics of turbofolk took it to task for its emphasis on glamour and "false brilliance," it is not necessary to view these features of its presentation as only a false picture of everyday life. The glamour of entertainment can also be taken as a wish for the possibility of a better life, especially under conditions that combine to prevent such a possibility. Although neofolk functioned principally as compliant regime culture in the period under investigation, it also contained the potential to become autonomous culture. It is not beyond possibility that the regime recognized this potential—just as neofolk's turbo variant was beginning to create documents of the time through Keba and serious competition for the dance-pop it imitated through Ceca—and moved to cut it off.

No autonomous cultural form can be completely destroyed, as long as its audience continues to expect things from it. Belgrade's rock and roll culture was successfully marginalized to some extent, and its public made to feel isolated, but this did not neutralize the culture. Rather, it made the music a more powerful source of identity against the regime, albeit for a minority urban public. Although it is still too early to predict the fate of the turbofolk culture, two things should be clear: It may change form, but it is unlikely to disappear; and if the culture is genuinely popular enough to survive without state sponsorship, it is able to become an autonomous cultural form. Ministers of Culture present and future may believe that they can have a powerful influence on such events, but culture rarely operates in the way its would-be organizers expect. The Serbian regime has given clear evidence of this: it has acted—twice—to destroy cultural alternatives in the field of music. Instead it has produced resentful remnants.

5

The Destruction of Sociability

Negative economic consequences, severe ones, can be expected to accompany periods of war and instability. In the case of Serbia, the economic chaos and social disorder brought on by the destruction of SFRJ
served the political purposes of the regime and were consequently permitted to fester until they altered the shape of everyday social life. Although SFRJ had been in economic crisis before political crises provoked
the violent demise of the country, events in Serbia after the breakup of
the country developed beyond the boundaries of "mere" crisis. Massive
hyperinflation saw the destruction of the national currency as a secure
means of exchange, and people were systematically separated from whatever savings they had in hard currency. The period of hyperinflation can
be fairly described as one of economic chaos and rapid impoverishment
of the population. The hyperinflationary period lasted only briefly, but
the period that followed saw a continuation of instability and unpredict-

ability in people's pursuit of everyday needs. Poverty became generalized to the extent that the average monthly salary wavered at around half the amount necessary to acquire basic necessities, and other material difficulties made the pursuit of these necessities more complex and difficult.

The instability and unpredictability of everyday life had broad social consequences, which, at least in the short term, served the interests of the regime. First, ground-level obstacles to everyday activity warred against both memory and political involvement by deflecting attention that might be directed toward public events onto private concerns such as the acquisition of food. Second, economic crisis altered both the distribution of wealth and the structure of the population in Serbia. Hundreds of thousands of people, mostly young urbanites, emigrated to other countries, and the resources of the urban middle class were depleted to the point that observers began to speak of the disappearance of that class.[1] The period of hyperinflation saw a massive transfer of wealth from the urban to the rural population and from private to public hands, while sanctions and economic insecurity encouraged the development of a new criminal elite. Third, shortages of money and provisions, and the need to dedicate considerable activity to the pursuit of basic necessities, narrowed people's space for autonomous action and choices in everyday life. Not only did most people lack disposable income to spend on anything other than necessary items, but instability and insecurity made planning and scheduling untenable. Fourth, collective isolation and economic insecurity eroded sociability and contacts between individuals. Finally, the repeated defeat of efforts to secure the means of everyday life made conditions of "normality" inaccessible to most people and encouraged further isolation, resignation, and passivity.

To the degree that economic conditions in Serbia have had the social consequence of making everyday life uncertain and unstable, they have enhanced the control of the regime over the public sphere. The continuation of the regime in power depends in good part on the feeling that options are unavailable and that autonomous action is impossible. Economic chaos, universal compulsory poverty, shortages, and isolation all contributed to enhancing that feeling.

1. See, for example, Mladen Lazić's concluding essay in Lazić, Mrkšić, Vujović, Kuzmanović, Gredelj, Cvejić, and Vuletić (1994), as well as the article by Sreten Vujović in the same volume.

Economic Conflict Before the Fall

In the period before the country's demise, the economic situation of SFRJ was not enviable. The rapid industrial development of the Communist era had been financed principally through international credits, to which Yugoslavia enjoyed enhanced access as a result of its intermediate position between Europe's eastern and western blocs. As was the case with many other less-developed countries, Yugoslavia's indebtedness ballooned as international banks offered more credit following the petroleum price increases of the 1970s, and the country suffered severe economic consequences as credit tightened and earlier loans came due in the 1980s.[2] The rapid collapse of the country's prosperity exposed poor management and distribution of resources and enhanced conflict among the constituent republics. The economic collapse of the latter half of the 1980s made an independent contribution to the collapse of SFRJ, motivating and illustrating points that would be made as nationalist rhetorics emerged in Yugoslavia's republics.

The economic situation in SFRJ was not, however, unbearable. The last prime minister of the country, Ante Marković, had embarked on an ambitious and generally successful program of economic restructuring, privatization, and convertible currency. Although nationalist governments in the republics did much to obstruct Marković's program and had begun to initiate boycotts and punitive tariffs against one another by 1990, the program generated a wave of private business starts, brought inflation under control, and saw an increase in personal earnings. In this period as well, although republican governments attempted to enhance their economic independence,[3] the economies of the republics remained significantly interdependent. Petar Đukić described the degree of interdependence: "[In 1987], during the period of highest production, 18.7% of purchases coming to Serbia and Montenegro came from other republics, and only 8.64% from other countries. 13.37% of deliveries from

2. An effort to relate the debt pressures of less-developed countries directly to rising ethnic and national tensions is developed by J. 'Bayo Adekanye, "Structural Adjustment, Democratization, and Rising Ethnic Tensions in Africa" (unpublished paper presented at the conference on Media and the Transition of National Identities, Oslo, January 1995).

3. In 1988, Marijan Korošić described this process as creating a "fragmentary Yugoslav market," in his *Jugoslavenska kriza* (Zagreb: Naprijed, 1988), chaps. 2 and 6.

Serbia and Montenegro went to other republics, while 8.82% went to other countries."[4] At the same time, earnings in Yugoslavia increased, exceeding levels in other Communist countries in Europe, but not quite approaching levels in the countries of Western Europe. In 1989, the gross national product of Yugoslavia averaged U.S. $2,100 per capita.[5]

Actual war between the republics was preceded by extended economic conflicts between them. Nationalist economists (and noneconomists) in the various republics developed theses holding the other republics responsible for Yugoslavia's debt crisis, for claiming a disproportionate share of the country's resources, and for "underdeveloping" the others.

The Federal Fund for Financing Accelerated Development of Economically Underdeveloped Republics and Autonomous Provinces, established in 1965, became an object of intense political debate. The investments made by the fund were half as productive as the Yugoslav average in generating return on investments and one-third as productive as investments in Slovenia. Many of its projects were abandoned before completion, failed to begin production, or operated well below capacity; often these projects failed to increase employment or income in the areas where they were built as these areas lacked access to transportation and did not have adequately skilled workforces. In addition, an increasing share of the fund's resources went to Kosovo by the 1980s; in the period 1986–88, contributions to the fund by Serbia proper and Vojvodina accounted for only 65 percent of Kosovo's share of financing from the fund.

4. Petar Đukić, *Iskušenja ekonomske politike: Hronologija života pod sankcijama* (Belgrade: Grmeč AD—Privredni pregled, 1995), 15. However, according to Korošić (1988), 73, trade within republics had increased from 59.6 percent of all trade in Yugoslavia in 1970 to 69.0 percent of all trade in 1980, while trade among republics had decreased from 27.7 percent to 21.1 percent of all trade in the same period.

5. Dejan Anastasijević, "Kratak pregled propadanja," *Vreme*, no. 211, 7 November 1994, p. 47. Distribution of this wealth varied, however. In the most industrially developed republics of Slovenia and Croatia, average earnings in 1986 were 145 percent and 107 percent, respectively, of the Yugoslav average. In the somewhat less developed regions of Vojvodina and Serbia proper, earnings were 93 percent of the Yugoslav average. In the less developed republics of Bosnia-Hercegovina and Montenegro, earnings were 87 percent and 81 percent of the average, respectively, while in the poorest portions of the country, Kosovo and Macedonia, earnings were 73 percent and 70 percent of the average, respectively. These figures represent an increase in inequality of income distribution from 1965, when earnings in the wealthiest republic of Slovenia were 124 percent of the Yugoslav average and in the poorest republic of Macedonia 83 percent. Korošić (1988), 133.

The fund issue then became tied to the ongoing state of emergency, which Serbia had declared in Kosovo, and which Slovenia and Croatia opposed. Wishing neither to finance Serbia's policies in Kosovo nor to continue in what they regarded as a wasteful attempt at transfer of wealth to poorer regions, the governments of Slovenia and Croatia ceased making payments to the fund in 1990.[6]

Political conflicts took on economic dimensions as Serbia declared a boycott of Slovenian goods in December 1989, to which Slovenia responded in kind in February 1990. Tensions increased as the Serbian regime printed massive quantities of money in an effort to artificially and briefly alter economic conditions as the elections of December 1990 approached.[7] An accelerated tariff war between Slovenia, Croatia, and Serbia effectively demolished the Yugoslav market. The country itself began its definitive collapse in June 1991, as Slovenia and Croatia declared independence.

Hyperinflation After the Fall

Economic conflicts between the republics, and especially the illegal issue of currency by the Serbian regime, had already erased most of the positive results of Ante Marković's economic reforms by 1991. The loss of markets and resources in other republics added massive unemployment to the troubles of Serbia's economy as the borders of new states became front lines. Additional consequences of the breakup of SFRJ applied further pressure to the economy in Serbia: The violent conflicts in the seceding republics amounted to a costly war for Serbia, which it carried out at the same time that it lost a large portion of its military equipment and personnel as well as the tax and trade base that paid for it; international

6. The activities of and political conflicts around the fund are described in detail by Bombelles (1991), 449–65.

7. According to Mladan Dinkić, the amount of money issued was "equivalent to nearly half of the entire monetary issue which was projected for all of 1991." Mladan Dinkić, *Ekonomija destrukcije: Velika pljačka naroda* (Belgrade: VIN, 1995), 32. As the maneuver became known and criticized, pro-regime media in Serbia charged that Slovenia and Croatia had also engaged in manipulation of the money supply before their elections were held. Dinkić explains (65–70) that the charges may well have been true, but that the dimensions of manipulation in Serbia were far greater than in the other republics.

actors sought to punish Serbia for its involvement in the wars of succession as sanctions were declared by the European Union in 1991, then by the United Nations in 1992; as newly independent republics established their own currencies and monetary systems, the Serbian economy became flooded with "worthless" Yugoslav dinars from Slovenia and Croatia, which placed further pressure on the money supply that already exceeded the hard-currency reserves of the national bank; and the Serbian regime continued to try to "buy social peace" by printing currency to cover pensions and paychecks, the effective equivalent of writing massive numbers of bad checks.

As a result of these incidental and intentional pressures, the inflation that Ante Marković had set out to control returned with a vengeance. By the beginning of 1992, monthly rates of inflation reached 50.6 percent for February and 42.0 percent for March and exceeded 100 percent by June. The monthly rate of inflation was never below 100 percent in 1993 and fell below 200 percent only in April, when it hit 114.1 percent. By the last quarter of 1993, genuine hyperinflation had set in. From a monthly rate of inflation of 1880.6 percent in August, inflation hit 20,190.1 percent by November. (See Fig. 9.) Petar Đukić summarized the period:

> During the course of 1993, the dinar objectively lost the meaning and all the functions of money, and its place in trade, payments, savings, and other activities was spontaneously taken by the remains of available foreign currency. In great measure economic actors (producers and traders) returned to barter as a primitive form of exchange of goods, which carried predictable negative consequences. Monetary and market chaos, achieved by enormous emission of currency, explosion of prices, and exchange rates, nearly put an end to all forms of real economic activity. Speculation became an obligatory part of the behavior of economic actors, citizens, banks, and the state.[8]

At the height of the hyperinflation in January 1994, the monthly rate of inflation averaged 313,563,558.0 percent, a barely imaginable figure, which meant that the daily rate of inflation averaged 62.02 percent for that month,

8. Đukić (1995), 17.

Fig. 9. During the period of hyperinflation in 1993, a street-corner currency dealer offers to exchange large-denomination dinar notes for single dollars. The dealers' constant murmurs of "*devize*" ("foreign currency") to passersby entered the soundscape of Belgrade as a running "zzzzzz" sound. Photo courtesy of *Vreme*.

and the hourly rate of inflation averaged 2.03 percent.[9] Under these conditions, prices reached dazzling sums. A kilogram of potatoes that cost 4,000 dinars on 10 November 1993 cost 8,000,000,000,000,000 dinars on 17 January 1994.[10] Goods that were sold for prices controlled directly by the state also became more expensive. A 600-gram loaf of bread sold for 12,500 dinars on 2 November 1993 and for 4,000,000,000 dinars on 22 December of the same year.[11]

9. The figures for rates of inflation from 1992 to 1994 are from Mlađan Dinkić (1995), table 2. By way of comparison, Petar Đukić (1995), 15, lists the yearly rate of inflation in 1989, when Ante Marković initiated his anti-inflation program, at 2,665 percent, and the yearly rate in 1993 at 353,088,324,829,858 percent.

10. Dinkić (1995), table 9-B.

11. Dinkić (1995), table 9-A. The printing and replacement of currency, and the withdrawal of old currency from circulation, occurred with speed that almost matched the rapidity of rising prices. On 21 September 1993, the national bank issued a currency note in the amount of 10,000,000,000 dinars. Nine days later, a revaluation of currency

Statistical expressions of the rate of inflation and comparisons of prices in dinars do not tell the whole story of the economic chaos in the period of hyperinflation. In their everyday lives, people lost the feeling of security that whatever money they earned or had saved could help them to fulfill their elementary needs, and they lost the sense that the next day, or the next hour, would find them with adequate money to acquire needed goods, or even that such goods would be available. People could spend an entire day searching for food and other necessities. A young professional woman in Belgrade described the period:

> All day we did nothing but search for basic materials for survival. I had to go through the whole city based on rumors—that bread had appeared somewhere on Banovo brdo, that there was milk on Kalenić pijaca. Just so my children would have something to eat. Prices did not matter at all, sometimes people would just write a check—ten billion, a hundred billion, it did not matter if the price was fifty times your salary. Because by the time you got your salary and the check was cashed, it was a hundredth of your salary. My salary in November was 30 pfennigs, less than a mark. But money did not exist, you just wrote checks as long as you could find something to buy.

Often, too, people would buy useless or unnecessary items in the hope of selling or trading them later, simply to be able to get something for their money before it lost all value.

In the general confusion over prices and the value of money, some astounding bargains were occasionally available. Many Belgraders told me of making endless international telephone calls, knowing that when the huge bill arrived, it could safely be set aside until the day it was due—at which time it could be paid for with the equivalent of a few cents.

---

was announced in which six zeroes were removed from the amounts of banknotes, as ordinary calculations became challenging and confusion likely. The zeroes quickly returned, so that on 23 December the extraordinary 500,000,000,000-dinar note was issued. Eight days later, revaluation of currency saw the elimination of another nine zeroes. The last banknote issued during the period of hyperinflation was on 14 January 1994, in the amount of 10,000,000 dinars. Demonstrating the regime's understanding of the monetary chaos, SPS spokesperson Borisav Jović declared in September 1993 that "the cause of poverty in Serbia is the great quantity of money which citizens have at their disposal." Quoted in *Vreme*, no. 167, 3 January 1994, p. 73.

Another friend described the apartment he had purchased with his wife in 1990, at which time monthly payments on the mortgage amounted to nearly their entire income. In 1993, "I paid off the entire apartment, for about the price of a pack of cigarettes." With devaluations occurring sometimes more than once in the course of a day, price comparisons or strategic waiting could sometimes pay off. A Belgrade auto mechanic described the price changes occurring in one afternoon: "All the stores changed their prices. But they did not all change them at the same time. So you could get some things very cheaply if you went to the right place at the right time. I remember I went with some friends to a *kafana* and we sat and ordered four beers. The waiter told us we should look at the price list but we said no, just bring the drinks. When he came back, the price was 75 German marks, for four beers. So we ordered another round. Two hours later, when we finally paid, the eight beers we had were five German marks." Enjoying such bargains, however, carried severe conditions. The consumer had to have access to hard currency, which progressively fewer people had. And the consumer had to have the time, resources, and strength to dedicate exclusively to shopping. Shopkeepers, aware of the risk of losing money on the sale of goods, were often inclined to withhold them from the market until the period of hyperinflation passed.

Average consumers enjoyed few of the dubious benefits of hyperinflation. Stronger social actors, however, were able to generate tremendous benefit. As dinars came to be worth less in fact than the paper they were printed on, hard currency, especially in the form of German marks, came to be the only real measure of value.[12] It is possible to view the period of hyperinflation as masking a process in which most people who had some savings in hard currency were relieved of them.

One dimension of this process has to do with the acquisition of food and other everyday goods. Because salaries and pensions generally covered only a small fraction of the cost of survival, people who had foreign currency were compelled to exchange small amounts every day for dinars, with which they could try to purchase food. This hard currency ended up either in the network of street dealers and the organizations that supplied

12. In a remark perhaps illustrative of the globalization-of-culture thesis, an American living in Belgrade told me that the most reliable way of following exchange rates was to check the price of a "Quarter-pounder" at the Belgrade McDonald's—which was always equivalent to two German marks.

and controlled them or eventually in state banks. Alternatively, especially in times of shortage when suppliers refused to sell goods for dinars, people could buy items only for hard currency. The money spent in this manner constituted a transfer of wealth from the urban to the rural population in the event that it was spent to buy food from peasant producers and from private to public hands in the event that it was spent on "big-ticket" items available only from state-owned corporations.

Another dimension of the process involves the trade in apartments. Urban residents in Serbia were most likely to have received the "right to live" (*stanarsko pravo*) in apartments they did not own, but that belonged instead to the companies for which the people worked, the district governing body, or the state Housing Fund. Under these conditions, residents had the right to live in their apartments throughout their lives, but not to sell them or to will them to others. While hyperinflation was in force, the state offered people the right to purchase the apartments in which they lived. The hard-currency prices fell from week to week, so that many residents purchased their apartments at the time when the price fell to the point that it was equal to the amount of their hard-currency savings. The transfer cost the state owners of the apartments very little in the short run—what residents purchased from the state was a future interest in their apartments that would come into force at an indeterminate time. This process gained the state institutions a great deal—in exchange for this future interest, they often received the entire hard-currency savings of the residents.

Large numbers of people, especially older people, were also relieved of their hard currency by two dubious banks that emerged at the time of hyperinflation. Jugoskandik, established by the previously unknown businessman Jezdimir Vasiljević,[13] and Dafiment, founded by convicted embezzler Dafina Milanović,[14] offered huge rates of interest for deposits in hard currency. Early depositors in these banks could profit handily from the scheme, and the owners of the banks achieved celebrity status—Vasiljević as the flamboyant *Gazda Jezda* (Jezda the Boss), and Milanović as the populist "Great Serbian Mother." Toward the end of their periods

13. A short biography of Jezdimir Vasiljević, along with a description of his unique business projects, appears in Dinkić (1995), 161–94.

14. A brief biography of Dafina Milanović, along with a narrative of the rise and fall of Dafiment, appears in Dinkić (1995), 195–238.

of celebrity, however, it became clear that the high rates of interest offered by these banks were financed principally by the new deposits arriving in them. This method of financing is known in the annals of fraud as a "pyramid scheme" and is notable for two characteristics: It can bring appreciable profit to early participants, but this profit can be obtained only at the expense of later participants; and its operation cannot be sustained for long. Jugoskandik's operations ceased on 8 March 1993, when Jezdimir Vasiljević fled Serbia, leaving Jugoskandik with unpaid obligations to its depositors amounting to around 312 million German marks. The panic that followed Jugoskandik's collapse assured that Dafiment could not operate much longer either. Dafiment held on a short while longer, closing in April 1993. The lost deposits at Dafiment amounted to 1,054,621,720 German marks.

From the economic point of view, the period of hyperinflation achieved several results. On the one hand, various claims, both legitimate and fraudulent, worked to deprive people of their hard-currency savings. Members of the middle classes came to be increasingly dependent on salaries and pensions and in some cases on remittances from relatives living abroad or on work in the "gray economy." The loss of disposable income among this group effectively reduced the degree of social autonomy they enjoyed; most or all of their resources came to be directed toward meeting basic material needs. Perhaps more important than the economic effects of hyperinflation were the social effects. Psychologically, the impossibility of meeting everyday needs fostered a sense of defeat and resignation among people whose attempts to assure the means of survival were regularly thwarted. On the level of sociability, the lack of adequate food and other resources prevented individuals from inviting others to their homes (where they had nothing to offer) and from visiting others in their homes (where they had nothing to bring).

Perhaps most important, however, hyperinflation and monetary chaos made the sense of normality untenable. Unable to plan for events even in the near future and compelled to constantly think and maneuver to carry out elementary tasks, people thought about their basic needs—and not about the dictatorial monopoly of power or about the wars going on at the same time. Speaking with many Belgraders about their memories of 1992 and 1993, I found people more inclined to mention lines for food, changing exchange rates, and shortages than the wars in Croatia and Bosnia-Hercegovina. Both categories of events affected them, but the economic crisis was more likely to affect them personally. As long as individuals were severely hindered in their private lives, the regime maintained its ability to act unobstructed in the public sphere.

After Hyperinflation: Lower-Level Instability

Hyperinflation came to an abrupt end on 24 January 1994. Economist Dragoslav Avramović was brought in to head the Yugoslav National Bank (*Narodna banka Jugoslavije—NBJ*) and declared a severe program of monetary reconstruction. The "old" dinars—the most recent edition of which had come into circulation ten days earlier—were to be replaced by a new "super dinar," its circulation restricted to correspond to NBJ's hard currency reserves and its value tied to the German mark at a ratio of 1:1. In the first several months of the monetary reconstruction, inflation appeared to remain in check, and the "super dinar" appeared to maintain its value, even as pensions and salaries increased. The elderly Avramović received heavy promotion in regime-controlled media as the savior of the economy, affectionately nicknamed "Avram" or "the super granddad" (*super-deka*). His folksy assurances, based on the price of fried smelts at street vendors' stands, that inflation was not returning served both to promote his endearing public image and to foster a new confidence in the national currency.

Avramović's apparent success, however, could not disguise the continuing instability of SRJ's economy. In the first place, although the monetary reconstruction he initiated came to be regarded as generally successful, it also seemed to confirm the suspicion that hyperinflation had occurred as a result of deliberate policy, and not as a result of economic inevitability: It began when the regime started printing currency it could not finance and ended when the practice ceased. Beyond this, Avramović's personal assurances that he would restrict the supply of money conflicted with the motivations of key actors in the regime, who knew that economic conditions were unlikely to improve and continued to have reason to want to "buy social peace" by paying unfinanced pension and salary increases at politically strategic moments.[15] As popular as he was

15. Directors of regime-controlled businesses also had little motivation to maintain the value of the dinar. As long as the official rate of exchange remained at 1:1, any

when his tight-money program began, his power was not equal to that of regime politicians who controlled most political, police, and business institutions. In fact, he was unceremoniously dismissed as the governor of the national bank in 1996, in a conflict over a new attempt by the regime to further inflate the money supply.

Most important, however, the consequences of hyperinflation were already well in place. Citizens' hard-currency savings had been largely eliminated, and salaries and pensions remained below the minimum required to meet everyday needs. Within a year, prices began to increase again, and the "street value" of the dinar began to fall. It became apparent that the much-promoted "economic miracle" of 1994 would last only briefly and that Avramović's reforms promised, at best, continued instability and unpredictability, albeit at a lower level than in the previous two years. Table 14 presents the value of the German mark in dinars, which nearly doubled during the period of observation:

The slow, steady fall in the value of the dinar did not approach the shocking proportions it had attained during the hyperinflationary period of the previous two years. Its more predictable instability and weakness, however, cast doubt on the regime's euphoric claims that it had successfully acted to rein in inflation and secure a stable currency.

In fact, despite the regime's self-congratulatory assessment of the strength of the "super dinar," the German mark remained the only stable measure of value in Serbia. Although Prime Minister Mirko Marjanović claimed in his 1995 report to the parliament that there had been no inflation in 1994,[16] the policies of his government belied the claim. As early as January 1995, Marjanović's government released a statement declaring

---

decrease in the "street value" of the dinar enhanced the competitive position of state-owned businesses. Because only state-owned businesses could purchase German marks at the official rate and all other businesses paid the "street price," hard-currency purchases by state-owned businesses cost less—an advantage that increased as the difference between the official and "street" rates of exchange increased.

16. According to Marjanović, "At the end of 1994 prices were at the same level as at the beginning of the year, which means that the rate of inflation was zero. The gross national product increased by 6.2 percent, the social security of citizens was significantly strengthened, salaries were increased elevenfold, and pensions eightfold." Quoted in Unsigned (attributed to Tanjug), "Marjanović: Vlada narodnog jedinstva u istom sastavu i u narednom periodu," *Politika*, 9 April 1995, p. 1. If his claim were true, 1994 would probably represent the largest increase in income unaccompanied by inflation known in economic history.

Table 14. "Street value" of the German mark in dinars Belgrade, October 1994–June 1995

Date	Buy/Sell
3 October 1994	1.20/1.40
10 October 1994	1.20/1.40
17 October 1994	1.20/1.40
24 October 1994	1.40/1.60
31 October 1994	1.20/1.40
7 November 1994	1.20/1.50
14 November 1994	1.30/1.50
21 November 1994	1.40/1.50
28 November 1994	1.40/1.60
5 December 1994	1.50/1.70
12 December 1994	1.60/1.90
19 December 1994	1.60/1.90
26 December 1994	1.60/1.70
2 January 1995	1.40/1.60
9 January 1995	1.50/1.70
16 January 1995	1.60/1.80
23 January 1995	1.60/1.80
30 January 1995	1.60/1.80
6 February 1995	1.60/1.80
13 February 1995	1.70/1.85
20 February 1995	1.75/1.85
27 February 1995	1.75/1.90
6 March 1995	1.80/1.90
13 March 1995	1.80/1.90
20 March 1995	1.80/2.00
27 March 1995	2.10/2.30
3 April 1995	2.00/2.20
10 April 1995	2.00/2.20
17 April 1995	2.00/2.20
24 April 1995	2.00/2.20
1 May 1995	2.00/2.20
8 May 1995	2.00/2.20
15 May 1995	2.05/2.20
22 May 1995	2.10/2.20
29 May 1995	2.10/2.30
5 June 1995	2.10/2.30
12 June 1995	2.25/2.50
19 June 1995	2.20/2.40
26 June 1995	2.20/2.50

NOTE: The figures are taken from the weekly table of exchange rates, which appeared in the magazine *Vreme*. Throughout the period, the official rate of exchange remained 1:1.

its intentions to "return prices to the level they were at on 25 July of last year."[17] More than a month later, the regime's principal print media outlet weakly claimed that "prices are continuing to return to the level of last July."[18] A bit more than a month after that, federal Prime Minister Radoje Kontić declared the intention of the government to "maintain the exchange value of the dinar at the level of last December."[19] Because the value of the German mark ranged between 1.50 and 1.90 dinars in December, Kontić's statement represented the first public admission by a representative of the regime that regime officials had neither succeeded, nor did they intend to attempt, to hold to the official rate of exchange.

Inflationary pricing presented a different set of challenges. The order had indeed gone out to reduce prices to the level of the previous July, an order that apparently held force at least for state-owned companies. In some cases, companies responded by withdrawing goods from the market, so that the period following the order saw shortages of both milk (but not dairy derivatives such as yogurt and cheese, which were subject to different regulations) and cooking oil.[20] Others responded somewhat more creatively, as did the "Zastava" automotive factory, which produced the Yugo. In February 1995, the price of the popular "Yugo koral 55" model remained at 8,700 dinars, the same price as in April 1994, but "Zastava" did not have any "Yugo koral 55" models to sell. It did have, however, the "modified" model "Yugo koral 55 C," at a price of 12,700 dinars.[21] The 4,000-dinar difference could be freely interpreted by consumers either as the cost of the letter "C" or as a reflection of the rate of inflation in the period since the price of the car was set.

The instability of the dinar and its extreme reliance on an artificial relation to the German mark became apparent in the last week of March 1995. Beginning at noon of Friday, 23 March, the value of the dinar fell

17. Zoran Jeličić, "Država zabranjuje cene," *Vreme*, no. 221, 16 January 1995, p. 21.

18. M. S., "Reč je data," *Večernje novosti*, 19 February 1995, p. 2.

19. Unsigned, "Očuvan dinar," *Večernje novosti*, 26 March 1995, p. 12.

20. The director of the cooking oil factory "Dijamanta," Savo Knežević, stated during the course of an earlier shortage that he had no idea why cooking oil was not available, claiming "There is enough cooking oil not only for the needs of the citizens of Yugoslavia but also for export. Where all the excitement about cooking oil is coming from is not clear to me. Oil leaves the factory on schedule, and where it ends up on its way to the consumer—the responsible agencies should find out." Quoted in Unsigned, "Test vremena," *Vreme*, no. 209, 24 October 1994, p. 31.

21. Unsigned, "Slovo," *Vreme*, no. 225, 13 February 1995, p. 31.

precipitously. On Sunday, the value of the German mark rose from Friday's 2.20 dinars to between 4 and 5 dinars. Intervention by state banks brought the value nearly back to its Friday level, so that by Monday morning the German mark was selling for 2.50 dinars.[22] Prices of highly valued imported goods rose accordingly; over the weekend a kilogram of coffee rose from 25 to 40 dinars. Goods generally smuggled onto the market, such as motor fuel and cigarettes, either quickly rose in price or were available only for German marks.[23]

Shops closed for "inventories" over the weekend and reopened with new price lists. The higher prices attributed to the swift fall in the value of the dinar remained in place after the dinar had in good measure recuperated. In a manner similar to the way "Zastava" found that a change in nomenclature offered a good method to raise prices, other businesses found that renewed panic about the value of the dinar offered a good method to respond to (or produce!) inflation. The regime attempted once again to respond to the renewed evidence of inflation with administrative measures. In a bulletin shortly after the "currency attack" weekend, the federal cabinet described its intentions:

> In yesterday's session, the cabinet considered the work of investigative agencies which, in the period from 24 to 27 March, when an attempted attack on the exchange value of the dinar occurred, surveyed the behavior of publicly- and privately-owned firms. According to their findings, it was demonstrated that a certain number of production and trade organizations during those days, without basis, for speculationary or psychological reasons, raised prices and withdrew goods from sale. Rigorous measures have been taken against those organizations, and they have been ordered to return their prices to the level of 24 March.[24]

Thus over the course of a single weekend, the regime's price policy altered dramatically. No longer did spokespeople pronounce the goal of

22. Dimitrije Boarov, "Crna devizna oluja," *Vreme*, no. 232, 3 April 1995, p. 11.

23. A sample of price changes in Novi Sad over the weekend is offered in Unsigned (attributed to Beta), "Marka u Novom Sadu dostigla 2,8 dinara," *Naša borba*, 27 March 1995, p. 20.

24. Quoted in Zoran Jeličić, "Danke državne banke: Dvorska istraga," *Vreme*, no. 234, 17 April 1995, p. 17. The order was reported from an agency bulletin in Unsigned (attributed to Tanjug), "Špekulativne cene moraće da se vrate," *Politika*, 13 April 1995, p. 1.

returning prices to their (preinflationary) level of July 1994, but now declared their intention to return them to the level of March 1995.

This effort to return prices to an earlier level did not meet with any greater success than before. By the second week of May, the regime-controlled *Večernje novosti* was repeatedly announcing new deadlines for the return of prices, accompanied by threats.[25] At best, the proclamation of administrative measures for the control of prices, which were later ignored, provided a means for the regime to continue to claim that it had "beaten down" inflation while the continued presence of inflation remained obvious to consumers.

On the financial level, the continued instability of currency and prices after hyperinflation offered some benefit to the regime. Immediately after the March weekend that saw the rapid fall and partial rise of the dinar, economist Mlađan Dinkić offered his prediction of who would benefit from the dinar's fall and eventual devaluation:

> In this first phase there is no place for ordinary citizens because they do not have money (because they are not receiving their salaries). So the German marks will probably be purchased by the debtors' lobby who can then pay off their debts for a third of the amount that they borrowed. When the state officially announces a devaluation of the dinar at a slightly lower level than the price on the street, citizens will be compelled to sell their marks to banks, to cover the period until they receive their paychecks. In that way the state will get new hard currency very cheaply and renew its hard-currency reserves.[26]

Whether the prediction was likely to be borne out or not, the basic assumptions behind it are emblematic of the posthyperinflation period: As in the hyperinflation period, the potential benefits of instability were more likely to be available to powerful institutions than to ordinary citi-

25. For example, on 8 May, *Novosti* announced a threat by "coordinating minister" Dragan Tomić that if prices were not at the level of 24 March by 10 May, "we will be compelled to force them to be returned by sanctions." When 10 May came, *Novosti* promised that prices would be lowered "by the end of the week." See R. M., "Rok—10. maj," *Večernje novosti*, 8 May 1995, p. 3, and S. Vuković, "Paravan za poskupljenja," *Večernje novosti*, 10 May 1995.

26. Quoted in T. Jakobi, "Priprema za devalvaciju?" *Naša borba*, 28 February 1995, p. 6.

zens, and again as in the hyperinflation period, basic goods were often likely to be available only to people with access to hard currency.

The period of hyperinflation remains unique, along with the chaos and severe insecurity that accompanied it. The subsequent period, however, institutionalized some of the qualities that made that period important socially as well as economically. Prices and exchange rates remained unstable, and salaries and pensions remained insufficient to meet basic needs. The brief panic in March also revealed that lack of confidence in the value of the dinar remained a feature of everyday life. However, because all these phenomena occurred at a lower level than they had a short time before, they were experienced with a degree of resigned acceptance, if not with measured confidence.

Universal Compulsory Poverty

Another phenomenon that emerged strongly in the period of hyperinflation and persisted afterward was poverty. Whereas average earnings before the destruction of SFRJ had not been extremely high, they had been high enough to provide citizens with money to cover their basic needs and also some disposable income. In the period of hyperinflation, earnings fell well below the minimum necessary to cover basic needs, and people were compelled to use hard currency, either from their savings or from remittances received from relatives abroad, to cover living expenses. The period following hyperinflation did see increases in salaries and pensions. These increases, however, were not large enough to bring earnings back up to a survival level. Dejan Anastasijević summarized the earnings picture: "[T]he average earnings per person was at the middle of last year ten times less than in the same month of 1990. The people who are by today's measures paid above average salaries (the highest earning group) receive about the same salary which the least well paid people received in 1990. The average Yugoslav today earns five times less than in 1990—which means that the majority of families are not in a condition to live normally from their own earnings."[27] Under these conditions, disposable income took on the status of a distant memory. The average family not only did not have space in which to choose how to spend the money it

27. Dejan Anastasijević, "Kratak pregled propadanja," *Vreme*, no. 211, 7 November 1994, p. 47.

earned, but was compelled to find additional money each month to meet basic needs. As the economic autonomy of individuals and families receded into the past, the range of activities, goods, and contacts available to them also became more constrained.

The generalization of poverty had two important political consequences. In the first place, cultural, informative, and social options taken for granted under normal circumstances were no longer available. In the second place, the marginal economic positions of most individuals made them uniquely sensitive to even small changes in the economic situation. Economist Aleksandra Pošarac set forward the dilemma:

> The establishment and development of civil society requires free, economically independent, self-conscious, and autonomous citizens. It would be difficult to describe the citizens of Serbia in those terms at this moment, as more than a third of them are not in a condition to meet their basic needs, while another third is "potentially poor" as a result of their small distance from the poverty line. That means that any change in the given situation: an increase in the price of utilities and municipal services, the end of the system of paid layoffs and firing of workers, a real fall in earnings and other receipts the level of which exceeds current possibilities, more rigorous enforcement of UN sanctions and the consequent reduction of black market activity (which could also result from a strengthening of repressive measures of the state against actors on the black market), reduction in the activity of the private sector and so on—can seriously threaten the fragile basis on which the standard of living of citizens is maintained.[28]

As long as people lived under these conditions of basic economic insecurity, they were not free to engage in activity that would positively alter their social or cultural condition. Instead they remained tied to the everyday struggle to satisfy their basic material needs.

There are two ways of expressing this situation in statistical terms. One way is to look at the percentage of earnings families spent on food. Table 15 presents those figures for 1994. People who spent more than 100 percent of their earnings on food, of course, were compelled to find sources

28. Quoted in Zoran Jeličić, "Srbija na kolenima," *Vreme*, no. 220, 9 January 1995, p. 11.

Table 15. Percentage of family earnings spent on food

Percentage of Earnings	Proportion of Respondents
Less than 33	11.0
From 33 to 50	7.3
From 50 to 66	19.9
From 66 to 100	44.7
More than 100	17.1

SOURCE: Dejan Anastasijević, "Kratak pregled propadanja," *Vreme*, no. 211, 7 November 1994, p. 48.

other than earnings to cover this expense. For some this meant selling possessions, using savings, or depending on remittances from abroad.[29] For others this meant working in the "gray economy" of smuggled goods and goods and services exchanged "under the table."[30] For many, the only possibility was to reduce the amount of food they consumed.[31]

Another way of expressing the economic position of ordinary citizens is to compare average earnings with the monthly statistical report of the cost of basic expenses called the "consumers' basket" (*potrošačka korpa*). In the last six months of 1994, salaries averaged 287 dinars, and the *potrošačka korpa* was valued at an average of 550 dinars, or 1.9 average salaries.[32] In January 1995, the average salary was 263.91 dinars, and the *potrošačka korpa* was valued at 596.33 dinars, meaning that a family of four would have to receive 2.3 average salaries to meet its basic needs.[33] The

29. According to research by the sociologist Stjepan Gredelj, one-sixth of retired persons in Serbia received remittances from relatives in other countries in 1994. Quoted in Dejan Anastasijević, "Tihi lapot," *Vreme*, no. 210, 31 October 1994, p. 19.

30. *Naša borba* reported that "half of all households in Yugoslavia have at least one member 'employed' on the gray market, and in the hyperinflationary year of 1994, 54% of the gross national product was realized in the gray economy." By 1994, the percentage of gross national product realized in the gray economy had fallen to 32 percent, according to the same report. Bojana Jager and Tanja Jakobi, "Korumpirana država, birokratija pere ruke," *Naša borba*, 3 February 1995, p. 6.

31. According to research on the economic conditions of pensioners by Stjepan Gredelj, "Every third older person complains that they have lost weight in the past months (an average of 6.5 kilograms per person)." In Dejan Anastasijević, "Tihi lapot," *Vreme*, no. 210, 31 October 1994, p. 19.

32. Gordana Đukić, "Otkud toliko mesa," *Naša borba*, 8 February 1995, p. 9.

33. Unsigned, "Prosečna januarska plata 263,91 dinar," *Naša borba*, 24 February 1995, p. 16.

average salary in February 1995 was 272.12 dinars, and the value of the *potrošačka korpa* was 599.28 dinars, or 2.2 average salaries.[34]

Average salaries are of course only a crude expression of the monthly earnings available to each family or individual. On the one hand, the figure does not express how many people receive more or less than the average or how many people receive salaries of any amount in any particular family. Nor does the figure account for income from sources other than earnings or unreported income earned in the "gray economy." Perhaps more important, considering the high rate of unemployment in Serbia during this period, it entirely leaves out of the picture people who do not receive a salary. Their earnings were considerably lower—so although the average salary in December 1994 was 290.69 dinars, the average amount received by workers on "forced vacation" in that month was 72 dinars.[35] In addition to this, another complication arises from the fact that many people who were working often did not receive their salaries when they were due or received them only after several months' delay.

Some portions of the population were more severely affected than others by the decline in living standards experienced in Serbia. In the first place, declining earnings had a greater impact on members of the urban population, who were more likely to acquire all their food by purchasing it. Members of the rural population were often able to substitute items they produced themselves for items they were no longer able to purchase.[36] Second, the general shortage of jobs strongly affected younger members of the population, who if they were employed were most likely to be sent on "forced vacation" as the least-senior workers in their companies, and who if they were not employed faced poor prospects of being hired. Economic difficulty was "distributed" in a manner that cast the greatest difficulty on those groups least likely to support the regime.

A unique set of problems faced pensioners. On the one hand, they found themselves, after a lifetime of earning generally much higher salaries, on fixed incomes, the only predictable element of which was that they were low. Beyond that, they did not discover what amount of money

34. Unsigned (attributed to Tanjug), "Prosečne zarade u februaru 272,12 dinara," *Naša borba*, 24 March 1995, p. 16.

35. Gordana Đukić, "Otkud toliko mesa," *Naša borba*, 8 February 1995, p. 9.

36. Differences in the decline in standards among these two populations are explored in detail in Sreten Vujović, "Promene u materijalnom standardu i načinu života društvenih slojeva," in Lazić, Mrkšić, Vujović, Kuzmanović, Gredelj, Cvejić, and Vuletić (1994).

they would receive until pensions were delivered. The delivery date of pensions was itself uncertain. In just one week in March 1995, *Večernje novosti*'s headlines on the topic read: "Checks tomorrow?" (27 March), "Checks from Friday?" (28 March), and "Checks tomorrow or Wednesday" (31 March).[37] In question was the payment of the first half of pensions, which were due to be paid in February.

On the other hand, many pensioners had once enjoyed a certain prosperity, and their poverty was relative. More likely than not, they lived in apartments or houses they either owned or where they had an uncontested right to remain. Often their children and grandchildren lived in the same place. Also more likely than not, they possessed valuable durable goods that are often taken as markers of prosperity—automobiles, television sets, household appliances, and similar items.[38] These facts point to the contradictory position of older people in this period in Serbia: they were poor and recently had not been.

Especially among older people, the swift and definitive decline in their standards of living and reasonable expectations engendered apathetic resignation. Stjepan Gredelj's research on living conditions among retired people found that very few were of the opinion that their situation was likely to change or that it would change meaningfully with a change in political regimes. Dejan Anastasijević summarized the feeling of hopelessness among this group: "To the question of what they could do to improve their lives, the largest number (37 percent) answered that they did not know, or answered that they could not do anything (14 percent). Despite the significant efforts of the regime to persuade people that sanctions are the cause of all their troubles, only 3 percent believe that their lives would be easier if sanctions were lifted."[39] Pensioners may have been more likely than other groups in the population to offer such assessments as a result of the unique constraints under which they lived, which are described in part above. However, the feeling that no appealing possibilities existed was probably not unique to one group, but was rather a consequence of the daily defeat encountered by all groups in their attempts to live normally.

37. D. J., "Čekovi sutra?" *Večernje novosti*, 27 March 1995, p. 3; A. J., "Čekovi od petka?" *Večernje novosti*, 28 March 1995, p. 3; A. J., "Čekovi sutra ili u sredu," *Večernje novosti*, 31 March 1995, p. 3.

38. They may not have had sufficient resources to purchase fuel, parts, and repairs to run this equipment, however.

39. Dejan Anastasijević, "Tihi lapot," *Vreme*, no. 210, 31 October 1994, p. 21.

Universal compulsory poverty, then, achieved two strategic purposes that operated to the benefit of the regime. First, on the material level, it effectively demolished the economic autonomy of most people. If all people's earnings, or in some cases more than the amount of their earnings, were directed toward acquiring such basic necessities as food, then a whole range of other potential activities was eliminated. These activities included travel, the pursuit of information, and the organization of social events that encouraged interpersonal contact. Second, on the psychological level, confronted with conditions of poverty and inefficacy, people came to think of themselves as poor and inefficacious. These two levels combined to the effect that individuals were compelled to dedicate their thinking and efforts to achieving normal conditions in their private lives and discouraged both materially and psychologically from attempting to engage in the public sphere.

Another Form of Instability: Electricity "Restrictions" and Shortages

Not only brute economic facts diminished people's ability to work, plan, and socialize. Everyday life was particularly affected in winter, when the supply of electricity became irregular and unpredictable. In the winter of 1994–95, shortages of electrical energy and breakdowns in the electrical system provoked a round of reductions and "restrictions" in the energy supply to homes and businesses. Users of electric energy found themselves without power for scheduled intervals lasting between two and six hours and also subject to unscheduled outages that lasted for an unpredictable amount of time. The official report of the electric utility "Elektrodistribucija Srbije" claimed, after the restrictions ended: "The reductions lasted a total of 48 days, during which time reductions occurred on five days in November, 28 days in December, and 15 days in January."[40] "Elektrodistribucija's" assessment accounts only for planned reductions scheduled by the agency. In addition to these, several days saw unplanned power outages the agency did not include in the report.

During these months, such elementary activities as work, the gathering of information from electronic media, social activity requiring electric

40. The quotation is attributed to "responsible people in Elektrodistribucija" by M. Perović, "Za otklanjanje kvarova do tri godine," *Politika*, 27 March 1995, p. 17.

appliances (such as dining), and the planning of future activities came to be subject to the uncertain and unpredictable supply of electricity. Among the groups most affected by the irregular supply of power were people whose employment depended on the functioning of machines, parents of young children, and older individuals, especially if they lived in apartments on high floors of their buildings.

A material basis certainly existed for the supply of electric energy to be unstable. The power system had deteriorated significantly in a short period. Serbia had exported electric energy before the breakup of SFRJ, both to other republics in SFRJ and to other countries. After the breakup of the country, "Elektrodistribucija" was among the companies transformed from a "socially owned company" (*društveno preduzeće*) to a "publicly owned company" (*javno preduzeće*); its semiautonomous management was placed under direct regime control. In the subsequent years, "it was demonstrated once again how it is possible to destroy in a few years what took decades to build."[41] The regime reduced the cost of electric energy as part of its general approach of "buying social peace," indirectly encouraging citizens to increase consumption. At the same time, it did not invest in new construction or in maintenance of the system. By the time the deterioration of the electric energy system became obvious, international sanctions made the acquisition of materials and technical assistance far more difficult and expensive, and the rapid spread of poverty made any effort to increase the cost of electric energy politically dangerous. Taken together, these factors made the condition of the system precarious by 1994 and also made any improvement in that condition unlikely.

As the cold season set in early in 1994, unplanned outages already began occurring in October. By November, "Elektrodistribucija" was instructing its users to reduce energy consumption by 15 percent from the amount they used in the same month of the previous year and informed consumers that subsequent reductions of 20 percent, 25 percent, and finally 30 percent could be on the way.[42] As December arrived, those restrictions became formal, with kilowatt-hours above the prescribed level charged at a higher price, accompanied by threats that people who chronically exceeded their quota would have their power shut off.[43]

41. Dragoslav Nedeljković, "U mraku se bolje vidi," *Vreme*, no. 216, 12 December 1994, p. 16.
42. J. Putniković, "Repriza mraka iz '83," *Borba*, 23 November 1994, p. 12.
43. J. Putniković, "Juče počelo očitavanje brojila," *Borba*, 2 December 1994, p. 28.

Scheduled outages began in November. In Belgrade, each district of
the city was divided into four "groups," as newspapers and television
news reports announced at what hour the outages would begin. From
outages lasting two hours once a day, the frequency of restrictions increased, so that by early December two-hour outages were announced
for twice a day. The length of the scheduled outages also increased, so
that by the end of December they lasted four hours, and the possibility
was put forward that they might be increased to six hours. People who
lived near hospitals, embassies, and the state television headquarters were
spared outages.

The announcement and scheduling of outages led people to actively
inquire about what "group" they were in and about the schedule of outages for the day. Motivating this curiosity was the assumption that if a
person knew the schedule of restrictions and the "group" status of others,
then everyday activities could be planned. Toward the beginning of the
period of outages, Svetislav Jovanov reflected on this fact in a newspaper
essay: "Instead of 'how are you,' 'have you received your paycheck,'
'what's up with Bosnia,' or even 'are they lifting those sanctions,' people
ask, in broad daylight, in meaningful tones, with calculation and worry,
'what group are you?' . . . Depending on the schedule of outages people
plan visits (ordinary visits become 'restriction visits'), business meetings,
children's birthdays, outings, and probably (God forgive me) funerals as
well."[44] As time went on, however, people paid less attention to the
schedule of restrictions. It became apparent first that the schedule was
followed irregularly and second that as many unplanned as planned outages occurred. Suggestions began to be made that dispatchers were at
fault, and they were suspected of deliberately ignoring the schedule and
acting independently by shutting off districts at will.[45] More probably,
the deteriorated condition of the system, combined with the pressure put
on it by repeated shutting off and turning on, caused more breakdowns
than usual, a situation not helped by the efforts of some people to evade
restrictions by technical means or to sabotage electric equipment to prevent scheduled outages.

Everyday activities became difficult if not impossible to plan under
conditions of uncertain electric supply. Workers and businesses whose

44. Svetislav Jovanov, "Koja si grupa," *Borba*, 28–30 November 1994, p. 32.
45. J. Putnikovic, "Pored redovnih i havarijska gašenja," *Borba*, 21 December 1994,
p. 24.

work depended on electric equipment found themselves unable to work at unpredictable times and for unpredictable lengths of time. In the winter weather, people whose homes were heated by electric energy were compelled to find other places to go. People could not invite others to their home for meals, as they could not be certain that they could prepare the meals or, if they lived on the upper floors of buildings, that guests would have an elevator to bring them to their homes. Belgrade took on a surreal appearance as residents became accustomed to carrying flashlights with them whenever they left their homes and leaving candles in strategic places in their homes.

For people not seriously threatened by the lack of electric energy, the situation took on a comical air. Nikola Burzan commented in *Borba* that Serbia was "at this moment the most romantic country in the world—we all live by candlelight."[46] The independent newsweekly *Vreme* came out on 12 December 1994 with a photo of Mirjana Marković's book *Noć i dan* (*Night and day*) on the cover and a free candle to read it by. Petar Luković sardonically associated the electric outages with contemporary MTV style in an essay titled *Srbija unplugged*.[47] Political responses could be equally sardonic. The Social-Democratic League of Vojvodina (*Liga socialdemokrata Vojvodine*) offered the following statement on the situation: "Darkness has conquered these lands not only figuratively, but now we are in actual darkness. Of course, once again, the people are undisciplined because they demand electric energy. Recently they wanted heat when it was cold, and now they would like light when it is dark. What a strange world."[48] Similarly, a Democratic Party spokeswoman found a bright spot in the darkness of electric outages, claiming, "the only good thing about not having electricity is that then there is no television to tell us that we have electricity."[49]

People strongly affected by the outages could not afford such irony, however. Among these were people charged with the care of young children, two of whom are quoted in a survey in the daily paper *Borba* on their situation:

46. Nikola Burzan, "Rasplet zapleta ili zaplet raspleta," *Nedeljna borba*, 24–25 December 1994.

47. Petar Luković, "Srbija unplugged," *Vreme*, no. 216, 12 December 1994, pp. 8–9.

48. D. V., "Mračna krčma," *Borba*, 7 December 1994, p. 22.

49. Gordana Čomić, quoted in Ž. S., "Mrak na prepad," *Borba*, 10 November 1994, p. 20.

My son and daughter-in-law move every day from their apartment to mine and back to be able to offer their eight-month old baby the most basic comfort, bathing, and warm food. Who will pay us for the broken household appliances which are breaking down more quickly because of these unreasonable outages? I know the answer—nobody.

I am simply afraid of what will happen in two or three months when my child is born. I cannot imagine how I will bathe my baby in a cold apartment, how I will feed it and all the rest. This is a return to the Middle Ages, and not a step on the way to the third millennium as the calendar says.[50]

Other responses to the electric outages could be less passive. The Council of Independent Trade Unions (*Veće samostalnih sindikata*) of Novi Sad warned that outages had "gone beyond the limit," that "the patience of citizens is at an end," and that it could not prevent "social unrest of wide proportions."[51] A spokesman for a medical workers' union had a more novel proposal: "The workers at 'Elektroprivreda Srbije' should be offered reciprocal medical services as long as they turn off our electric power. They should be given only necessary urgent care. No electricity—no medical care."[52] Neither "social unrest" nor medical workers' strikes materialized, however, as outages continued to weaken the everyday social position of ordinary people.

Electric outages did provide rhetorical ammunition for oppositional groups, as the everyday inconvenience experienced by most people came to be expanded into a general metaphor of "darkness." Depending on the orientation of the critic, this "darkness" implied the efforts of the regime to silence independent media outlets (informative darkness), official corruption and the continuing war in Bosnia-Hercegovina (moral darkness), the replacement of urban culture with neofolk "kitsch" (cultural darkness), or the irresponsibility of regime agencies epitomized by "Elektrodistribucija" (literally keeping people in the dark). The uncertain supply of electric power can be seen as having functioned in two ways. On the

50. Quoted in N. J., "Povratak u srednji vek," *Borba*, 19 December 1994, p. 22.
51. Unsigned (attributed to Tanjug), "Prete 'socijalni nemiri širih razmera,'" *Borba*, 20 December 1994, p. 24.
52. Dragan Arsić, quoted in M. Milišić, "Koliko struje, toliko lečenja," *Borba*, 20 December 1994, p. 24.

one hand, as a practical matter, the situation constituted one more means by which the everyday lives of individuals were made more precarious and everyday activities made more time consuming, thereby freeing the hands of the regime in the public sphere as private needs consumed more of the attention of most individuals. On the other hand, the arbitrary and unpredictable nature of the outages, and the inconveniences they caused, seemed to offer a mnemonic by which people could understand under what sort of regime they lived and associate their everyday experience with other events.

Help from Outside: How Sanctions Help Authoritarian Power

As economic and other crises continued, the regime adopted the official position that the "unfair and undeserved" sanctions imposed against SRJ by the United Nations were at the root of the troubles citizens faced. There can be no doubt that the loss of access to international markets and international assets worked some damage to the economy in Serbia and Montenegro, although the question of how much damage these losses inflicted remains unresolved.[53] The official thesis that all the economic troubles faced by SRJ resulted from sanctions, however, was implausible. In the first place, the primary markets for most goods produced in SRJ were in other republics that had once been part of SFRJ, and the hostile relations between these republics and SRJ probably assured that these markets would have been lost with or without sanctions. Second, the economy had been in poor condition and in need of major reform before sanctions took effect. War and the refusal of the regime to consider economic reform had predictable consequences, which may have been enhanced but were certainly not caused by sanctions.

The consequences of sanctions had dimensions not directly related to the general performance of the economy, however. These consequences may well have mattered more to the regime than the more directly economic ones, especially as the preceding analysis has indicated that the economic well-being of citizens was not foremost in the mind of regime leaders. Slobodan Milošević could preside undisturbed over the impover-

53. Various estimates of the losses to SRJ as a result of sanctions are discussed by Dimitrije Boarov, "Tek ćemo izgubiti 100 milijardi dolara," *Vreme*, no. 241, 5 June 1995, p. 19.

ishment of the population of Serbia, while he enjoyed several opportunities offered by sanctions for the consolidation and continuation of his rule. These opportunities worked on the levels of ideology, communication, and everyday life.

On the ideological level, sanctions permitted the regime to encourage the homogenization of public opinion, drawing on the feeling of national pride and spite shared both by supporters and opponents of the regime. The perception that "the world" had turned against Serbia offered space for regime-controlled media to attack the set of institutions they liked to refer to as "the so-called international community."[54] Resentment of sanctions was general, even among people who regarded the regime as responsible for their introduction. The perception was also widely articulated that sanctions embodied a one-sided perception of the war in Bosnia-Hercegovina, a perspective also promoted in regime-controlled media.[55]

Beyond these general perceptions, sanctions permitted regime-controlled media to attribute all the difficulties people experienced to external sources. This principle applied to psychological as well as economic difficulties. In an essay in *Večernje novosti*, ostensibly a review of translations of American "pop psychology" books, all the difficulties and sadness of everyday life are associated with a single cause:

Our people, in spite of their lack of money, more and more often buy books on applied psychology, expecting that these books will show them the path to a happier life. However, in these books there is no solution for sanctions, which affect us all, nor for lack of money, milk shortages, lost savings, or electric outages. . . .
Ailing Americans have the means to treat themselves, while people

54. This was not, however, the sentiment expressed on one banner carried by a participant in the student protests in Belgrade in 1992. The banner read "The world is not anti-Serbian, Sloba is anti-world" (*Svet nije antisrpski, Sloba je antisvetski*).

55. RTS produced few full-length dramatic films during the period of research. It did produce one film, *Dnevnik uvrede '93* (Diary of an insult '93), which purports to chronicle the experiences of a retired couple in the period of hyperinflation. In one scene, a domestic quarrel reaches its denouement with the (pro-regime) husband telling his wife, "You are worse than Clinton, Kohl, and the European Union!" Presumably, the audience was expected to regard the outburst as a justifiable expression of wounded national masculine pride, although in the theater where I saw the film people responded with laughter.

here, handicapped by the "care" of the international community and by sanctions, are deprived of that ability![56]

As long as all difficulties, from economic troubles to psychological depression, could be attributed to "the international community," the regime was rhetorically relieved of all responsibility.

Sanctions also provided means by which perceptions of the regime could be manipulated. In October 1994, in recognition of the Serbian regime's ostensible break in relations with the Bosnian Serb entity, the United Nations Security Council voted a limited suspension of sanctions on travel, sports, and culture for one hundred days. The official ecstasy that greeted this move was accompanied by assertions that "the world is ever more openly recognizing that we were in the right,"[57] and Slobodan Milošević awarded himself a peace prize.[58] The atmosphere of self-congratulation that accompanied the Security Council vote offered the regime the opportunity to present the audiences of regime-controlled media with what appeared to be its first-ever success in international policy, an opportunity it took with enthusiasm.[59]

On the level of communication, sanctions isolated those individuals who were interested in receiving information from and sharing information with others beyond the borders of SRJ. International media, contacts in other countries, and travel had long been primary sources of alternative ideas and independent information and an option that had distinguished SFRJ from other Communist countries from the time it made passports available to citizens in 1965. The evaporation of these channels of communication had two important consequences: The regime was able to control the information available to citizens more easily, and the regime was particularly able to control information about other former

56. Dragana Savić, "Šta poručuju sve popularnije knjige iz primljene psihologije: Udri brigu na veselje," *Večernje novosti*, 6 February 1995, p. 13.

57. Slobodan Jovanović, quoted in Unsigned, "Prvi i najtiražniji," *Večernje novosti*, 16 October 1994, p. 5.

58. D. Stojić, "Povelja mira Slobodanu Miloševiću," *Večernje novosti*, 8 October 1994, p. 4.

59. More nationalist regime clients did not share in the official enthusiasm, however. Biljana Plavšić's comment on the reopening of the Belgrade airport reflected an earlier (and later) official view of the international community: "The airport will only serve for planes to land, so that various groups for human rights and spies can come to Belgrade and send out information about violations of human rights." Quoted in *Vreme*, no. 210, 31 October 1994, p. 59.

Yugoslav republics, because the autonomous channels of communication that offered alternative information had effectively disappeared.[60]

Another variety of communication—trade—also changed shape as a result of sanctions. With most imports and exports legally precluded, smuggling became big business. The dimensions of smuggling of certain high-demand items, especially motor fuel and cigarettes, required the knowledge and cooperation of both the customs service and the police, who undoubtedly received some consideration in return. Two consequences arose from this situation. On the one hand, a new criminal class quickly achieved tremendous wealth, earned in a manner that assured their dependence on agencies of the regime. In some areas of international trade, this new criminal class came to supplant legitimate export-import companies, which were legally precluded from doing business. On the other hand, people became dependent on the activities of this new criminal class to the extent that they purchased goods that were available only from other countries. In this way, any person became complicit with the regime and the new class of smugglers any time he or she did something as ordinary as purchasing gasoline; many became complicit as they sought employment with smugglers who constituted the most active businesses in the country.

Finally, in the sphere of everyday life, sanctions tightened the control of the regime over the range of options people had available to meet their daily needs. Particularly in the area of work and business, several developments strengthened the dominance of state-owned corporations over the opportunities people had available: Independent businesses that relied on international clients or international trade had their avenues effectively cut off; in effect, state-owned companies and smugglers shared a monopoly over these fields; international sources of capital and technical assistance were unavailable to people hoping to start independent businesses, leaving potential startups with the option of seeking independent domestic capital (which was scant) or capital from the regime (which threatened their autonomy); and people who had worked in local offices of international companies before the sanctions took effect found them-

60. Fortunately, some exceptions to this rule existed. The "Zamir" computer network provided e-mail links between antiwar groups in Belgrade, Zagreb, Sarajevo, and Priština through a computer in Austria, which the local antiwar organizations dialed by modem to send and receive messages. And at least in Belgrade, some smuggled Croatian publications (*Arkzin, Globus, Feral Tribune, Start*) were available from courageous street vendors, albeit irregularly and at high prices.

selves without work, as the companies that employed them were severely restricted in the activities they could carry out. Taken together, these factors meant that the autonomous private sector of business and employment developing over the previous decade was severely reduced in size, as the autonomy of the people who participated in this sector was also reduced. As alternatives outside the geographic boundaries of the country and the economic boundaries of the state diminished, the degree of control enjoyed by the regime intensified.

Beyond this, to the degree that sanctions made a contribution to the impoverishment of people in SRJ independent of the contribution made by the regime and the war, they deepened the psychological and material effects of the general economic situation, which are discussed in the previous sections of this chapter. As an added dimension, sanctions contributed the factor of isolation. In this regard especially, sanctions can be considered to have had a greater "punishing" effect on people who relied on and valued connections with the outside world than on regime supporters who resented the "interference" of international factors or on nationally minded people who believed that Serbia could get along nicely without the cultural, political, or economic contributions of other countries. For all these reasons, the symbolic efforts of international actors to punish the Serbian regime with sanctions succeeded only in offering the regime a wider variety of means to consolidate and continue its power. At the same time, these efforts diminished the space in which people could develop social positions autonomous from the regime and cut off a variety of autonomous sources of information and exchange.

Economic and other material difficulties bring the story of the destruction of alternatives in Milošević's Serbia toward its end. In the previous chapters of this book, efforts to make alternatives unavailable in political institutions, cultural expression, and public information were detailed. The concern in this section is with some more fundamental details of everyday life. Whether the matter at hand is the price of basic goods, the value of currency, the adequacy of salaries to cover basic needs, or the supply of electric energy, the basic subject touched by all these themes remains the same—the possibilities available to people to carry out elementary everyday activities related to survival and, consequently, the degree of independence and autonomy individuals have available to them in everyday life. In Serbia, a variety of obstacles assured that carrying out such everyday activities was difficult and that the degree of autonomy enjoyed by individuals was hence extremely restricted.

The point has already been made in the preceding discussion that the assortment of difficulties and obstacles that individuals faced placed both material and psychological barriers between them and the public sphere. The various categories of activity that were made more difficult—from work to trade and from the security that money will have some exchange value to the assurance that homes will be heated and lit—all bear on the sense that a person lives under conditions that can be described as "normal" and in the context of which choices can be made and activities carried out.

The cumulative effect of instability, impoverishment, and restriction was that "normality" became a scarce commodity. Deprived of this fundamental backdrop for social activity, autonomous means of social exchange, both economic and interpersonal, broke down. It is in this regard that the group of sociologists directed by Mladen Lazić came to speak of the effect of a series of catastrophic events as "the destruction of society."[61] Similarly, Silvano Bolčić described the breakdown of a variety of ordinary means of social activity in Serbia as a process of "decivilization."[62] Whether one accepts these apocalyptic definitions of the situation or not, in the period in which economic crisis and international isolation reigned in Serbia, the dependence of most people on the regime was deepened, the space available to people for autonomous action and decision was restricted, and the social consequences of these facts were profound.

Did the constellation of factors limiting the social autonomy of citizens help the regime? In the short run, the question has to be answered affirmatively. The parents who spent all day trying to purchase food for their children or the pensioners who moved from neighborhood to neighborhood in the course of a day hoping to find a heated space were certainly thinking about their own needs and difficulties. They were not thinking about whether they approved of the wars carried out in their name in neighboring republics or about the monopoly of administrative and corporate positions by a single political party. Nor were they, if their interest was strongly dominated by the pursuit of basic necessities, likely

61. Lazić, Mrkšić, Vujović, Kuzmanović, Gredelj, Cvejić, and Vuletić (1994).
62. Silvano Bolčić, "O 'svakodnevnici' razorenog društva Srbije početkom devedesetih iz sociološke perspektive," in Prošić-Dvornić (1994), 139–45.

to pursue or exchange information about such questions as they might under more "normal" conditions.

Whether such material restrictions on everyday activities can sustain the free hand of the regime in the long run, however, remains an open question. Unlike the fields of everyday life discussed in other chapters of this study, the areas discussed here affect everybody, including people who have no interest in political parties, musical culture, or information media. The general impoverishment experienced by people in Serbia has had a unique impact on them, because the majority of people who have become poor in the last several years were not poor previously. In that sense, the degree of dissatisfaction and outrage people may express could be greater. To some extent, that potential may have been blunted through 1995, when the regime had war and sanctions as an all-purpose explanation for the difficulties citizens faced. Since then, a peace agreement has been signed and sanctions have been suspended. The economic situation has not changed, but when people begin to take an active interest in the factors that caused it and the parties that benefit from it, the political situation might change.

6

Conclusion: Destroying and Maintaining Alternatives

> I don't have much faith in political action. . . . The people who got into politics were mostly those who could not accomplish anything anywhere else. Even back in grade school I was able to observe those few and mostly unfortunate people who went into politics with the hope that maybe there, by means of power over others, they could feed their egos and their pockets. In my basic system telling stories was always more important and more powerful, if you like a more subversive act than any kind of straight political action. I have always believed that life itself can best break open the rigidity and stupidity of the system.[1]

This study promised to answer the question, "How does the Serbian regime survive?" with several variations on the answer "By making alternatives to its rule unavailable." In different fields of everyday life, it succeeded to a different degree. Although the cumulative result of the destruction of alternatives has been to preserve the regime in power, the variation in outcomes in different fields makes it possible to theoretically engage the material that has been presented in the previous chapters. This final chapter, then, attempts to assess the destruction of alternatives as a political and social phenomenon, to present some ideas about the conditions on which the destruction and preservation of alternatives rely, and finally to emphasize the conditions that need to exist for the destruction of alternatives to be overcome.

1. Rajko Grlić, in Milivoj Đilas, "U Hrvatskoj je nesreća na vlast" (interview), *Feral Tribune*, 22 June 1998, p. 48.

One of the best-known definitions of sociology was put forward by C. Wright Mills, who defined it as the field that investigates "the interplay of man [*sic*] and society, of biography and history, of self and world."[2] The interplay, clearly, does not have in every instance the same degree of reciprocity or intensity. The destruction of alternatives in Serbia involved, in each of the cases explored in this study, some form of engagement of the state against society. It is hardly surprising to note, then, that this engagement succeeded best in those fields of everyday life that are most amenable to manipulation and control on the part of the state and most susceptible to state intervention. By using its complete control of the electoral and legislative process, aided by near-complete control of information media and a good deal of luck in the ineptitude of its opponents, the regime did succeed in preventing the emergence of a credible democratic political opposition. By manipulating the value and supply of currency, the regime did succeed in financing itself through the savings of its citizens and in engineering a transfer of financial power away from the centers of potential opposition. The regime did not generally succeed in preventing people who wanted to be informed from being informed, and its efforts to intervene in the musical tastes of its citizens left it discredited and embarrassed.

All these observations may seem obvious and a bit trivial: of course the interventions of the regime succeed best in areas in which states are expected to act and have experience acting; of course people maintain control over areas of their private lives, which states have little capacity to alter. Examined another way, however, these observations suggest that exactly in those areas of private life, the areas of their lives in which people are engaged every day, resides a power that, at least potentially, allows people to resist what appears to be a strong and controlling political establishment. Cultural attachments and dispositions can and do survive without regard for political pressures and can and do (sometimes) work against these political pressures.

There are two potential ways of interpreting this observation. On the one hand, it is possible to conclude, as many in Serbia have, that the only consistent and credible sources of resistance to the regime are underground musicians and independent journalists. From there it is not a big step to decide that there exists no opposition with the potential to funda-

2. C. Wright Mills, *The Sociological Imagination* (New York: Oxford University Press, 1959), 4.

mentally alter living conditions at all. Such a conclusion is tempting, in that it is apparently consistent with events as they have developed and is also consistent with the depressing fatalism bound to emerge from any sustained consideration of contemporary Serbia. However, it is a poor analysis that takes conditions as they are and endeavors to interpret them as permanent.

I therefore propose to offer an alternative interpretation. This alternative involves comparing the fields of the destruction of alternatives examined in this book to develop a general theory of social resistance. The theory developed out of this effort should offer a sense of what potential exists for a powerful resistance to develop in Serbia and a more general sense of where to look for sources of ground-level social power in other nationalist-authoritarian environments. These environments are not so unique or isolated that they are not comparable to contemporary liberal democracies; a sociological tradition also exists in liberal states, which emphasizes the "controlled consumption"[3] and "repressive tolerance"[4] of these environments, and which locates their alternatives in the spaces of everyday culture.[5] Contemporary nationalist authoritarianism is, however, distinct in the sense that the states in which it emerges have well-developed cultural conflicts whereas the institutions through which these conflicts might find expression are weak. Any analysis of change in such societies, then, has to involve culture to a greater degree, and formal politics to a lesser degree, than comparable analyses of liberal states.

What Succeeds and What Does Not

All the republics of the former Yugoslavia already had cosmopolitan artists and audiences, independent journalists, antinationalists, and antiwar actors. To some degree, it could even be argued that such groups had been encouraged and cultivated by the old Communist regime during its relatively liberal period, although even if this is not necessarily the case they were tolerated to a greater degree than they came to be with the rise

3. Henri Lefebvre, *Everyday Life in the Modern World* (New York: Harper and Row, 1971).
4. Herbert Marcuse, *One-Dimensional Man: Studies in the Ideology of Advanced Industrial Society* (Boston: Beacon Press, 1964).
5. Michel de Certeau, *The Practice of Everyday Life* (Berkeley and Los Angeles: University of California Press, 1984).

of nationalist authoritarianism. When the social atmosphere that nurtured these groups faded and their social base became smaller, their survival and continued activity became more difficult, but not impossible.

On the other hand, none of the republics of the former Yugoslavia had any developed tradition of organized political opposition or peaceful competition between parliamentary parties offering a diversity of ideological and programmatic choices. A liberal parliamentary system can be said to have been developing in Serbia during the period between its independence in 1878 and the beginning of World War I, but the traces of this were largely erased in the post–World War I royal dictatorship and the post–World War II Communist monopoly of power. In the case of political opposition, then, the regime had a relatively easy task: rather than working to diminish an existing social force, it worked to prevent a new social force from emerging.

Various forms of cultural resistance had an ongoing tradition and a social base. Democratic politics certainly had a potential social base, but it was unorganized and its consolidation was systematically undermined. The regime found it easier to keep away something that was not there than to destroy something that was, and the antiregime groups in society found it less difficult to maintain a movement that already existed than to create a new one.

In addition, the regime was able to act on the political legacy of the Communist political monopoly that preceded it. Under the Communist regime, people had become accustomed both to the absence of an institutional opposition and to the intervention of the state in a variety of areas, such as economic management, business administration, and employment, which directly affected the livelihood of citizens. By contrast to other Communist regimes, however, the relatively liberal Yugoslav regime did not develop a habit of repressive intervention into the area of culture. The interventions of the SPS regime, both in promoting new "nationally appropriate" cultural forms and in hindering the diffusion of other forms, appeared as something unprecedented and inconsistent with recent Serbian political tradition—this political tradition was authoritarian, but under Tito's successors, at least, it was weakly authoritarian. To many who had learned to live with the system, political authoritarianism may well have become tolerable, but these same people might not be so easily persuaded to tolerate the move to cultural authoritarianism.

War, international isolation, and economic crisis combined to undermine the social base even of such resistant groups that had some tradition and established existence. In the period since Milošević established his regime, the population of Serbia has changed. It has changed in numbers: a good portion of the young, urban, and educated population has made its way to other countries, and an influx of rural refugees from Croatia and Bosnia-Hercegovina has made its way to Serbia. It has changed in character: The economic autonomy of the middle classes has eroded. The SPS regime has left Serbia older, more rural, less educated, and poorer, and consequently less open to cultural and political activity that might open up democratic possibilities. At the same time, the involvement of the regime, directly and through its surrogates, in the wars in Croatia and Bosnia-Hercegovina has created an international image of Serbia associated with aggression and war crimes. This image is not likely to change quickly and is bound to hinder the development of international contact and cooperation that could encourage democratic development.

Demographic Correlates of Nationalist Authoritarianism

In politics and in culture, in economics and in attitudes, the destruction of alternatives also concerns the distribution of benefits to the groups that acquiesce in the continuation of the regime and the isolation and frustration of the groups that do not. In most cases, there is a kind of homology across the different fields of the destruction of alternatives. The electoral base of SPS is principally older, nonurban, and less educated; these groups are also least likely to feel aggrieved by the demolition of urban and cosmopolitan culture, least likely to be affected by the disappearance of professional and educational opportunities, and least likely to have lost hard-currency savings in the hyperinflationary panic to acquire food and other basic necessities.

Are they, however, the groups most likely to be persuaded and mobilized by nationalist rhetorics? Here the evidence, both from Serbia and elsewhere, is not entirely clear. Certainly in the early period of nationalist mobilization in Serbia and in the returns of the first elections, a pattern seems apparent: The more developed northern part of the country and the urban centers offered the least support to the regime in elections and the least support to its projects in responding to military mobilization. It would be easy to use such evidence to draw conclusions about urban and mixed populations as a "progressive class" and to argue for the backwardness and gullibility of the rest.

Such an argument would not be without resonance—it stands at the center of much contemporary liberal political thought—and it would not be without provenance—Marx's description of the progressive character of the bourgeois revolution remains one of the more memorable and influential passages of his *Communist Manifesto*. Marx developed the argument to predict the origin of the next revolution, and as Theda Skocpol established, was (along with most theorists of revolution) demonstrably wrong in his prediction and in his identification of the locus of revolutionary change.[6] The point here is not to turn the tables or to make the case for the existence of a new or different "progressive" or "revolutionary" class. Revolutionary change is hardly the goal of most ordinary people in Serbia, who have likely experienced enough of the effort to create revolutions in their lifetimes. Rather, social categories are not absolutely constitutive of political orientations—except as they reflect actual conditions. We can discuss the demographic bases of support for the regime, but we cannot establish that the groups that make up these bases will inevitably support this regime or similar ones.

Developments in the period since the research for this study was conducted offer some alternative suggestions, in fact. In local and municipal elections in 1996, SPS lost in every urban center in Serbia—not only in Belgrade and not only in the northern region, but in every urban center—a fact the regime was forced to recognize after eighty-eight days of continuous citizens' protests. Several changes grew out of the period of protests. Opposition-led city governments turned local television stations into the first nonregime television stations to be seen in the interior of the country; Belgrade's Radio B-92 teamed up with independent local stations across the country to form an independent radio network. Splits in the editorial staff of the regime-dominated newspapers *Blic* and *Večernje novosti* made those papers (*Novosti* for a short time, and the portion of the *Blic* staff that split off to publish *Demokratija*) a source of more diverse news distributed outside Belgrade. The elections and protests of 1996–97 not only brought oppositional governments to provincial cities, but also resulted in the availability of independent news outside Belgrade. Although the opposition coalition that won the 1996 elections quickly disintegrated, most obviously in the city of Belgrade, several of the

6. See her argument in the preface and introduction of Skocpol, *States and Social Revolutions: A Comparative Analysis of France, Russia, and China* (New York: Cambridge University Press, 1979).

provincial cities that had previously been thought to be Milošević strongholds have maintained their opposition coalitions in power.

Similarly, in 1997, a significant political challenge to the regime came from an unexpected source. A split in the SPS satellite party in Montenegro led to the apostasy of the prime minister, Milo Đukanović, who was elected to the presidency of Montenegro later the same year on a reform platform, in a coalition with several opposition parties. Whereas folk wisdom and legend have characterized Montenegro as the natural home of the most extreme Serbian nationalism, Đukanović's behavior in power has not been consistent with that stereotype. He has sought to resolve disputes and to open border traffic with neighboring Croatia, has included Albanian and Muslim ethnic parties in his coalition, and has actively opposed Milošević's military adventures in Kosovo.

None of the foregoing suggests that southern Serbia or Montenegro is naturally inclined (or becoming naturally inclined) to opposition, any more than urban intellectuals are naturally so inclined. The areas that handed SPS its biggest electoral defeats were once his strongest bases of support, and the urban population that provides a home to the rock and roll culture also provides a home to the nationalist intellectuals gathered around the Serbian Academy of Sciences and Arts and the Serbian Writers' Union. Civil society in the urban centers is not all sweetness and light, and provincial culture is not all nationalism and backwardness. The character these parts of the society display depends on the concrete possibilities available. Although the regime focused on the destruction of alternatives in the major cities, they seem to have re-emerged elsewhere.

Cultivating Alternatives

If the distinction between open and authoritarian perspectives is not strictly tied to where people live (although it is certainly related), what is at its core? Key to the distinction between those willing to live with the regime and those straining to live in spite of it is a difference in outlook—and differences in outlook are wide in contemporary Serbia. The 1996 and 1997 election protests indicate that something occurred in some places to shift the balance away from generally pro-regime outlooks and toward a greater openness. What was it?

The outlooks of individuals—like nationalism—are cultivated, not naturally or biologically determined. Events in contemporary Serbia suggest that they are not necessarily cultivated over a very long term and that they do not necessarily put down firm roots. Mobilization to establish the nationalist authoritarian regime succeeded most where alternative sources of information were unavailable. Nationalist authoritarian political parties succeeded best where political alternatives did not have a large public presence. The nationalist authoritarian intervention into music gained the greatest popularity where musical alternatives were not available. For the most part, these places were remote from the major urban centers. When that situation changed, other conditions changed along with them.

The presence of alternatives depends on two crucial factors: the degree of control exercised by the regime over various aspects of everyday life and the degree of people's access to environments beyond their immediate experience, whether this is defined as information about the local scene, information about political events, or a regional or international perspective.

It is even possible that alternatives expand and multiply more quickly than efforts at destruction can keep up with them. For the most part, it is safe to say that if people have alternatives available, they make use of them. However, it is safer to say this for some groups than for others and safer under some conditions than under others. What is crucial is that the basic tools—information, contact, autonomy—be available to people inclined to use them.

Conclusion: It Takes a Global Village

The destruction of alternatives is a struggle of the state against the society, in which the state seeks to assure that alternatives to its rule remain unavailable, while social actors try to keep channels of information, expression, and everyday activity open. The state is ahead in this struggle as long as the access of social actors to these goods is severely limited. This struggle, however, cannot be "won" by either side. Not even the most authoritarian state can achieve the level of control necessary to make everything unavailable. At the same time, inexhaustible abundance has never been available to anybody, and certainly never to the citizens of a poor and isolated state. The best that either side can hope for is for the balance of repression or openness to remain in its favor long enough to have a lasting influence. To date, despite the meaningful efforts of citizens, chronicled in this book, to maintain open avenues of contact, the regime has generally kept the upper hand. How can the balance be shifted in favor of citizens? How can the source material of alternatives be made available?

If one current has run through all the cases and arguments presented here, it is that the regime has worked in a variety of ways to close doors while at least some portion of the population has sustained an effort to keep them open. One of the key objects in this struggle is which side will control the understanding of what is implied by "openness." To the supporters of nationalist authoritarianism, openness is openness to domination and consequently betrayal of the nation. To its opponents, openness is cosmopolitanism, in the rooted sense: the belief that the people in a place are also part of a global culture and that the world belongs also to them (even if they are in internationally isolated Serbia). The conflict between the two perspectives was nicely summarized in a poster that appeared in the Belgrade student protest of 1992: *Svet nije antisrpski, Sloba je antisvetski* ("The world is not anti-Serbian, Sloba [Milošević] is anti-world").[7]

What does it mean to be "pro-world"? Regime-controlled media attempted to disqualify the massive protests of 1996–97 by showing pictures of participants in those protests carrying foreign, especially American and German, flags. The pictures were intended to demonstrate the regime's argument that the protests were engineered by, and served the interests of, states that it perceived as hostile to Serbia. If one were to take the image literally, it implied that some group of (certainly unrepresentative!) citizens had gone so far as to fly a "hostile" flag on the streets of the capital. In her magazine column, Mirjana Marković characterized the flags as fitting with other types of real and imaginary weapons: "In the hands of those disturbed, disinformed, uninformed, manipulated, unsatisfied, angry, curious people were put foreign flags, stones, bombs, and pots."[8]

The photos were not manufactured: those flags were in fact carried in

7. I am indebted to Mirjana Stevanović, in whose photos of the student protest I had the opportunity to read this and other slogans.
8. Quoted in *Odraz B-92*, 20 January 1997. There were no bombs used in the protests, contrary to Mirjana Marković's claim. The reference to pots is to a nightly action on the part of the protesters. Every evening at 7:30, when the principal daily news program was broadcast on the regime-controlled television station, protesters banged on pots and otherwise made noise to symbolically drown out the sound of the program.

the protests, but they were not the only flags protesters carried. In addition to flags with the emblems of various countries, protesters also carried flags with the emblems of, among others, the Ferrari automobile company, the Chicago Bulls basketball team, and Jack Daniels whiskey. The combination bespeaks a different understanding than the one presented by the regime-controlled media. The protesters seemed to suggest with their flags that the countries of the world, its entertainment spectacles, and commercial products, share a value—and that the places and pleasures of the world, the taste of its bourbon, and the strategies of Michael Jordan belong to them also. The flags represent not a declaration of (dis)-loyalty, but a demand for the right to be included in the world and in all the world has to offer. As the banner that went before the daily procession through the streets of Belgrade read, *"Beograd je svet!"* ("Belgrade is the world")—or at least demands to be able to see itself as part of it.

As the examples in this book have shown, this openness is difficult to maintain in an atmosphere of enforced separation and isolation. Efforts on the part of various international groups and individuals to show support and to maintain contact have helped in whatever small degree to support it. When access to public opinion in Serbia is limited, it makes a difference that the European Parliament and the Committee to Protect Journalists are interested in the regime's moves against independent media, that international scholars are interested in soliciting work and visits from domestic observers, that globally marketed musicians are interested in performing in the country. Politically, all these things mean that the regime's control over everyday life is not absolute. Psychologically, they mean that the citizens under the rule of regime are not, after all, alone in the world. Small gestures from outside can potentially have important consequences.

Contact, support, and exchange of information have to be maintained and expanded. Nationalist authoritarianism came to power easily, in a climate of fear, uncertainty, and isolation. The rhetoric and activity of nationalist authoritarianism sought to make orientalist stereotypes into self-fulfilling prophecy. So far, the prophecy has neither been fully realized nor fully negated. It can be realized only if the regime is able to remain in power. The regime can remain in power only as long as it can maintain the uncertain climate of impossibility, isolation, and inevitability. The global capacity to share culture, share ideas, and share information can accomplish a lot to make that climate difficult to maintain, and it can accomplish a lot to make it difficult to create again.

Bibliography

Daily, Weekly, and Monthly Periodicals

Arkzin
Borba
Duga
Feral Tribune
Naša borba
NIN
Odraz B-92 vesti
Politika
Republika
Ritam
Talas
Telegraf
Ukus nestašnih
Večernje novosti
Vreme
Vreme novca
Vreme zabave
YU rock magazin

Books and Research Articles

Adorno, Theodor W. 1981. *Prisms*. Cambridge, Mass.: MIT Press.
Adorno, Theodor W., Else Frenkel-Brunswik, Daniel J. Levinson, and R. Nevitt Sanford. 1982. *The Authoritarian Personality*. New York: Norton.
Albahari, David, ed. 1983. *Drugom stranom: Almanah novog talasa u SFRJ*. Belgrade: Istraživačko-izdavački centar SSO Srbije.
Allport, Gordon. 1954. *The Nature of Prejudice*. New York: Addison-Wesley.
Anderson, Benedict. 1991. *Imagined Communities: Reflections on the Origin and Spread of Nationalism*. 2d ed. New York: Verso.
Ang, Ien. 1985. *Watching Dallas: Soap Opera and the Melodramatic Imagination*. London: Methuen.
Ash, Timothy Garton. 1990. *The Uses of Adversity: Essays on the Fate of Central Europe*. New York: Vintage.
Atkinson, Paul. 1990. *The Ethnographic Imagination: Textual Constructions of Reality*. New York: Routledge.
Babic, Branislav. 1992. *Ko je taj čovek!* NIS: Sorabla Disk.

————. 1994. *Reci pravo*. Novi Sad: Prometej.

Banac, Ivo. 1984. *The National Question in Yugoslavia: Origins, History, Politics.* Ithaca: Cornell University Press.

Banac, Ivo, ed. 1992. *Eastern Europe in Revolution.* Ithaca: Cornell University Press.

Barton, Allen H., Bogdan Denitch, and Charles Kadushin, eds. 1973. *Opinion-Making Elites in Yugoslavia.* New York: Praeger.

Becker, Howard S. 1963. *Outsiders: Studies in the Sociology of Deviance.* New York: Free Press.

Berelson, Bernard. 1949. "What Missing the Newspaper Means." In Paul Lazarsfeld and Frank Stanton, eds., *Communication Research 1948–9* (New York: Duell, Sloan and Pierce).

Biro, Mikloš. 1994. *Psihologija postkomunizma.* Belgrade: Beogradski krug.

Biserko, Sonja, ed. 1993. *Yugoslavia: Collapse, War, Crimes.* Belgrade: Center for Antiwar Action and Belgrade Circle.

Bloch, Ernst. 1988. *The Utopian Function of Art and Literature: Selected Essays.* Trans. Jack Zipes and Frank Mecklenburg. Cambridge, Mass.: MIT Press.

Blumer, Herbert. 1969. *Symbolic Interactionism: Perspective and Method.* Berkeley and Los Angeles: University of California Press.

Bogdanović, Bogdan. 1994. *Grad i smrt.* Belgrade: Beogradski krug.

Bolčić, Silvano. 1994. "O 'svakodnevnici' razorenog društva Srbije početkom devedesetih iz sociološke perspektive." In Mirjana Prošić-Dvornić, ed., *Kulture u tranziciji* (Belgrade: Plato).

Bombelles, Joseph T. 1991. "Federal Aid to the Less Developed Areas of Yugoslavia." *East European Politics and Societies* 5 (Fall), 439–65.

Bookman, Milica Žarković. 1994. *Economic Decline and Nationalism in the Balkans.* New York: St. Martin's Press.

Bourdieu, Pierre. 1984. *Distinction: A Social Critique of the Judgment of Taste.* Cambridge, Mass.: Harvard University Press.

Bourgois, Philippe. 1996. *In Search of Respect: Selling Crack in El Barrio.* New York: Cambridge University Press.

Brajović, Nino, ed. 1994. *Mala lokalna televizija.* Special edition of *Novinarstvo*, nos. 2–3.

Breslauer, George W., ed. 1991. *Dilemmas of Transition in the Soviet Union and Eastern Europe.* Berkeley: Center for Slavic and East European Studies.

Breuilly, John. 1993. *Nationalism and the State.* 2d ed. Chicago: University of Chicago Press.

Bryant, Jennings, and Dolf Zillman, eds. 1994. *Media Effects: Advances in Theory and Research.* Hillsdale, N.J.: Lawrence Erlbaum Associates.

Brzezinski, Zbigniew. 1967. *The Soviet Bloc: Unity and Conflict.* Cambridge, Mass.: Harvard University Press.

Carey, James W. 1989. *Communication as Culture: Essays on Media and Society.* Boston: Unwin Hyman.

Carsten, F. L. 1967. *The Rise of Fascism.* Berkeley and Los Angeles: University of California Press.

Centre for Contemporary Cultural Studies. 1978. *On Ideology.* Birmingham, England: Centre for Contemporary Cultural Studies.

Chambers, Iain. 1985. *Urban Rhythms: Pop Music and Popular Culture.* New York: St. Martin's Press.

———. 1986. *Popular Culture: The Metropolitan Experience.* New York: Routledge.

Cohen, Lenard. 1978. "Devolutionary Socialism: The Political Institutionalization of the Yugoslav Assembly System, 1963–1973." Ph.D. dissertation, Columbia University.

———. 1989. *The Socialist Pyramid: Elites and Power in Yugoslavia.* Oakville, Ontario: Mosaic Press.

———. 1995. *Broken Bonds: Yugoslavia's Disintegration and Balkan Politics in Transition.* 2d ed. San Francisco: Westview Press.

Čolović, Ivan. 1985. *Divlja književnost.* Belgrade: Nolit.

———. 1994a. *Bordel ratnika.* Belgrade: XX Vek.

———. 1994b. *Pucanje od zdravlja.* Belgrade: Beogradski krug.

———. 1995. "Fudbal, huligani, i rat," *Republika* (1–15 June).

Čolović, Ivan, and Aljoša Mimica, eds. 1992. *Druga Srbija.* Belgrade: Plato, Beogradski krug i Borba.

Curran, James, Michael Gurevitch, and Janet Woollacott, eds. 1979. *Mass Communication and Society.* Beverly Hills: Sage.

Cushman, Thomas. 1995. *Notes from Underground: Rock Music Counterculture in Russia.* Albany: SUNY Press.

David, Filip. 1994. *Fragmenti iz mračnih vremena.* Belgrade: Beogradski krug.

de Certeau, Michel. 1984. *The Practice of Everyday Life.* Berkeley and Los Angeles: University of California Press.

Denitch, Bogdan. 1994. *Ethnic Nationalism: The Tragic Death of Yugoslavia.* Minneapolis: University of Minnesota Press.

Dinkić, Mlađan. 1995. *Ekonomija destrukcije.* Belgrade: VIN.

Dragićević-Šešić, Milena. 1994. *Neofolk kultura: Publika i njene zvezde.* Novi Sad: Biblioteka clementi.

Đukić, Petar. 1995. *Iskušenja ekonomske politike: Hronologija života pod sankcijama.* Belgrade: Grmeč A.D.-Privredni pregled.

Džuverović, Borisav, Srećko Mihailović, and Slobodan Vuković. 1994. *Izborna upotreba medija.* Belgrade: Institut društvenih nauka.

Fischer, Claude S. 1976. *The Urban Experience.* New York: Harcourt Brace Jovanovich.

———. 1982. *To Dwell Among Friends: Personal Networks in Town and City.* Chicago: University of Chicago Press.

Fiske, John. 1987. *Television Culture.* New York: Routledge.

Frei, Norbert. 1993. *National Socialist Rule in Germany: The Führer State, 1933–1945.* London: Blackwell.

Frith, Simon. 1983. *Sound Effects: Youth, Leisure, and the Politics of Rock 'n Roll.* London: Constable.

———. 1988. *Music for Pleasure: Essays in the Sociology of Pop.* New York: Routledge.

Frith, Simon, ed. 1988. *Facing the Music.* New York: Pantheon.

Frith, Simon, and John Street. 1992. "Rock Against Racism and Red Wedge: From Music to Politics, From Politics to Music." In Reebee Garofalo, ed., *Rockin' the Boat: Mass Music and Mass Movements* (Boston: South End Press).

Frith, Simon, and Andrew Goodwin, eds. 1990. *On Record: Rock, Pop, and the Written Word*. New York: Pantheon.

Gans, Herbert J. 1962. *The Urban Villagers: Group and Class in the Life of Italian-Americans*. New York: Free Press.

———. 1974. *Popular Culture and High Culture: An Analysis and Evaluation of Taste*. New York: Basic Books.

Garofalo, Reebee, ed. 1992. *Rockin' the Boat: Mass Music and Mass Movements*. Boston: South End Press.

Gati, Charles. 1990. *The Bloc That Failed: Soviet-East European Relations in Transition*. Bloomington: Indiana University Press.

Gellner, Ernest. 1983. *Nations and Nationalism*. Ithaca: Cornell University Press.

Gerbner, George, Larry Gross, Michael Morgan, and Nancy Signorielli. "Growing Up with Television: The Cultivation Perspective." In Jennings Bryant and Dolf Zillman, eds., *Media Effects: Advances in Theory and Research* (Hillsdale, N.J.: Lawrence Erlbaum Associates).

Gitlin, Todd. 1980. *The Whole World Is Watching: Mass Media in the Making and Unmaking of the New Left*. Berkeley and Los Angeles: University of California Press.

———. 1990. "Who Communicates What to Whom, In What Voice, and Why, About the Study of Mass Communications." *Critical Studies in Mass Communications* 7 (June).

Glenny, Misha. 1993. *The Fall of Yugoslavia: The Third Balkan War*. New York: Penguin Books.

Goati, Vladimir. 1992. "Višepartijski mozaik Srbije." In Miroslav Pečuljić, Vladimir Milić, Vladimir Goati, Srbobran Branković, and Miladin Kovačević, *Rađanje javnog mnjenja i političkih stranaka* (Belgrade: Centar za javno mnjenje i marketing "Medium").

Goati, Vladimir, Zoran Slavujević, and Ognjen Pribićević. 1993. *Izborne borbe u Jugoslaviji, 1990–1992*. Belgrade: Radnička štampa.

Goffman, Erving. 1961. *Asylums: Essays on the Social Situation of Mental Patients and Other Inmates*. New York: Anchor Books.

Goldfarb, Jeffrey. 1978. "Social Bases of Independent Public Expression in Communist Societies." *American Journal of Sociology* 4.

Golubović, Zagorka. 1988. *Kriza identiteta savremenog jugoslovenskog društva*. Belgrade: Filip Višnjić.

Gould, Julius, and William Kolb, eds. 1964. *A Dictionary of the Social Sciences*. New York: Free Press.

Grossberg, Lawrence, Cary Nelson, and Paula Treichler, eds. 1992. *Cultural Studies*. New York: Routledge.

Hall, Stuart, Chas Critcher, Tony Jefferson, John Clarke, and Brian Roberts. 1978. *Policing the Crisis: Mugging, The State, and Law and Order*. London: Macmillan.

Hall, Stuart, David Held, Don Hubert, and Kenneth Thompson. 1996. *Modernity: An Introduction to Modern Societies*. Oxford: Blackwell.

Hall, Stuart, and Tony Jefferson, eds. 1976. *Resistance Through Rituals: Youth Subcultures in Postwar Britain*. Birmingham, England: Centre for Contemporary Cultural Studies.

Haraszti, Miklós. 1987. *The Velvet Prison: Artists Under State Socialism.* New York: Farrar, Straus and Giroux.

Hebdige, Dick. 1979. *Subculture: The Meaning of Style.* London: Methuen.

Heller, Agnes. 1993. *A Philosophy of History in Fragments.* Oxford: Blackwell.

Henry, Tricia. 1989. *Break All Rules! Punk Rock and the Making of a Style.* Ann Arbor: UMI Research Press.

Hobsbawm, E. J. 1990. *Nations and Nationalism Since 1780: Programme, Myth, Reality.* Cambridge: Cambridge University Press.

Hobsbawm, E. J., and Terence Ranger, eds. 1983. *The Invention of Tradition.* Cambridge: Cambridge University Press.

Hoggart, Richard. 1957. *The Uses of Literacy.* London: Chatto and Windus.

Horkheimer, Max. 1974a. *Critique of Instrumental Reason.* New York: Seabury.

———. 1974b. *Eclipse of Reason.* New York: Seabury.

———. 1982. *Critical Theory: Selected Essays.* New York: Continuum.

Horkheimer, Max , and Theodor W. Adorno. 1972. *Dialectic of Enlightenment.* New York: Continuum.

Ignatieff, Michael. 1993. *Blood and Belonging: Journeys into the New Nationalism.* New York: Farrar, Straus and Giroux.

Inkeles, Alex, and David H. Smith. 1974. *Becoming Modern: Individual Change in Six Developing Countries.* Cambridge, Mass.: Harvard University Press.

Iyengar, Shanto. 1991. *Is Anyone Responsible? How Television Frames Political Issues.* Chicago: University of Chicago Press.

Iyengar, Shanto, and Donald R. Kinder. 1987. *News That Matters: Television and American Opinion.* Chicago: University of Chicago Press.

Janjatović, Petar, ed. 1994. *Pesme bratstva i detinstva: Antologija rok poezije SFR Jugoslavije, 1967–1991.* Belgrade: Nova.

Jelavich, Barbara. 1983. *History of the Balkans.* New York: Cambridge University Press.

Joksimović, Snežana, Ratka Marić, Anđelka Milić, Dragan Popadić, and Mirjana Vasović. 1988. *Mladi i neformalne grupe: U traganju za alternativom.* Belgrade: Istraživačko-izdavački centar SSO Srbije and Centar za idejni rad SSO Beograda.

Jowitt, Kenneth. 1971. *Revolutionary Breakthroughs and National Development: The Case of Romania, 1944–1965.* Berkeley and Los Angeles: University of California Press.

Kaplan, Robert D. 1993. *Balkan Ghosts: A Journey Through History.* New York: St. Martin's Press.

Katz, Elihu, and Tamar Liebes. 1984. "Once upon a Time in Dallas." *Intermedia* 12, no. 3.

———. 1985. "Mutual Aid in the Decoding of *Dallas.*" In Philip Drummond and Richard Patterson, eds., *Television in Transition* (London: British Film Institute).

Keane, John, ed. 1988. *Civil Society and the State: New European Perspectives.* London: Verso.

Knabb, Ken, ed. 1981. *Situationist International Anthology.* Berkeley: Bureau of Public Secrets.

Konstantinović, Radomir. 1991. *Filosofija palanke.* Belgrade: Nolit.

———. 1992. "Živeti sa čudovištem." In Ivan Čolović and Aljoša Mimica, eds., *Druga Srbija* (Belgrade: Plato, Beogradski krug i Borba).

Korošić, Marijan. 1988. *Jugoslavenska kriza*. Zagreb: Naprijed.

Kovač, Oskar, Ljubomir Madžar, Zoran Popov, and Dragoljub Stanišić. 1983. *Privredni razvoj Jugoslavije do 2000.: Makroekonomski model i projekcije*. Belgrade: Institut ekonomskih nauka.

Kuzmanović, Bora. 1994. "Socijalna distanca prema pojedinim nacijama (Etnička distanca)." In Mladen Lazić, ed., *Razaranje društva: Jugoslovensko društvo u krizi 90-tih* (Belgrade: Filip Višnjić).

Kuzmanović, Bora, ed. 1993. *Studentski protest 1992: Socialno-psihološka studija jednog društvenog događaja*. Belgrade: Institut za psihologiju.

Lalić, Lazar. 1995. *Tri TV godine u Srbiji*. Belgrade: Nezavisni sindikat medija.

Lampe, John R., and Marvin R. Jackson. 1982. *Balkan Economic History, 1550–1950: From Imperial Borderlands to Developing Nations*. Bloomington: Indiana University Press.

Laquer, Walter, ed. 1976. *Fascism, A Reader's Guide: Analyses, Interpretations, Bibliography*. Berkeley and Los Angeles: University of California Press.

Lazić, Mladen. 1994. "Društveni činioci raspada Jugoslavije." *Sociološki pregled* 28, no. 2.

———. 1994. *Sistem i slom: Raspad socijalizma i struktura jugoslovenskog društva*. Belgrade: Filip Višnjić.

Lazić, Mladen, Danilo Mrkšić, Sreten Vujović, Bora Kuzmanović, Stjepan Gredelj, Slobodan Cvejić, and Vladimir Vuletić. 1994. *Razaranje društva: Jugoslovensko društvo u krizi 90-tih*. Belgrade: Filip Višnjić.

Lefebvre, Henri. 1971. *Everyday Life in the Modern World*. New York: Harper and Row.

Lekić, Slaviša, ed. 1995. *SRJ '94: Ličnosti godine*. Belgrade: Agencijski centar Borba.

Lembo, Ron, and Ken Tucker. 1990. "Culture, Television, and Opposition: Rethinking Cultural Studies." *Critical Studies in Mass Communications* 7 (June).

Leppert, Richard, and Susan McClary. 1987. *Music and Society: The Politics of Composition, Performance, and Reception*. New York: Cambridge University Press.

Lokner, Branimir. 1994. *Kritičko pakovanje*. Belgrade: Vizija 011.

Luković, Petar. 1989. *Bolja prošlost: Prilozi iz muzičkog života Jugoslavije, 1940–1989*. Belgrade: Mladost.

Luković-Pjanović, Olga. 1990. *Srbi: Narod najstariji*. Belgrade: AIZ Dosije.

Manuel, Peter. 1993. *Cassette Culture: Popular Music and Technology in North India*. Chicago: University of Chicago Press.

Marcuse, Herbert. 1958. *Soviet Marxism: A Critical Analysis*. New York: Columbia University Press.

———. 1964. *One-Dimensional Man: Studies in the Ideology of Advanced Industrial Society*. Boston: Beacon Press.

———. 1968. *Negations: Essays in Critical Theory*. Boston: Beacon Press.

———. 1978. *The Aesthetic Dimension: Toward a Critique of Marxist Aesthetics*. Boston: Beacon Press.

Marković, Peđa J. 1992. *Beograd i Evropa: 1918–1941: Evropski uticaj na proces modernizacije Beograda*. Belgrade: Savremena administracija, d.d.

Mayer, Arno. 1988. *Why Did the Heavens Not Darken? The "Final Solution" in History*. New York: Pantheon.

McQuail, Denis. 1983. *Mass Communication Theory: An Introduction*. Beverly Hills: Sage.

Meštrović, Stjepan. 1994. *The Balkanization of the West*. New York: Routledge.

Meštrović, Stjepan, Slaven Letica, and Miroslav Goreta. 1993a. *Habits of the Balkan Heart: Social Character and the Fall of Communism*. College Station: Texas A & M University Press.

———. 1993b. *The Road from Paradise: Prospects for Democracy in Eastern Europe*. Lexington: University Press of Kentucky.

Milanović, Branko. 1994. *Protiv nacizma*. Belgrade: Radio B-92.

Milić, Anđelka. 1994. *Žene, politika, porodica*. Belgrade: Institut za političke studije.

Milić, Vladimir. 1992. "Socijalni lik političkog javnog mnjenja." In Miroslav Pečuljić, Vladimir Milić, Vladimir Goati, Srbobran Branković, and Miladin Kovačević, *Rađanje javnog mnjenja I političkih stranaka* (Belgrade: Centar za javno mnjenje i marketing "Medium").

Milinković, Branko, ed. 1994. *Govor mržnje: Analiza sadržaja domaćih medija u prvoj polovini 1993. godine*. Belgrade: Centar za antiratnu akciju.

Mills, C. Wright. 1959. *The Sociological Imagination*. New York: Oxford University Press.

Milošević, Slobodan. 1989. *Godine raspleta*. Belgrade: Beogradski izdavačko-grafički zavod.

Mukerji, Chandra, and Michael Schudson. 1991. *Rethinking Popular Culture: Contemporary Perspectives in Cultural Studies*. Berkeley and Los Angeles: University of California Press.

Negus, Keith. 1992. *Producing Pop: Culture and Conflict in the Popular Music Industry*. New York: Edward Arnold.

Nemanjić, Miloš. 1991. *Filmska i pozorišna publika Beograda: Socijalno-kulturni uslovi formiranja u periodu 1961–1984*. Belgrade: Zavod za proučavanje kulturnog razvitka.

Novaković, Relja. 1993. *Srbi: Ime Srbi kroz vreme i prostor*. Zemun: Izdavačko prometna agencija "Miroslav".

Okey, Robin. *Eastern Europe 1740–1985: Feudalism to Communism*. Minneapolis: University of Minnesota Press, 1986.

Ortega y Gasset, José. 1932. *The Revolt of the Masses*. New York: Norton.

Pajić, Kamenko. 1991. *9. mart 1991*. Sremčica: Kamenko.

Pečuljić, Miroslav. 1992. "U začaranom krugu politike." In Miroslav Pečuljić, Vladimir Milić, Vladimir Goati, Srbobran Branković, and Miladin Kovačević, *Rađanje javnog mnjenja i političkih stranaka* (Belgrade: Centar za javno mnjenje i marketing "Medium").

Pečuljić, Miroslav, Vladimir Milić, Vladimir Goati, Srbobran Branković, and Miladin Kovačević. 1992. *Rađanje javnog mnjenja i političkih stranaka*. Belgrade: Centar za javno mnjenje i marketing "Medium."

Perović, Latinka. 1995. "Beg od modernizacije." *Republika* (16–31 March).

Petrović, Ruža. 1985. *Etnički mešoviti brakovi u Jugoslaviji*. Belgrade: Institut za sociološka istraživanja Filozofskog fakulteta u Beogradu.

Popov, Nebojša. 1993. *Srpski populizam: Od marginalne do dominantne pojave*. Special supplement to *Vreme*, no. 135, 24 May.

Popović, Nenad D. 1968. *Yugoslavia: The New Class in Crisis*. Syracuse: Syracuse University Press.

Poulton, Hugh. 1991. *The Balkans: Minorities and States in Conflict.* London: Minority Rights Group.

Press, Andrea. 1991. *Women Watching Television: Gender, Class, and Generation in the American Television Experience.* Philadelphia: University of Pennsylvania Press.

Pribićević, Ognjen. 1993. "Politička kultura i demokratska stabilnost" In Vladimir Goati, Zoran Slavujević, and Ognjen Pribićević, *Izborne borbe u Jugoslaviji, 1990–1992* (Belgrade: Radnička štampa).

Prica, Ines. 1991. *Omladinska potkultura u Beogradu: Simbolička praksa.* Belgrade: SANU etnografski institut.

Prošić-Dvornić, Mirjana, ed. 1994. *Kulture u tranziciji.* Belgrade: Plato.

Prpić, Katarina, Blaženka Despot, and Nikola Dugandžija, eds. 1993. *Croatian Society on the Eve of Transition: Collected Papers.* Zagreb: Institute for Social Research.

Radway, Janice A. 1984. *Reading the Romance: Women, Patriarchy, and Popular Literature.* Chapel Hill: University of North Carolina Press.

Ramet, Sabrina. 1992a. *Balkan Babel: Politics, Culture, and Religion in Yugoslavia.* Boulder, Colo.: Westview Press.

———. 1992b. *Nationalism and Federalism in Yugoslavia, 1962–1991.* 2d ed. Bloomington: Indiana University Press.

Ramet, Sabrina, ed. 1994. *Rocking the State: Rock Music and Politics in Eastern Europe and Russia.* San Francisco: Westview Press.

Ramet, Sabrina, and Ljubiša Adamovich. 1995. *Beyond Yugoslavia: Politics, Economics, and Culture in a Shattered Community.* San Francisco: Westview Press.

Reich, Wilhelm. 1970. *The Mass Psychology of Fascism.* New York: Farrar, Straus and Giroux.

Republički zavod za statistiku. 1993. *Prevremeni izbori za narodne poslanike Narodne skupštine republike Srbije 1993, konačni rezultati.* Belgrade: Republički zavod za statistiku.

———. 1994. *Statistički godišnjak Srbije 1993.* Belgrade: Republički zavod za statistiku.

Rogin, Michael. 1987. *Ronald Reagan, the Movie, and Other Episodes in Political Demonology.* Berkeley and Los Angeles: University of California Press.

Rothschild, Joseph. 1974. *East Central Europe Between the Two World Wars.* Seattle: University of Washington Press.

———. 1989. *Return to Diversity: A Political History of East Central Europe Since World War II.* New York: Oxford University Press.

Rubin, Alan. 1994. "Media Uses and Effects: A Uses-and-Gratifications Perspective." In Jennings Bryant and Dolf Zillman, eds., *Media Effects: Advances in Theory and Research* (Hillsdale, N.J.: Lawrence Erlbaum Associates).

Ryback, Timothy. 1990. *Rock Around the Bloc: A History of Rock Music in Eastern Europe and the Soviet Union.* Durham: Duke University Press.

Said, Edward W. 1978. *Orientalism: Western Conceptions of the Orient.* New York: Pantheon.

Sanford, Nevitt, and Craig Comstock, eds. 1971. *Sanctions for Evil: Sources of Social Destructiveness.* San Francisco: Jossey-Bass.

Saveljić, Branislava. 1988. *Beogradska favela: Nastanak i razvoj Kaluđerice kao posledica bespravne stambene izgradnje u Beogradu.* Belgrade: Istraživačko-izdavački centar SSO Srbije.

Šćekić, Draško. 1994. *Sorabi: Istoriopis*. Belgrade-Podgorica: Sfairos & Timor.

Schudson, Michael. 1984. *Advertising: The Uneasy Persuasion, Its Dubious Impact on American Society*. New York: Basic Books.

Schuman, Howard, Charlotte Steeh, and Lawrence Bobo. 1985. *Racial Attitudes in America: Trends and Interpretations*. Cambridge, Mass.: Harvard University Press.

Schwartz, Barry. 1986. *The Battle for Human Nature: Science, Morality, and Modern Life*. New York: Norton.

Serafin, Joan, ed. 1994. *East-Central Europe in the 1990s*. Boulder, Colo.: Westview Press.

Seroka, Jim, and Vukašin Pavlović, eds. 1992. *The Tragedy of Yugoslavia: The Failure of Democratic Transformation*. New York: M. E. Sharpe.

Shillinglaw, Draga, ed. and trans. 1978. *The Lectures of Professor T. G. Masaryk at the University of Chicago, Summer 1902*. London: Associated University Presses.

Silj, Alessandro, ed. 1988. *East of Dallas: The European Challenge to American Television*. London: British Film Institute.

Simić, Andrei. 1973. *The Peasant Urbanites: A Study of Rural-Urban Mobility in Serbia*. New York: Seminar Press.

———. 1978. "Commercial Folk Music in Yugoslavia: Idealization and Reality." *Journal of the Association of Graduate Dance Ethnologists, UCLA* 2 (Fall–Winter).

Singleton, Fred. 1976. *Twentieth-Century Yugoslavia*. New York: Columbia University Press.

———. 1985. *A Short History of the Yugoslav Peoples*. Cambridge: Cambridge University Press.

Skocpol, Theda. 1979. *States and Social Revolutions: A Comparative Analysis of France, Russia, and China*. New York: Cambridge University Press.

Slavujević, Zoran. 1993. "Borba za vlast u Srbiji kroz prizmu izbornih kampanja." In Vladimir Goati, Zoran Slavujević, and Ognjen Pribićević, *Izborne borbe u Jugoslaviji, 1990–1992* (Belgrade: Radnička štampa).

Smith, Anthony. 1991. *National Identity*. Reno: University of Nevada Press.

Spengler, Oswald. 1928. *The Decline of the West*. New York: Knopf.

Stambolić, Ivan. 1995. *Put u bespuće*. Belgrade: Radio B-92.

Starr, S. Frederick. 1985. *Red and Hot: The Fate of Jazz in the Soviet Union*. New York: Limelight Editions.

Staub, Ervin. 1989. *The Roots of Evil: The Origins of Genocide and Other Group Violence*. New York: Cambridge University Press.

Street, John. 1986. *Rebel Rock: The Politics of Popular Music*. London: Blackwell.

Szemere, Anna. 1992. "The Politics of Marginality: A Rock Musical Subculture in Socialist Hungary in the Early 1980s." In Reebee Garofalo, ed., *Rockin' the Boat: Mass Music and Mass Movements* (Boston: South End Press).

Szemere, Anna. 1995. "Subcultural Politics and Social Change: Alternative Rock Music in Postcommunist Hungary." Paper presented at the conference of the International Association for the Study of Popular Music—USA, Nashville.

Tadić, Ljubomir. 1986. *Da li je nacionalizam naša sudbina?* Belgrade: Multiprint.

Talmon, Jacob L. 1952. *The Rise of Totalitarian Democracy*. Boston: Beacon Press.

Taylor, Jay. 1993. *The Rise and Fall of Totalitarianism in the Twentieth Century*. New York: Paragon House.

Thompson, Mark. 1995. *Proizvodnja rata: Mediji u Srbiji, Hrvatskoj, i Bosni i Hercegovini.* Trans. Vera Vukelić. Belgrade: Medija centar Radio B-92.

Todorović, Mijalko. 1986. *Političko biće, društvene krize.* Zagreb: Bibliotheca Scientia Yugoslavica.

Tomasevich, Jozo. 1955. *Peasants, Politics, and Economic Change in Yugoslavia.* Stanford: Stanford University Press.

Troitsky, Artemy. 1987. *Back in the USSR: The True Story of Rock in Russia.* Boston: Faber and Faber.

Tucker, Robert C., ed. 1972. *The Marx–Engels Reader.* New York: Norton.

Tuđman, Franjo. 1981. *Croatia on Trial: The Case of Croatian Historian Dr. F. Tuđman.* Amersham, England: United Publishers.

———. 1981. *Nationalism in Contemporary Europe.* New York: Columbia University Press.

———. 1989. *Bespuća povijesne zbiljnosti.* Zagreb: Matica Hrvatska.

Univerzitetna konferenca ZSMS. 1985. *Punk pod Slovenci.* Ljubljana: Univerzitetna konferenca ZSMS.

Verdery, Katherine. 1991. *National Ideology Under Socialism: Identity and Cultural Politics in Ceausescu's Romania.* Berkeley and Los Angeles: University of California Press.

Vujačić, Veljko. 1995. *Communism and Nationalism in Russia and Serbia.* Ph.D. dissertation. Department of Sociology, University of California, Berkeley.

Vujović, Sreten. 1994. "Promene u materijalnom standardu i načinu života društvenih slojeva. " In Mladen Lazić, ed., *Razaranje društva: Jugoslovensko društvo u krizi 90-tih* (Belgrade: Filip Višnjić).

———. 1995. "Stereotipi o gradu, nacionalizam i rat." *Republika,* no. 113 (1–15 April).

Vukić, Radivoj. 1994. *Svaštalice: Hronika ideološke konjunkture, 1991–1994.* Zrenjanin: Građanska čitaonica Banat.

Walser, Robert. 1993. *Running with the Devil: Power, Gender, and Madness in Heavy Metal Music.* Hanover: University Press of New England.

White, Stephen, John Gardner, George Schöpflin, and Tony Saich. 1990. *Communist and Postcommunist Political Systems.* New York: St. Martin's Press.

Wicke, Peter. 1990. *Rock Music: Culture, Aesthetics, and Sociology.* New York: Cambridge University Press.

Willis, Paul. 1990. *Common Culture: Symbolic Work at Play in the Everyday Cultures of the Young.* San Francisco: Westview Press.

Wolff, Larry. 1994. *Inventing Eastern Europe: The Map of Civilization on the Mind of the Enlightenment.* Stanford: Stanford University Press.

Yinger, J. Milton. 1982. *Countercultures: The Promise and Peril of a World Turned Upside Down.* New York: Free Press.

Živković, Marko. 1995. "The Turkish Taint: Dealing with the Ottoman Legacy in Serbia." Paper presented at the conference of the American Anthropology Association, Washington, D.C.

———. 1996. "Stories Serbs Tell Themselves (and Others) About Themselves: Discourses on Identity and Destiny in Serbia Since the Mid-Eighties." Dissertation prospectus, University of Chicago.

Index

Adžić, Blagoje, 18
Aksentijević, Pavle, 152–53
Albanian minority
  election boycott, 54 n. 74, 56–57
  political parties, 56
Amadeus, Rambo. See Pušić, Antonije
Anastasijević, Dejan, 182, 186
ANEM. See Association of Independent Electronic Media
Aranđelovac, 110–11
Arkan. See Ražnatović-Arkan, Željko
army. See military, Serbian; Yugoslav People's Army
Art TV, 66–67, 88
Association of Independent Electronic Media (Asocijacija nezavisnih elektronskih medija—ANEM), 68
authoritarianism. See also nationalist-authoritarian regimes
  outlook of supporters, 205–6
  survival from Communist era, 16
automobile prices, 179
Avramović, Dragoslav, 18, 176–77

B-92. See Radio B-92
Babić, Milan, 18, 41, 41 n. 45
Babić-Sneki, Snežana, 149–50, 160
Bajaga i instruktori (Bajaga and the Instructors), 112
Bajagić-Bajaga, Momčilo, 123, 145
Balašević, Đorđe, 107
Baletić, Branko, 89
banks, pyramid schemes, 174–75
Belgrade. See also demonstrations; rock and roll culture
  cultural changes, 105, 106, 141
  elections (1996), 204–5
  electrical outages, 146–47, 189
  ethnic diversity of population, 12–13
  housing, 106–7
  independent media, 16, 95–96
  migration from rural areas, 105–7
  National Museum, 73
  newsmagazines, 68–70
  newspapers, 63–65

population growth, 105–6
radio stations, 67–68, 131
rock and roll venues, 121 n. 40, 141, 145
social groups, 109 n. 15, 133
"struggle against kitsch," 155–56
support for SPS, 54
television stations, 66–67, 88
Terazije, 41–42, 43
Ušće, 42, 43
Biro, Mikloš, 57, 65
BK Telekom, 67, 88
Blic, 204
Bogdanović, Radmilo, 40, 41–42
Bokan, Dragoslav, 13–14
Bolčić, Silvano, 197
Borba: Vanredno izdanje (Borba: special edition), 91, 92–94, 95
Borba, 29, 43, 65. See also Naša borba
  association with Studio B, 67 n. 13
  attacks from regime, 83, 84–90
  availability outside Belgrade, 83
  in Communist era, 81
  coverage of demonstrations (1991), 82
  coverage of opposition parties, 82
  defense against state takeover, 89
  financial problems, 83
  independent views, 81–82
  legal registration of company and dispute over, 83, 84–86, 87–90
  price, 83
  privatization of company, 82–83
  protests of state takeover, 94–95, 99
  readership, 83–84
  regime takeover of, 62, 65, 90–92
  regime version, 75–76, 91–93, 94, 99
  stockholders, 82–83, 88–89
  surveys, 190–91
  war coverage, 82
Bosnia and Hercegovina
  elections (1990), 30–31
  nationalist parties, 27
  Serbian nationalism in, 28
  United States policy, 12
  Vance-Owen peace plan, 48, 100, 105, 132, 152, 154
  war, 46, 58–59, 72

Bosnian Serbs, 48, 152, 154
Boye (Colors), 111
Braća Karić bank, 67, 88
Brena, Fahreta Jahić–Lepa, 133
Brčin, Dragutin, 78–79, 85–86, 90, 91, 92, 100
Brkić, Milovan, 78
broadcast media. *See* radio; television
Budimirović-Bidža, Dobrivoje, 141
Burzan, Nikola, 190
businesses
    independent, 195–96
    privatization programs, 16, 167
    state-owned, 15–16, 54, 195

Čalija, Milivoje, 122
Ceca. *See* Veličković-Ceca, Svetlana
Cerović, Stojan, 7, 69
cities. *See* urban centers; urban culture
Clinton, Bill, speculation on German ancestry of, 12
Cobain, Kurt, 149
Cohen, Lenard, 15
Čolović, Ivan, 72, 128, 129–30, 131
Communist era
    contingency of ideology, 16–17
    differences from current Serbian regime, 10–12, 14
    disapproval of nationalism, 26
    end of, 29–31
    legacy to Serbian regime, 8–9, 11, 14–16, 23, 202
    neofolk music, 129, 131
    political and economic elites, 15
    state control of economy, 15–16
    state control of media, 15, 81
Communist Manifesto, 204
Communist Party. *See* League of Communists
cooking oil, 179, 179 n. 20
Ćosić, Dobrica, 18, 126–27, 126 n. 50
cosmopolitanism, 207–8
    in former Yugoslavia, 10–11
    of rock and roll culture, 107, 115–16, 143, 148–49
Council of Independent Trade Unions (*Veće samostalnih sindikata*) of Novi Sad, 191
Čović, Nebojša, 156
criminal elite
    association with turbofolk music, 135, 141, 143
    development related to sanctions, 166, 195
Croatia
    Drašković's association with regime, 38 n. 37
    economic conflicts with Serbia, 169
    elections, 30, 31, 53 n. 72
    folk music, 131

independent media, 79–80, 195 n. 60
music used for political purposes, 131, 131 n. 62
nationalist-authoritarian regime, 8, 27
opposition to Ante Marković, 32 n. 22
power of president, 37 n. 35
privatization, 16
regime during World War II, 30, 30 n. 19, 31
Serbian minority, 28, 30, 34 n. 32, 71
United States policy, 12
violence in, 38 n. 37
war in, 43–44, 46, 58–59, 62, 72, 73–74
Croatian Democratic Union (*Hrvatska demokratska zajednica—HDZ*), 30, 30 n. 19, 31
culture. *See* Ministry of Culture; music; urban culture
Ćurguz-Kazimir, Velimir, 64
currency. *See also* dinar
    hard, 173–74, 175, 177, 181, 182
Cushman, Thomas, 115, 122
Czechoslovakia, 29

Dačić, Ivica, 89
Dafiment, 174–75
daily life. *See* everyday life
Darkwood dub, 121–22, 147
democracy
    appearance of, 24–25
    negative attitudes toward, 57–58
    in period before World War I, 202
Democratic Center, 157–58
Democratic Party (*Demokratska stranka—DS*), 190
    in coalition, 75
    lack of nationalism policy, 34 n. 30
    meeting against darkness, 94–95
    shift to extreme nationalism, 56
    weakness, 50
Democratic Party of Serbia (DSS), 50, 75
demographic changes
    emigration of young people, 44, 56, 59, 114, 166, 203
    refugees from other republics, 203
Demokratija, 204
demonstrations
    in March 1991, 24, 37–43, 44, 62, 82
    in 1992, 43, 207
    in 1994 (meeting against darkness), 94–95
    in 1996, 62, 204, 207–8
    by regime supporters, 42
Đerić, Veronika, 88
deseterac metric scheme, 131, 131 n. 63
Đilas, Milovan, 141
dinar. *See also* inflation
    fall in value, 165, 170, 176–77, 179

instability, 177, 181–82
money supply, 170
super, 176
withdrawal and replacement of paper currency, 171 n. 11
Đinđić, Zoran, 50, 50 n. 65, 76
Dinkić, Mlađan, 181
Disciplina kićme (Discipline of the spine), 111
Dnevni telegraf, 65
Dišić, Vera, 88
Đogani, Gagi, 134
Đogani, Hamid, 133
Đokić, Zoran, 131, 134, 152
Đorđević, Bora, 110, 110 n. 17, 123, 123 n. 44, 145
Drašković, Vuk, 21. *See also* Serbian Renewal Movement
  association with Croatian regime, 38 n. 37
  demonstrations of March 1991, 38–39, 40, 41
  as deputy premier, 21 n. 1
  media coverage, 75, 76
  nationalist rhetoric, 33–34, 34 n. 31
DS. *See* Democratic Party
DSS. *See* Democratic Party of Serbia
Duga, 68–69
Đukanović, Milo, 205
Đukić, Petar, 167, 170

East-Central Europe
  end of Communist rule, 29
  rock and roll culture, 115
economy. *See also* dinar; inflation; poverty
  changes in distribution of wealth, 166, 174
  conflicts among republics, 168
  development programs, 168–69
  disruption that served purposes of regime, 175–76, 181–82, 187, 200
  effects of problems in everyday life, 172–74, 175–76
  effects of problems on pensioners, 185–86
  effects of sanctions, 192–96
  "gray," 184, 184 n. 30, 185
  interdependence of republics, 167–68, 192
  power of SPS, 58
  problems caused by breakup of Yugoslavia, 165–66, 169–72
  problems in urban areas, 185
  of SFRJ, 9 n. 10, 15, 28, 167–69
  shortages, 179
  state control of, 15–16
  unemployment, 185
educational levels, political divisions, 54, 203
Ekaterina velika (Catherine the Great), 119, 122, 124, 145, 146

elections
  abstention rates, 53
  boycotts by Albanian minority, 54 n. 74, 56–57
  manipulations of results, 53
  of 1990 (Serbia), 18, 25, 31, 32–37
  of 1990 (Yugoslav republics), 29–31
  of 1992 (Serbia), 46–47
  of 1993 (Serbia), 25 n. 5, 48–49, 52, 56–57
  of 1996 (Serbia; local), 204–5
electrical outages
  deterioration of distribution system, 188, 189
  opposition's reactions, 94–95, 191
  planned, 187–90
  residents' responses, 190–92
  unplanned, 146–47, 188, 189
Električni orgazam (Electrical Orgasm), 108–10, 110 n. 16, 116, 119, 121 n. 38, 129 n. 58
Elektrodistribucija Srbije, 146–47, 187, 188, 191
emigration of young people, 44, 56, 59, 114, 166, 203
epic poetry, 131, 131 n. 63
ethnic groups
  Albanians, 54 n. 74, 56, 56–57
  mixed marriages, 4
  public opinion on, 3–4
  in urban centers, 12–13
  in Vojvodina, 13 n. 15
European Union
  peace negotiators, 154
  sanctions against Serbia, 170
everyday life
  destruction of alternatives, 2, 6–7, 197–98, 200
  disruption that served purposes of regime, 166, 175–76
  effects of economic problems, 172–74, 175–76
  electrical outages, 146–47, 187–92
  instability of, 166
  lack of absolute control by regime, 208
  possibility of resistance in, 200–201
  reduction of sociability, 175–76
  restrictions on, 196–98
  sanctions blamed for difficulties in, 193–94

Fatherland Serbian Action (*Otadžbinska srpska akcija*), 76
Federal Fund for Financing Accelerated Development of Economically Underdeveloped Republics and Autonomous Provinces, 168–69

Federal Republic of Yugoslavia. *See* SRJ (*Savezna republika Jugoslavija*)
Feral tribune, 79–80
folk music. *See also* neofolk music; turbofolk music
  izvorni (authentic), 128 n. 56, 152, 161
  old city songs of Belgrade (*starogradske pesme*), 151–52, 151 n. 94
football chants, 129 n. 58

Galija, 123–24, 124 n. 45
Gavrilović, Ivan, 133–34
generational divisions, 43, 52–53, 203
German marks, 173–74, 177, 179–80
Germany, National Socialist regime, 2
Gile. *See* Gojković-Gile, Srđan
Gipsy Kings, 155
Glišić, Milivoje, 69
Goati, Vladimir, 35–36
Goffman, Erving, 98
Gojković-Gile, Srđan, 108, 109, 110 n. 16, 116
gray economy, 184, 184 n. 30, 185
Gredelj, Stjepan, 186
Grujić, Dragoslav, 52, 69

hard currency, 173–74, 175, 177, 181, 182
Haustor (Lobby), 112
HDZ. *See* Croatian Democratic Union
housing prices, 173, 174
Hungary, rock and roll culture, 115
hyperinflation, 165, 170–73. *See also* inflation
  consequences, 166, 174, 175–76, 177, 203
  as deliberate policy, 176–77
  end of, 176, 182
  transfer of wealth to rural residents, 174

Ignjatović, Slobodan, 89
Ilić, Mile, 141
Ilić, Miroslav, 152
incomes. *See also* poverty
  before breakup of Yugoslavia, 168, 182
  declines, 182–83
  needed for basic expenses, 184–85, 187
  proportion spent on food, 183–84
  remittances from abroad, 184
inflation. *See also* hyperinflation
  in 1995, 180–82
  benefits to regime, 181–82
  creative ways to raise prices, 179
  efforts to control, 177–79, 180–81
  regime's attempts to downplay, 91–92
information. *See also* media
  e-mail links, 195 n. 60
  motivations for seeking, 97–98
  regime's control of, 194–95

intellectuals
  criticism of turbofolk music, 151–52, 153
  nationalist, 11, 27–28
international community. *See also* sanctions
  assistance to independent media, 79
  Milošević's relations with, 154–55
  seen as enemy, 12, 193–94
  support for Serbian opposition, 208
  view of Serbian role in wars, 203
Internet, 68, 195 n. 60

Jagger, Mick, 138
Janjatović, Petar, 64, 111–12, 116–17
jazz, 107
Jerić, Vlada, 121–22
Jevrić, Nebojša, 68–69
Jevtić, Nenad, 147
JNA. *See* Yugoslav People's Army
Jošić, Zlatko, 122 n. 41, 124–25
journalists. *See also* media
  independent, 71–72, 78, 200
  political pressure on, 71–72
  violence against, 78
Jovanović, Slobodan, 77, 78 n. 43
Jovanov, Svetislav, 189
Jović, Borisav, 18, 40, 42
Jugoskandik, 174–75
JUL. *See* United Yugoslav Left

Kadijević, Veljko, 18
Kalajić, Dragoš, 68
Karadžić, Radovan, 50 n. 65, 130 n. 60
  relationship with Milošević, 18, 34 n. 32, 48, 154
Karić, Bogoljub, 88
Kašanin, Milenko, 146, 156
Kljajević, Goran, 84, 89
Kojadinović, Dragan, 81
Kojić–Keba, Dragan, 138–40
Kojić–Koja, Dušan, 111, 145
Kontić, Radoje, 84 n. 63, 179
Kosović, Nedeljko, 40, 41
Kosovo. *See also* Albanian minority
  economic development efforts, 168
  Serbian regime's policies, 26 n. 6, 27, 169, 205
  Serbian Resistance Movement (*Srpski pokret otpora*), 26
Kostić-Cane, Zoran, 119–20
Krajina
  epic poetry, 131
  Šešelj's forces, 44, 46
  Serbian media coverage of war in, 73–74
  Serb minority, 41, 41 n. 45
  war, 18
Kristali, 122

KST (*Klub studenata tehnike*; Technical Students Club), 121 n. 40, 124–25, 141, 142–43, 147
Kučan, Milan, 29
KUD Idijoti, 112, 113
Kupres, Radovan, 115
Kuzmanović, Bora, 4

Lalić, Lazar, 72
Lazić, Mladen, 15, 197
League of Communists—Movement for Yugoslavia (*Savez komunista–Pokret za Jugoslaviju—SK-PJ*), 25 n. 5, 87–88, 154
League of Communists of Serbia (*Savez komunista Srbije—SKS*), 25, 25 n. 5, 27, 28, 32
League of Communists of Yugoslavia (*Savez komunista Jugoslavije—SKJ*), 10–11, 16–17, 29, 81, 82, 87–88
Leningrad, 122
Leskovac district, 57
liberal political parties, 34, 34 n. 30
Lilić, Zoran, 85, 91–92
Ljubljana, rock and roll culture, 108, 109
Logar, Gordana, 83, 91, 92, 93
Lokner, Branimir, 123–24
Luković, Petar, 69, 117, 190

Macedonia, elections (1990), 30–31
magazines. *See also specific magazines*
    in Belgrade, 68–70
    nationalist, 62
    supportive of regime, 68–69
Mandić, Oliver, 123, 123 n. 44
Marjanović, Mirko, 177–79
Marković, Ante, 28–29, 31–32, 32 n. 22, 82, 167
Marković, Mihailo, 127
Marković, Mirjana
    book, 190
    criticism of opposition, 207
    disapproval of independent media, 87
    magazine column, 18 n. 28, 68, 207
    photographs in media, 17
    political differences with Milošević, 18 n. 28
    political party, 25 n. 5, 154
    as surrogate for Milošević, 18
Mark-plan agency, 65
Martić, Milan, 18, 41 n. 45, 46, 74
Marx, Karl, 204
Matković, Dušan, 42
Mayer, Arno, 13
media. *See also* newspapers; radio; television
    choice of, 62–63, 96–101
    freedom in former Yugoslavia, 61, 61 n. 2
    motivations for seeking information, 97–98

in other republics, 71, 79–80
    smuggled in, 195 n. 60
    uses and gratification approach, 96–97
media, independent. *See also* Radio B-92; Studio B
    availability, 63, 70, 97, 200, 204
    broadcast, 63
    criticism of, 78–79, 80–81, 87
    definitions, 86–87
    effects of sanctions, 194–95
    emotional functions, 98–99
    foreign assistance, 79
    limited to cities, 16, 54, 63, 95–96
    marginalization, 78–81
    Naša borba, 65, 95, 98
    in other republics, 79–80
    public suspicion of, 80–81, 100
    regime's attempts to silence, 62
    regime takeovers, 62, 65, 68, 90–92
    survival of, 95–96, 204
media, state controlled. *See also* newspapers; RTS
    attacks on foreigners, 79
    audiences, 99–100
    availability, 97
    coverage of opposition, 33, 37–38, 64, 71, 75–76, 207–8
    coverage of regime, 76–77
    fear of other republics promoted by, 71
    financial support from regime, 77–78, 97
    influence on public opinion, 100
    inherited from Communist era, 15, 62, 81
    magazines, 68–69
    Milošević's use of, 31–32, 33, 62
    nationalist-authoritarian views, 74–75
    newspapers, 63–65
    promotion of neofolk and turbofolk music, 104–5, 121 n. 39, 123, 138, 143–44, 153, 162
    promotion of peace plan in Bosnia, 154
    reports on national conflicts, 38, 38 n. 37
    role in preparations for war, 24, 44, 71, 72
    support for regime, 71
    use in 1990 elections, 33
    war coverage, 72
mental hospitals, 98
Mićunović, Dragoljub, 50, 50 n. 65
middle classes
    disappearance of, 166
    effects of inflation, 175, 203
Mijić, Dušan, 82–83, 84 n. 63
Milanović, Branko, 46
Milanović, Dafina, 141, 174–75
Milić, Vladimir, 52–53
Milinović, Branivoje, 40, 41

military, Serbian, 15. *See also* Yugoslav People's Army
  Milošević and, 24, 26, 31, 43
  resistance to service in, 44, 126
  violence against civilian demonstrators, 37, 43
Mills, C. Wright, 200
Milošević, Milan, 47–48, 69
Milošević, Slobodan. *See also* Serbian regime; SPS
  alliance with Šešelj, 18, 44, 46, 48
  association with neofolk music, 130
  as federal president, 17 n. 27
  government by executive power, 37
  lack of clear message, 26 n. 6
  lack of concern for economic problems, 192–93
  longevity in power, 1–2, 18–19
  peace prize, 194
  photographs in media, 17
  policy shifts on Bosnia peace plans, 48, 72, 100, 105, 152, 154
  popularity, 31
  as president of Serbia, 25, 37
  public personality, 9 n. 11, 17
  reactions to demonstrations, 38, 40
  relationship with military, 24, 26, 31, 43
  relations with international community, 154–55
  rise to power, 6, 25, 26–28, 31–34, 62, 81
  support from rural areas, 14, 54, 203
  support for Serbs in Kosovo and other republics, 26 n. 6, 34 n. 32, 48, 152
  use of Serbian nationalism, 6, 25, 27–28
  use of surrogates, 17–18
Ministry of Culture, campaign for true cultural values and "struggle against kitsch," 105, 155–57, 158, 159–60
Mirković, Dragana, 134, 153
Mladenović, Milan, 124, 145–46
money supply, 170. *See also* inflation
Monitor, 80
Montenegro
  economy, 167–68
  independent media, 80
  Milošević's takeover of government, 27
  opposition in power, 205
Mrđen, Ivan, 83
music. *See also* folk music; neofolk music; rock and roll culture; turbofolk music
  American, 149–50
  jazz, 107
  political divisions, 111, 117, 126, 136, 149–51, 200
  social divisions, 104, 105, 107–8

Naša borba, 65, 95, 98
nationalism. *See also* Serbian nationalism
  attitudes in former Yugoslavia, 4–6, 26
  rhetoric of Drašković, 33–34
nationalist-authoritarian regimes. *See also* Serbian regime
  in Croatia, 8
  openness seen as threat, 207
  organizing myths reflected in media, 74–75
  Serbian regime as, 8–10, 206
  in Slovakia, 8
  social conflicts and, 201
National Museum (Belgrade), 73
Naumović, Slobodan, 58
NBJ. *See* Yugoslav National Bank
ND. *See* New Democracy Party
Nemanjić, Miloš, 106
neofolk music. *See also* turbofolk music
  analogy to American country-and-western, 136 n. 74
  commercial success, 132–33
  in Communist era, 129, 131
  contemporary themes, 132
  criticism of, 107 n. 11, 152–53
  definition, 104 n. 2
  distinction from turbofolk, 135–36
  divisions from rock and roll culture, 108
  end of regime's support of, 105, 153–58, 159
  Islamic elements heard in, 107 n. 11, 152–53
  musical quality, 136
  opposition from rock and roll culture, 116, 119–20, 142, 143–44, 162–63
  origins, 127 n. 53
  popularity, 107–8, 110, 141, 163
  popularity among workers abroad, 107, 128 n. 55, 144
  promotion by regime, 125–26, 127–30, 136, 143–44, 162
  promotion by state-controlled media, 104–5, 121 n. 39, 123, 143–44
  satire of, 118–19
  seen as kitsch, 142, 155–57
  seen as primitive, 144
  songs dedicated to Milošević, 130
  urban audience, 128 n. 55, 141
  use as nationalist agitprop, 128–32, 133, 152
New Democracy Party (*Nova demokratija— ND*), 49
New Musical Express, 108
newspapers. See also *Borba*; *Politika*; *Večernje novosti*
  in Belgrade, 63–65
  prices, 83, 97

readership, 65, 96
readers as percent of Serbian population, 33
      n. 27
state subsidies, 97
Nezavisnost, 91
NIN, 62, 69, 86
Novi Sad, 11, 191
novokomponovana narodna muzika (newly com-
      posed folk music), 104 n. 2, 127 n. 53,
      141. *See also* neofolk music
Novosti. See *Večernje novosti*

Obojeni program (Color program), 122, 148
older people
      effects of economic problems, 185–86
      support for Serbian regime, 52, 203
Open Society Foundation, 79
opposition. *See also* demonstrations
      antiwar, 46, 47, 49, 58, 126, 195 n. 60
      cosmopolitanism, 207–8
      effects of war and economic disruption,
            202–3
      failure of, 59
      international support, 208
      labeled as traitors, 44
      lack of democratic experience, 202
      peaks of strength, 24
      political outlooks, 205–6
      potential for future, 198, 200–201
      reactions to electrical outages, 94–95, 191
      resignation of, 22
      rock and roll culture's association with, 111,
            117, 126, 136, 149–51, 200
      role in regime's longevity, 55–56
      social groups existing in SFRJ, 201–2
      social resistance, 201
      threat to regime, 59
      views of regime, 7–8
      view of wars in former Yugoslavia, 23–24
opposition political parties. *See also* elections
      of Albanian minority, 56
      coalitions, 75
      coverage in state-controlled media, 33, 37–
            38, 64, 71, 75–76, 82
      demonstrations against state television,
            38–39
      emergence of, 33
      improbability of coming to power, 53
      lack of power, 24–25
      lack of unity, 28, 35, 49–50, 53, 55–56
      legalization of, 32
      liberal, 34, 34 n. 30
      in Montenegro, 205
      role in parliament, 50–51
      social groups supporting, 52, 54, 204

support in urban areas, 53–54, 204
suppression of, 200
Otašević, Branka, 64

Pančić, Teofil, 11, 160–61
Panić, Milan, 18, 48 n. 61
paramilitary forces, in Krajina, 46, 46 n. 57
parliament, Serbian, 32. *See also* elections
      live television broadcasts, 51 n. 68
      role of opposition parties, 50–51
      special session following demonstrations
            (1991), 42
      SPS control of, 35–37, 46–47, 50, 53
Partibrejkers (Party breakers), 111, 119, 122,
      146–48
Partner polling agency, 3–4, 67
Pavlović, Milivoje, 77
peasants. *See also* rural Serbia
      as symbol of Serbian national identity, 13
peasant urbanites, 107
      popularity of neofolk music among, 107–8,
            163
Pečuljić, Miroslav, 54
Pekić, Borislav, 44
pensioners, 185–86
Perović, Latinka, 72
Pešić, Vesna, 51
PGP-RTS, 133, 143, 158
Pošarac, Aleksandra, 183
police force, Serbian, 15, 38–41, 78
political parties. *See also* opposition political
            parties; *and specific parties*
      generational differences in support for, 52–
            53, 203
      single-party rule, 15, 25
Politika, 63–64, 159
      in Communist era, 81, 81 n. 54
      coverage of events in other republics, 73
      coverage of opposition, 75–76
      coverage of regime, 76–77
      criticism of independent media, 80
      cultural correspondents, 64, 160
      radio and television stations associated with,
            67
      readership, 65
      regime takeover of, 62, 81
      role in preparation for war, 72
Politika ekspress, 64–65
Popović-Perišić, Nada, 155
poverty
      effects of sanctions, 196
      increase following breakup of Yugoslavia,
            165–66, 182–83
      political consequences of increase, 183, 187
      potential for political unrest caused by, 198
      psychological effects, 187, 198

Predić, Uroš, 73
Pribićević, Ognjen, 53–54
prices. *See* inflation
Priština, election participation by ethnic Albanians, 54 n. 74, 57
private sphere. *See also* everyday life
  as refuge, 103–4
  resistance in, 200–201
privatization
  in Croatia, 16
  SFRJ program, 167
Pušić, Antonije (Rambo Amadeus), 114 n. 26, 116–19, 122, 126, 144 n. 83
public opinion
  influence of state-controlled media, 100
  on other ethnic groups, 3–4
Pula, rock and roll culture, 109, 113
pyramid schemes, 174–75

Rabassa, Toza, 110–11
Radio B-92, 96
  antiwar activities, 126
  coverage of demonstrations, 40
  daily news program, 97
  government attempts to control, 40, 62, 68
  independent radio network, 204
  news published on Internet, 68
Radio Indeks, 62
Radio Novosti, 67, 143 n. 81
Radio Politika, 67
Radio Ponos, 131, 132, 134, 152
radio stations
  in Belgrade, 67–68
  independent, 67, 204
  local, 62, 67, 127 n. 53, 128
  rock and roll programming, 108
  state-run network, 63, 67
Radio Student, 108
Radmilović, Zoran, 118
Radović-Raka, Radovan, 141
Radulović-Futa, Aleksandar, 133
Radulović, Radomir, 88
Ramadanovski, Džej, 156
Ražnatović-Arkan, Željko
  associations with musicians, 110, 123 n. 44
  criminal activities, 48 n. 63
  political party, 48
  as surrogate for Milošević, 18
  wedding, 136–38, 141, 143
recording companies
  independent, 112
  state-controlled, 143, 158
  turbofolk, 133
Reljić, Dušan, 78
Republika Srpske Krajine, 73–74. *See also* Krajina

resistance, social, 201. *See also* opposition
Riblja čorba (Fish chowder), 110, 110 n. 17, 112
Rimtutituki, 119, 145
Ristić, Ljubiša, 18
rock and roll culture
  absence from television, 121 n. 39
  availability of recordings, 112–13, 114
  Belgrade venues, 121 n. 40, 141, 145
  cosmopolitan orientation, 107, 115–16, 143, 148–49
  counteridentity to folk music, 144–51, 163
  cultural space reduced, 104, 120–22, 140–41, 142–43, 144–51
  decline of, 119–23, 125, 132
  development of, 107, 108–9
  effects of breakup of Yugoslavia, 112–14
  effects of emigration of young people, 114
  hostility of regime toward, 126–27, 162
  increased media exposure, 158
  individualism, 111
  marginalization of, 104, 114–15, 121–22, 163
  move away from mainstream, 115, 122–23, 124–25, 148
  in 1990s, 116–23, 125, 126, 132
  opposition to neofolk and turbofolk, 116, 119–20, 142, 143–44, 162–63
  opposition to regime, 111, 117, 126, 136, 149–51, 200
  performers allied with regime, 123–24
  pirate market, 112–13
  pop style, 122, 123
  quality of bands, 108
  success in 1980s, 111–12, 115, 116, 162
  symbolism of, 115–16
  in urban centers, 109–10, 125, 126
Rolling Stones, songs covered by Serbian band, 138–40
Romania, 29
Rome, 74–75
RTS (*Radio-Televizija Srbije*), 38 n. 36
  audiences, 65, 66
  coverage of war, 71, 73
  critical coverage of opposition, 71
  political pressure on journalists, 71–72, 78
  promotion of neofolk, 143
  radio stations, 67
  regime's use of, 77
  rock and roll documentaries, 158
  role in preparations for war, 72
  state control of, 62
Rugova, Ibrahim, 56–57
Rundek, Darko, 112, 113 n. 22
rural Serbia
  effects of economic problems, 185
  migration to Belgrade from, 105–7

peasants as symbol of Serbian national identity, 13
political differences from urban areas, 53–54, 105
support for Milošević, 14, 54, 203
wealth transferred as result of inflation, 174
Russia, rock and roll culture, 115, 122

Sakan, Dragan, 156
sanctions
benefits to regime, 192–96
cultural isolation caused by, 115–16, 148–49, 166, 194–95, 196
declaration of, 170
development of criminal elite related to, 166, 195
economic effects, 192, 196
nationalist feeling increased by, 193
partial suspension of, 154–55, 194
SANU. See Serbian Academy of Sciences and Arts
Sarajevo, rock and roll culture, 109
Savezna republika Jugoslavija. See SRJ
Savić, Dragan, 92–93
Seattle, music from, 149–50
Serbia. See also Serbian regime; Serbian society
constitution, 32, 32 n. 24, 35
democratic period before World War I, 202
demographic changes, 44, 56, 59, 114, 166, 203
election law, 32
Serbian Academy of Sciences and Arts (Srpska akademija nauka i umetnosti—SANU), 11, 27
Serbian Chetnik Movement (Srpski četnički pokret), 44, 46
Serbian Communist Party. See League of Communists of Serbia
Serbian nationalism
Drašković's rhetoric, 33–34, 34 n. 31
hostility toward urban centers, 13–14
international community as enemy, 12, 193–94
peasants as symbol, 13
rhetoric in early 1990s, 11
role in Milošević's rise to power, 6, 25, 27–28
use of neofolk music, 128–32, 133, 152
view of enemies, 12, 18
view of nationalism in other republics, 12
Serbian Radical Party (Srpska radikalna stranka—SRS), 44, 46–47, 49, 75
Serbian regime
benefits of sanctions, 192–96
conflict with society, 2, 200, 206–7

coverage in state controlled media, 76–77
cultural orientation, 136, 162, 202
destruction of alternative power centers, 21–22, 24
destruction of alternatives in everyday life, 2, 6–7, 197–98, 200
differences from Communist regime, 10–12, 14
differences from Germany's National Socialist regime, 2
hostility to urban centers, 12–14
involvement in popular music culture, 104–5, 114, 156–57, 158, 159–60, 161–62
legacy from Communist regime, 8–9, 11, 14–16, 23, 202
means of maintaining power, 18–19
Milošević's rise to power, 6, 25, 26–28, 31–34, 62, 81
as nationalist-authoritarian, 8–10, 206
power of president, 37, 37 n. 35
rapid ideological and policy shifts, 16–17
role of opponents in longevity, 55–56
social groups supporting, 2, 9, 42, 51–59, 136, 203–4
supporters' views of, 7–8, 22, 59–60, 203–4, 205–6
U.S. opposition to policies, 12
war as means of maintaining power, 24, 37, 43–44, 58–59
Serbian Renewal Movement (Srpski pokret obnove—SPO), 34, 75
antiwar policies, 56
demonstrations against state television, 38–39
in government, 21 n. 1
parliament seats, 35
Serbian Resistance Movement (Srpski pokret otpora), 26
Serbian society. See also everyday life; urban centers
conflict with state, 2, 200, 206–7
destruction of, 59, 197, 206–7
divisions, 6–7, 51–52, 104, 105, 107–8
divisions by educational levels, 54, 203
effects of economic problems, 166, 175–76
generational divisions, 43, 52–53
groups supporting regime, 2, 9, 42, 51–59, 136, 203–4
increased isolation, 166
marriages between ethnic groups, 4
resignation and apathy in, 7, 59, 186
urban-rural division, 10, 53–54, 105
Serbian Unity Party (SSJ), 48
Šešelj, Vojislav
alliance with Milošević, 18, 44, 46, 48

media coverage of, 75
paramilitary forces, 46, 46 n. 57
in parliament, 44, 46, 47–48, 50–51
political party, 44, 46–47, 49, 75
prison sentence for insult in parliament,
    50–51
reaction to 1991 demonstrations, 44
view of urban culture, 46 n. 57
SFRJ (*Socijalistička federativna republika Jugos-*
    lavija), 4. *See also* Communist era
breakup of, 11, 32 n. 24
division of state property, 89 n. 80
economy, 9 n. 10, 15, 28, 167–69
ethnic and national attitudes, 4–6
freedom of media, 61, 61 n. 2
government debt, 167
last prime minister (Marković), 28–29, 31–
    32, 32 n. 22, 82, 167
modernization, 9 n. 10
multiparty elections (1990), 18, 29–31,
    32–37
paralysis of federal presidency, 28 n. 14
reform demands, 28–31
relative openness, 10, 162, 194, 201–2
social change in, 6, 201–2
state's loss of credibility in 1980s, 10
successor states, 89
Simić, Andrei, 107
SKJ. *See* League of Communists of Yugoslavia
Skocpol, Theda, 204
Škorić, Mira, 134
SK-PJ. *See* League of Communists—
    Movement for Yugoslavia
SKS. *See* League of Communists of Serbia
Slavujević, Zoran, 28, 31, 33, 35
Slovakia, 8
Slovenia
breakup of Yugoslavia, 31, 32 n. 24
Communist Party, 16–17
conflicts with Serbia, 27, 29, 169
multiparty elections (1990), 29
power of president, 37 n. 35
Serbian media coverage of, 74
smuggling, 195, 195 n. 60
Sneki. *See* Babić-Sneki, Snežana
Social-Democratic League of Vojvodina (*Liga*
    socialdemokrata Vojvodine), 190
Socijalistička federativna republika Jugoslavija.
    See SFRJ
Socialist Party of Serbia. *See* SPS
society. *See* Serbian society
Socijalistička partija Srbije. See SPS
Šolević, Miroslav, 18
Soros Foundation, 12
Soros, George, 79, 79 n. 47
Soviet Union, rock and roll culture, 115, 122

Sovrlić, Branka, 134, 134 n. 72
SPO. *See* Serbian Renewal Movement
sports teams, 155
SPS (*Socijalistička partija Srbije*)
control of parliament, 35–37, 46–47, 50, 53
demonstrations by supporters (March
    1991), 42
economic power, 58
election losses, 25–26, 204–5
elections of 1990, 32–35
elections of 1992, 46–47
elections of 1993, 48–49, 57
generational differences in support, 52, 203
membership increases, 58
property used by, 87–88
single-party rule, 15, 25
support from less educated, 54, 203
support in rural areas, 14, 54, 203
use of state-controlled media, 71, 77, 81 n.
    54
weak support for, 1
SRJ (*Savezna republika Jugoslavija*; Federal Re-
    public of Yugoslavia)
constitution, 24–25
Ćosić as federal president, 126 n. 50
legitimacy as successor to SFRJ, 89
Milošević as federal president, 17 n. 27
Srpska reč, 78
SRS. *See* Serbian Radical Party
SSJ. *See* Serbian Unity Party
Stakić, Vladimir, 159–60, 161
Starčević-Stari, Zoran, 133, 138, 140
state-owned industries, 15–16, 195
privatization programs, 16, 167
workers in, 54
Stojadinović, Ljubodrag, 76
Stojković, Danilo, 118
student protests. *See* demonstrations
Studio B, 67
coverage of demonstrations, 40
criticism of, 80–81
daily news program, 97
equipment stolen from, 67 n. 14
founding, 67 n. 13
government attempts to control, 40, 62, 88
radio station, 67, 68
regime takeover, 62, 68
rock and roll programming, 121 n. 39
Šumadija, 13
Szemere, Anna, 115

Tadić, Ljubomir, 156
Tanjug news agency, journalists fired from, 78
Tasić, Dragoljub, 94
Telegraf, 69

television news
  audience, 33 n. 27, 67, 96, 99
  authority of, 99, 100
  coverage of demonstrations, 41
  coverage of opposition parties, 33, 37–38
  live broadcast of parliament, 51 n. 68
  photographs of Milošević shown, 17
  as primary source of news, 65–66
television stations. See also RTS; Studio B
  absence of rock and roll programs, 121 n.
    39
  in Belgrade, 66–67, 88
  broadcasts of neofolk videos, 121 n. 39, 123
  independent, 204
  local, 66, 204
  state-controlled, 38 n. 36, 63, 66–67, 70
  Yutel, 62
Thompson, Mark, 61, 65, 72, 100
Timotić-Zlaja, Zlatko, 133
Tirnanić, Bogdan, 64, 160
Tito, Josip Broz, 10
Tomić, Dragan, 77, 86–87
Trninić, Mirjana, 83, 84
Trofrtaljka, Mica, 118
Tucaković, Marina, 133
Tuđman, Franjo, 18
  election victory, 30, 31
  public manner, 9 n. 11
  relations with Serbian minority in Croatia,
    30
  on World War II, 30, 30 n. 19
turbofolk music
  association with glamor and luxury goods,
    133–35, 138
  association with regime and criminal elite,
    135, 138, 141, 143–44
  critics, 134 n. 72, 141, 142, 151–54, 161,
    163
  defenders, 160–61
  definition, 104 n. 2
  development, 105, 133
  distinction from neofolk, 135–36
  end of regime's support of, 153–56, 159–60,
    161–62
  folk elements in, 134, 135–36
  future of, 163–64
  Islamic elements heard in, 134 n. 72,
    152–53
  opposition from rock and roll culture, 142,
    143–44
  origin of term, 114 n. 26
  precursors, 145
  promotion by state-controlled media, 138,
    143–44, 153, 162
  themes of songs, 134
  western pop influences, 133

TV Palma, 66–67, 88, 121 n. 39, 123, 133,
    142, 143 n. 81
TV Pink, 66–67, 88, 121 n. 39, 123, 133, 143
    n. 81, 158 n. 110
TV Politika, 67, 121 n. 39

UKS. See Union of Serbian Writers
unemployment, 185
Union of Serbian Writers (Udruženje književ-
    nika Srbije—UKS), 11, 27–28
United Nations, 154. See also sanctions
United States
  music from Seattle, 149–50
  opposition to Serbian policies, 12
United Yugoslav Left (Jugoslovenska udružena
    levica—JUL), 25 n. 5
urban centers. See also Belgrade
  disappearance of middle class, 166
  economic changes, 166, 185
  emigration of young people from, 44, 56,
    59, 114, 166, 203
  ethnic diversity in, 12–13
  hostility of regime toward, 12–14
  independent media limited to, 16, 54, 63,
    95–96
  lack of support for regime, 126
  municipal elections (1996), 204–5
  neofolk music in, 128 n. 55
  peasant urbanites, 107–8, 163
  political differences from rural areas, 53–54,
    105
  rock and roll culture, 109–10, 125, 126
  support for opposition political parties, 53–
    54, 204
urban culture. See also rock and roll culture
  changes in Belgrade, 105, 106
  in former Yugoslavia, 9 n. 10, 10–11
  isolation caused by sanctions, 115–16, 148–
    49, 166
  Šešelj's view of, 46 n. 57
  social groups, 109 n. 15, 133

Vance-Owen peace plan, 48, 100, 105, 132,
    152, 154
Vanity Fair, 17
Vasiljević, Jezdimir (Gazda Jezda), 141,
    174–75
Vasić, Miloš, 39, 40
Večernje novosti (Evening news), 64, 88, 138,
    145, 155, 156, 193–94
  articles copied by Borba, 92–93
  articles on neofolk celebrities, 143 n. 81
  coverage of opposition, 75–76
  coverage of regime, 77
  criticism of independent media, 80
  nationalist authoritarian myths in, 74–75

ownership, 82 n. 57
radio station associated with, 67
readership, 65
report on *Borba* dispute, 85
reports on inflation, 181
splits among staff, 204
war coverage, 72, 73–74
Veličković-Ceca, Svetlana, 134, 136–38, 141,
    143, 144
Vico, Ratomir, 86, 87, 91, 100
Vojvodina
    electrical outages, 190
    ethnic German population, 13 n. 15
    Milošević's takeover of government, 27
Vreme, 3–4, 69–70, 78, 190
Vreme zabave, 113
Vučelić, Milorad, 144
Vujačić, Veljko, 6, 72
Vujović, Sreten, 66, 70

wars in former Yugoslavia
    antiwar groups in Serbia, 46, 47, 49, 58,
        126, 195 n. 60
    in Bosnia and Hercegovina, 46, 58–59, 72
    costs for Serbia, 169
    coverage by state-controlled media, 72
    in Croatia, 43–44, 46, 58–59, 62, 72, 73–74
    economic conflicts preceding, 168
    economic effects, 192
    international view of Serbia, 203
    as means of preserving power, 24, 37, 43–
        44, 58–59
    official Serbian positions on, 48, 58 n. 80,
        72, 105, 132, 152, 154
    opposition's view of, 23–24
    refugees, 203

role of state-controlled media in prepara-
    tions, 24, 44, 71, 72
Women's Movement for the Preservation of
    Yugoslavia (*Pokret žena za očuvanje Jugos-
    lavija*), 42
workers abroad, 107 n. 11
    popularity of neofolk music among, 107,
        128 n. 55, 144
World War II
    Croatian regime, 30, 30 n. 19, 31
    Tuđman's view of Holocaust, 30 n. 19

Yugo automobiles, 179
Yugoslavia, Federal Republic of. *See* SRJ (*Sa-
    vezna republika Jugoslavija*)
Yugoslavia, former. *See* SFRJ (*Socialistička fed-
    erativna republika Jugoslavija*)
Yugoslav National Bank (*Narodna banka Ju-
    goslavije—NBJ*), 176–77
Yugoslav People's Army (*Jugoslovenska
    narodna armija—JNA*), 37, 38 n. 37, 43,
    44
Yutel television, 62

Zagreb
    elections, 53 n. 72
    missiles fired at, 73–74
    rock and roll culture, 109
ZAM (*Zabava miliona*), 133
Zastava automotive factory, 179
Zebić, Jovan, 90
Žena, 17
Živković, Marko, 152–53
Zmijanac, Vesna, 144
Zvoncekova bilježnica (Zvoncek's notebook),
    110